❧ ANOTHER CITY UPON A HILL ❧

PORTUGUESE IN THE AMERICAS SERIES

*Portuguese-Americans and
Contemporary Civic Culture
in Massachusetts*
Edited by Clyde W. Barrow

Through a Portagee Gate
Charles Reis Felix

*In Pursuit of Their Dreams:
A History of Azorean Immigration
to the United States*
Jerry R. Williams

Sixty Acres and a Barn
Alfred Lewis

*Da Gama, Cary Grant,
and the Election of 1934*
Charles Reis Felix

Distant Music
Julian Silva

*Representations of the Portuguese
in American Literature*
Reinaldo Silva

The Holyoke
Frank X. Gaspar

Two Portuguese-American Plays
Paulo A. Pereira and Patricia A. Thomas
Edited by Patricia A. Thomas

Tony: A New England Boyhood
Charles Reis Felix

*Community, Culture and the Makings
of Identity: Portuguese-Americans
Along the Eastern Seaboard*
Edited by Kimberly DaCosta Holton
and Andrea Klimt

The Undiscovered Island
Darrell Kastin

*So Ends This Day: The Portuguese
in American Whaling 1765-1927*
Donald Warrin

*Azorean Identity in Brazil and the
United States: Arguments about History,
Culture, and Transnational Connections*
João Leal
Translated by Wendy Graça

Move Over, Scopes and Other Writings
Julian Silva

*The Marriage of the Portuguese
(Expanded Edition)*
Sam Pereira

Home Is an Island
Alfred Lewis

Land of Milk and Money
Anthony Barcellos

The Conjurer and Other Azorean Tales
Darrell Kastin

Almost Gone
Brian Sousa

*Land, As Far As the Eye Can See:
Portuguese in the Old West*
Donald Warrin and Geoffrey L. Gomes

ANOTHER
CITY
UPON
A HILL

⸂A New England Memoir⸃

JOSEPH A. CONFORTI

Tagus Press UMass Dartmouth Dartmouth, Massachusetts

PORTUGUESE IN THE AMERICAS SERIES

Tagus Press at UMass Dartmouth
www.portstudies.umassd.edu
© 2013 Joseph A. Conforti

Manufactured in the United States of America
General Editor: Frank F. Sousa
Managing Editor: Mario Pereira
Copyedited by Naomi J. Burns
Designed by Mindy Basinger Hill
Typeset in New Caledonia LT Std

Tagus Press books are produced and distributed for Tagus Press by
University Press of New England, which is a member of the
Green Press Initiative. The paper used in this book meets their
minimum requirement for recycled paper.

For all inquiries, please contact:
Tagus Press at UMass Dartmouth
Center for Portuguese Studies and Culture
285 Old Westport Road
North Dartmouth MA 02747–2300
Tel. 508–999–8255
Fax 508–999–9272
www.portstudies.umassd.edu

Library of Congress Cataloging-in-Publication Data

Conforti, Joseph A.
Another city upon a hill: a New England memoir / Joseph A. Conforti.
pages   cm.—(Portuguese in the Americas series)
Includes bibliographical references.
ISBN 978-1-933227-56-6 (pbk.: alk. paper)—
ISBN 978-1-933227-57-3 (ebook)
1. Conforti, Joseph A. 2. Portuguese Americans—Massachusetts—Fall River.
3. Italian Americans—Massachusetts—Fall River.
4. Fall River (Mass.)—Social conditions. 5. Fall River (Mass.)—History.
6. Fall River (Mass.)—Biography. I. Title.
F74. F2C66 2013
974.4'85—dc23   2013009669
5   4   3   2   1

For GEORGE "SNEAKER" MCDONALD,
DON MONTLE, *and the late* MANNY LIMA,
the best of Fall River, and for
BILL STUECK, *the best of friends*

❧ *Contents* ❧

Acknowledgments xi

Prologue 1

ONE Spindle City 7

TWO Family Migrations 30

THREE Street and Tenement 53

FOUR "Up the Flint" 76

FIVE Faith 102

SIX Aspirations 125

SEVEN Native Ground, Again 152

EIGHT Leaving 173

Epilogue 193

A Note on Sources 199

Notes 201

Illustrations follow page 124.

❧ *Acknowledgments* ❧

This memoir is a personal story, but also, as the title suggests, it's a story about a New England place. My Fall River, Massachusetts, was distinctive in ways that I try to convey to the reader. I am grateful to Frank Gaspar, who read a draft of this memoir and pointed out that the personal narrative was too often in the background to the story about Fall River. My friend, the distinguished poet Wesley McNair, suggested something similar two years earlier. He gave it to me straight, as a good friend should. Had I listened to him, it would have saved me a lot of grief. But it proved a challenge to wean my writing away from what I was taught growing up: you don't speak about family and especially yourself in public. I also want to thank Tom Grady for reading two drafts of this memoir and offering critical evaluations that gave me a basis to revise and greatly improve my narrative. Phil Silvia Jr. read the first chapter to make sure I had my historical facts straight.

I thank Darrell Reinke, my former colleague at Rhode Island College who pulled up stakes and returned to his tiny Idaho hometown. More than thirty years ago, we explored surprising similarities in our widely divergent backgrounds. Across the continent and years we have tried to keep the conversation going.

Several years ago I needed a respite from academic writing. Howard Rosenfield, a psychiatrist (though not mine) and a fiction writer, encouraged me to explore writing a memoir. I am grateful for his persistence. My local academic friends, now all retired from the University of Southern Maine and other institutions, have offered encouragement over lunch during the time I worked on this memoir. Joe Grange, Jim Leamon, Dick Maiman (who helped with photographs), John Woolverton, and Oliver Woshinsky have served as an inspiration by their continuing pursuit of research and writing. Also Victoria Bonebakker, now retired from the Maine Humanities Council, has been a good friend, a wonderful collaborator, and a stimulating lunchtime conversationalist. With family roots in New Bedford, she has been very interested in the progress of this memoir.

At the University of Massachusetts at Dartmouth, Frank Sousa has been a constant source of encouragement during the process of review and revision. Mario Pereira has quickly responded to my numerous questions about producing and publicizing the book. The university has a strong connection to my family. Many of my nieces and nephews are alumni. One of my brothers graduated from a predecessor institution, Durfee Tech, and so did a cousin who went on to become academic vice president of the university. It never occurred to me when I started writing that this family connection made the university the appropriate publisher of this memoir.

At the Fall River Historical Society, Michael Martins expressed a strong interest in my work. I am grateful for his help with photographs.

I especially want to thank my brothers John, Bill, and "Doc" and my sister "Betts" for answering my constant queries, reading a draft of early chapters about our growing up, correcting errors that crept into my memory, and suggesting areas where I needed a more balanced perspective. I trust my daughter Antonia, an only child, will gain a broader understanding of the background to her life from this memoir. I also hope she acquires some insight into what she has meant to her parents. Once again my wife Dorothy patiently supported me while I scraped this book off the brain, to paraphrase the great Herman Melville. Her love and her values have shaped my life in countless ways. I have dedicated previous books to her, a small token of my love. This book I dedicate to three Fall River men who took me under their wings, and to a highly accomplished diplomatic historian who also happens to be my most loyal friend since our undergraduate days at Springfield College.

Note: Perhaps it is my historian's training, but I am skeptical of memoirs that reconstruct detailed dialogue thirty, forty, or fifty years after it has occurred. My memoir is not a dialogue-driven work. I have included exchanges that I overheard or I was party to and that I remember vividly and, I believe, accurately. I have slightly changed only two names to protect persons' privacy.

❧ ANOTHER CITY UPON A HILL ❧

"I'm not going! I'm not going! I'm not going!" I screamed, as I fell to my knees and tears streamed down my cheeks. This outburst was not a stubborn child's tantrum. I was a forty-two-year-old college professor with a family and a mortgage. For three nights running I had awakened with a start at 3:00 a.m. I bolted out of bed, rushed down the stairs of our white Cape Cod house with green shutters in Cranston, Rhode Island, and began nervously pacing around an obstacle course of packed boxes. In a matter of minutes my wife once again stood face-to-face with me in the dark. And again we retreated to the family den in the back of the house so as not to awaken Antonia, our fifteen-year-old daughter, sleeping upstairs.

"I have already said my goodbyes," Dorothy calmly reminded me. "Well, that's ok. I'm not going." "Your name will be mud in New England," she prodded me. "I'm still not going." "But the house is sold, and we've bought another one in Maine." "We haven't signed any final papers. I'm not going, I tell you," my voice nearly at a shriek. I knew that I might be squandering an opportunity that I would regret for the rest of my life. I'll deal with that possibility later, I told myself.

This crisis erupted during the third week in June of 1987, days before we were to exit Rhode Island, our move paid for by my new employer, the state university in Portland, Maine. During the preceding February, just as I was promoted to full professor at Rhode Island College in Providence, I had tendered my resignation. I gave up tenure, and so did Dorothy, an associate professor at the college, for the uncertainty and snowbanks of Maine.

I had interviewed twice, in January and February, the only times I had visited Maine. I had always considered the state, when I thought about it at all, as New England's Siberia. By the second month of winter, Portland was under siege from the snow. I had not seen banks of plowed snow more than six feet high since New England's crippling "Blizzard of '78." In Portland, icicles were also measured in feet. Many residents had forgone gutters, I learned, to avoid ice dams from melting and freezing snow. Icicles hung from rooflines, like the stalactites in caves that we learned about in grammar school. Then there were the homemade signs nailed to telephone poles: "Roof Shoveling, Call ——." Even in southern New England I hated winter. "Thank God another January is over," I used to say each year as I counted the days until the Red Sox began spring training. Now I was venturing to a place where the temperature averaged ten degrees below Providence and six feet of snow fell in a typical winter.

There were compensations, I had concluded, when I accepted my new position. With ten thousand students, the University of Southern Maine was a rapidly growing institution. It was located in a booming area anchored by a beautiful city that *New England Monthly* magazine had recently named the best place to live in the entire six-state region. After a national search, I had been chosen as the director of a new interdisciplinary graduate program with a focus on the study of New England. My doctorate was in American studies; I held a joint appointment in the history and English departments at "RIC"; and my research and publications focused on colonial New England. "You're our man," the chairman of the search committee had indiscreetly said to me after the first round of daylong interviews. "You'll hear from us soon."

I was not eager to leave Rhode Island, where most of Dorothy's family lived and where we both had job security. I had only responded to the Maine advertisement to see if I would be offered the position. Then, offer in hand, I would approach the RIC administration and ask for a modest raise to my low salary. Such a practice was common among research universities, which regularly tried to poach outstanding professors. I was soon reminded that I labored far from that grove of academia.

Between my interviews in Maine, I went to see RIC's academic vice president. He and I had a good relationship. When he first arrived on campus in 1983, we had spent three days together at a conference at Carnegie Mellon University in Pittsburgh. We represented RIC, which was one of eleven colleges and universities from across the country engaged in a yearlong study of undergraduate education. At the time of our visit to Pittsburgh, the RIC administration had recently approved my early tenure and promotion to associate professor after only four years rather than the customary seven. Thus, I was shocked by what happened during my meeting with the vice president.

He occupied a spacious office in one of the uniform tan-and-clay-colored brick buildings that defined the not unattractive 1960s campus. The vice president sat behind a large mahogany "power" desk. I didn't ask for a pay raise, though RIC might have kept me for a lousy three thousand dollars. I had become increasingly intrigued with the Maine position, but I was unsure the new program would take wing. I gave the vice president the details about the job that would soon be offered to me and then requested a one-year leave of absence.

I thought he might say something like "We'd be sorry to lose you." Or perhaps, "If things don't work out after one year, we'd gladly welcome you back." After all, RIC would lose my wife too, a highly respected member of the faculty. Instead, he turned on me. "You can't go out and find a job and expect me to put a safety net under you."

"Look," I said, "this is an opportunity, but it carries high risk. I'll have to build something from the foundation up. Besides, I have two faculty positions to consider — my wife's and mine."

"A leave of absence will set a bad precedent, faculty trawling for jobs and then asking me to provide security," he countered. The vice president made it sound as if RIC's most immobile faculty, tenured senior professors, regularly received job offers. I was actually fortunate. I had certain credentials that appealed to a search committee trying to fill an unusual position.

The vice president was showing me the door—and, in effect, Dorothy too. I left his office humiliated, stung by his dismissive words. At that moment, I knew I had to leave RIC for good.

When the second series of interviews with faculty and administrators was completed a month after my initial visit to Maine, I persuaded myself that the new position was custom tailored for me. Never mind that I possessed not a minute of administrative experience, which I had viewed as an academic sand trap for someone who loved teaching and scholarly research and writing. My new position entailed hazards beyond my lack of administrative experience. The master's program claimed no students, faculty, or curriculum. It would require writing major grant proposals for program development. Such grant writing, like auto mechanics, had escaped my graduate education. I confronted an additional problem: I would have to earn tenure again, and do so within three years. After surviving three Maine winters, I might be sacked.

Then there were the family issues. Dorothy would have to get her career back on track. At a very awkward age, Antonia would have to adjust to a new high school.

In February, I tossed all these challenges in the shade, aided by a substantial increase in salary. By late June, they seemed staggering. I had been far from the best student in my family. I had grown up in the 1950s and '60s as a "jock" in down-on-its-luck Fall River, Massachusetts, once a mighty textile manufacturing center. While navigating through my teens, I had frittered away far too many hours on the ball fields and street corners of the city's Flint section—a timeworn mill village in Fall River's East End. Immersion in sports had enabled me to temporarily give the slip to my older brothers' daunting academic shadow. Whether as an undersized athlete in high school or as a poorly prepared student in college and graduate school or simply as an offspring of Flint Village, I always felt I had to work harder, always had to prove myself. In snowbound Portland I would have to do it again, with the stakes higher than ever.

After my third panic-filled night, Dorothy sent up a flare for help. She called a friend who worked at Bradley Hospital, a psychiatric center in East Providence. He said he would approach a young psychiatrist whom he liked if I were willing to go. Dorothy turned to me. "Bud Bloom says that he might be able to quickly arrange a visit with a psychiatrist at Bradley. Do you want to go?" "Yes." Bud apparently made it sound to the psychiatrist as if I might leap from my five-story campus office building. We received an appointment for early the next morning.

Another night of distress followed, and then we set off for the hospital. I remained baffled by my sudden paralysis as the day for departing Rhode Island drew nearer. I filled out some forms and then Dorothy and I were directed into what seemed like a small conference room. Within minutes, the boyish-looking psychiatrist strode in briskly, followed by an even younger man, a social worker I learned after introductions. The psychiatrist asked me to explain what was happening. When I finished he posed a series of questions. "How long have you been married?" "Seventeen years." "How long have you been at your current job?" "Nine years." "Do you abuse alcohol or drugs?" "No."

Having established what I gathered were the basic elements of stability in my life, he pivoted with the fourth question. "What happened to you on your first day of school?" I had an instant flashback to my neighborhood Brown School, filled with mostly working-class Portuguese and Italian kids. "I cried and clutched my mother."

This moment resembled a historical discovery, the realization of a narrative thread that enabled me, after months or years of research, to braid complementary strands of evidence into a coherent story. I had a mini-panic attack on my first day at Brown School in 1950—a fear of leaving the protectiveness of my mother, even though my two older brothers would be on the scene of separation. I now recalled other near or minor panic attacks when faced with major change, such as leaving Fall River for college, when I had teetered on the verge of reenacting in some way what happened at five years of age.

There was still more self-discovery during this brief encounter with a skilled psychiatrist. He explained how in his practice he found that people who cried on their first day of school were less able as adults to cope with life's major turns: a divorce, a death, a relocation, or a new job. "Where are you from?" he asked. "Fall River." "You live in Cranston. Do you see? The first time you tried to get away you only made it about twenty miles."

My panic attacks vanished after the session with the psychiatrist. Of course, I continued to feel anxious about what awaited me—along with Dorothy and Antonia—in Maine. I departed Rhode Island for the North Country, the only one of my parents' children to leave Fall River or its close quarters. Dorothy and Antonia rode in one car. I followed in the other with our beloved Beagle—and not me—tranquilized in the backseat for the three-hour drive to Portland.

One visit to a psychiatrist, however adept he proved to be, could not enable me to fully understand let alone resolve long-standing conflicted feelings about my background and about Fall River. I had lugged my love-hate affair with the city away to college side by side with my brand-new Olympia typewriter. I then hauled my interior conflicts off to graduate school followed by an ultimately unsustainable "rest stop" twenty-five miles from Fall River. In the trek to Maine, I gained geographical and emotional distance from my safe, familiar world. I was all but compelled to take the measure of the attachments I had left behind. Long, subzero Maine winter nights led inward, and I pondered how I had been borne along on life's unpredictable currents. "You brood too much," Dorothy often observed. "You're such a brooder" was her alternate refrain. Butting heads with such Puritan sages as Cotton Mather and Jonathan Edwards year after year held consequences for me. In fact, I came to realize that my academic specialization on Puritanism and colonial America represented a search for the "real" New England and an escape from the ethnic Catholicism of my youth in Fall River. I am getting ahead of myself, however.

This memoir represents the story I now tell myself in quest of the kind of understanding about the past and the present that a psychiatrist imparted to me twenty-five years ago. Most personal memoirs entail a story of self-discovery. But they usually record much more. Tug one narrative thread and another springs loose. Here I single out one of those threads in the stories that make up this memoir: a narrative about Fall River, more than just another run-of-the-mill New England industrial city. Distinctive Fall River shaped who I am, yet it was a place that I tried to "run away" from, like the cellar rats in my childhood triple-decker, for years.

I now know and accept that though I have long left Fall River, the city has not left me. Fall River is more than a storehouse of memories and formative experiences. The city is in my bones. Its rolling hills and granite mills, and its forests of triple-deckers and tribes of ethnic Catholics—these things that filled my world are still in the blood.

I need to start with a sketch of how Fall River became Fall River. After all, I am a historian by trade, and I can't simply crawl out of my skin. I need to rough out the Fall River story because we baby boomers were never told what happened to the diminished city we inherited. Above all, I need to boil down Fall River's distinctive story because the city's history is so intertwined with my own. In the 1890s, my Azorean and Calabrian grandparents wagered their lives in what was then the cotton cloth capital of America. My parents, siblings, and nearly all of my numerous aunts, uncles, and cousins chose to live in or next door to the city of "hills, mills, and dinner pails," as Fall River came to be known. Most summoned the determination to successfully make their way in a place that had fallen on hard times beginning in the 1920s. I fully expected to join them. No wonder I initially managed to stray barely half an hour away.

SPINDLE CITY

Too many stories about Fall River begin with Lizzie Borden, who has often seemed to own the franchise on the city's history. It is more fruitful to start with the Quequechan River, at scarcely two miles long, one of the more modest but hardworking millstreams in all of industrial New England. The Quequechan flowed through the heart of Fall River; it also coursed through my early life. We lived near the heart of Flint Village, the city's largest mill district, which overspread the Quequechan's rock-ribbed banks and mud flats in Fall River's East End. I crossed the river hundreds of times, on foot or in a car, before I left Fall River for college. During the summer I worked in steamy mills along the Quequechan to help pay college expenses. After I graduated I taught for two years in a Portuguese Catholic school, Espirito Santo, which squatted on the north bank of the Quequechan. From kindergarten to eighth grade, the school was filled with the children of immigrants and kids who had been born in the Azores.

In 1954, when I was nine years old, an engineering report summarized the consequences of Fall River's historic abuse of the river: "It is our opinion that the quality of the water in the Quequechan River is unfavorable for anything but the roughest industrial usage and furthermore is an ever-present health menace to the inhabitants of the City of Fall River." I was too young to be aware of this report. But my brothers and I did not need engineering consultants to tell us that we lived less than a half mile from a sludgy, toxic millstream.

The Quequechan partially redeemed itself in downtown Fall River, where it made a dramatic plunge toward Mount Hope Bay. The Pocasset Mill, a six-story granite cotton manufactory built in 1846, had harnessed the power of the Quequechan's "Great Falls," which plummeted sixty-eight feet into what became the center of Spindle City. In 1928, one of Fall River's most devastating fires had reduced the mill to rubble, exposing the falls to public view. The Pocasset Mill's ruins were still visible in the 1950s and '60s, as Fall River antiquities that recalled an era when the city rode the rapids of industrial capitalism to national distinction. The falls bestowed some welcomed natural dignity on downtown Fall River. On every childhood visit to Main Street, the falls lured my brothers or my friends and me. We marveled at the power of the Quequechan and tossed stone residue of the Pocasset Mill into the cascading river's foam. The falls, the mill ruins, and their location in the center of the city gently reminded us that Fall River had not always been down-at-the-heels — had not always been as spent and listless as the unhurried water that flowed through Flint Village. I need to tell the story of such mementos of boyhood that echo through Spindle City's past.

I knew one major historical fact growing up: the strange name Quequechan is an English version of the Pocasset Indian word for "falling water" and "Fall River" is an adaptation of that translation. But I grew up unaware of what happened along our millstream. "Quequechan" actually designated a river that flowed over eight falls in less than a half a mile as it descended precipitously into Mount Hope Bay. The multiple falls transformed the humble Quequechan's geography, defining it as a distinctive, exploitable New England site. The river offered significant waterpower for industrial use at a coastal location with ocean access to major textile markets in New York City and Philadelphia. Little did I realize growing up that geography awarded Fall River another major advantage over expanding industrial centers north of Boston, along the Merrimack River. Baled southern cotton and mid-Atlantic coal for steam-powered mills could be more easily and cheaply delivered to Fall River than to major inland industrial cities. To reach Lowell and Lawrence, Massachusetts, and Manchester, New Hampshire, for example, ships had to travel around Cape Cod's extended arm. The early cotton manufacturers who clustered along the Quequechan discovered an additional competitive edge Fall River wielded over interior textile centers to the north: a more humid climate that increased the elasticity of cotton fibers, reducing breakage and slowdowns in production.

Geography dealt Fall River yet another hand that shaped the city's history, particularly its industrial trajectory. The Quequechan flowed near a long-disputed borderland, first contested by Plymouth Colony and Rhode Island, and then by Massachusetts and the Ocean State. After nearly two centuries of on and off wrangling and shifting boundary lines, the U.S.

Supreme Court finally settled the historic quarrel with a ruling in 1861. A year later Fall River, Rhode Island, was annexed to its larger Bay State namesake, forming the city's extensive South End. I hadn't a glimmer that this transformative annexation had taken place because no one ever mentioned it while I lived in Fall River. Yet I did develop some sense that with its proximity to Providence and Newport, Fall River was a kind of cultural satellite of the Ocean State, not just a cultural backwater of the Bay State. Most important, I would later learn, Fall River followed the Rhode Island industrial model of numerous small to midsized mills rather than the large planned textile centers that the well-financed, famous Boston Associates constructed in Lowell and Lawrence. These titans of industrial New England ceded to more common men a stream of less than two miles with a clunky, unpronounceable name.

The families who ushered Fall River into the industrial age left their imprint on the city long after their textile empire expired. When I was growing up, Borden and Durfee, the Romulus and Remus of industrial Fall River, retained one shred of their historic entitlement: their family names were still plastered across the city on mills, businesses, schools, streets, and houses in the "Highlands," Fall River's Nob Hill. The names of other pioneering Fall River industrialists, such as Chace, Davol, and Flint, persisted on mills. Except for Lizzie Borden and the Durfee for whom our high school was named, I knew nothing about Fall River's textile nabobs and neither did my brothers nor my friends. We simply possessed a bare-bones narrative that once prominent Yankee families had called the shots in Fall River, lived lavishly, made a hash of things, and then forsook the broken city. My Durfee High School yearbook from 1963, when I graduated, contains photographs or just names of the more than the six hundred members of my class. There is one Borden, two Durfees, and no Braytons, Chaces, Davols, or Flints. In my Fall River, descendants of families who founded and industrialized the city were almost as extinct as early New England's once prolific Great Auk. Who were these people whose historical privilege lingered over our lives?

The scrappy Yankees who rose to the top of Fall River's industrial order were pale reflections of the Boston Associates, who ascended from merchant princes to wealthy industrialists to Boston Brahmins. The enterprising families of middling means who set in motion Fall River's evolution into Spindle City were descendants of settlers from the old Plymouth Colony and especially from Rhode Island. They gave birth to a factory town that looked toward the Ocean State and away from the manufacturing communities of the Boston Associates. Early industrial Fall River was neither a planned nor a paternalistic place—a birthmark that continued to define the city even after it swelled into an industrial colossus rivaling Lowell and Lawrence as well as Manchester, New Hampshire.

Members of the Borden and Durfee families, large clans whose offspring lived both in Fall River and in nearby Rhode Island, initiated and aggressively pursued local industrial development. They, along with Chaces, Flints, and Braytons, were unable to follow the example of the Boston Associates. The Bordens, Durfees, and their affiliated local industrialists constituted families on the rise headed by enterprising men on the make. In a word, they were self-made individuals, not merchant princes or Brahmins in waiting.

The Borden-Durfee textile dynasty originated with men accustomed to callused hands and dirt under their fingernails. Angling for advantage, they combined their capital and augmented their ambition by repeated marriages between the two families. Consider Colonel Richard Borden (1795–1874) and Major Bradford Durfee (1788–1843), both of whom clung to their militia titles. Colonel Borden was married to a Durfee. In turn, Major Durfee, who descended from the Rhode Island Bordens, wed his second cousin—Colonel Borden's widowed sister Phoebe—in 1809. Borden was a ship carpenter who built vessels along the Taunton River. He also engaged in local trade, carting foodstuff and firewood to markets in Rhode Island. Major Durfee was a blacksmith and a ship carpenter.

In 1821, the colonel and the major, along with other investors, raised the modest sum of $24,000 to establish the Fall River Iron Works at the lowest falls of the Quequechan River, where it emptied into Mount Hope Bay. The Iron Works manufactured a variety of products for ships, including nails and hoops for whale oil barrels. The colonel, the major, and their partners soon expanded their investments to cotton mills on the falls of the Quequechan; they also established the American Print Works for dyeing cloth. The ingenious Durfee served as an untrained engineer, supervising the construction of cotton mills and dams that advanced the emerging empire of his Borden brother-in-law and their fellow investors along the Quequechan.

Tragically, Major Durfee died in 1843 from the effects of ferociously fighting a raging fire that consumed the center of Fall River. After his wife Phoebe Borden Durfee died in 1841, the major had married Mary Brayton. She inherited his estate. Mary Brayton Durfee turned her financial affairs over to her brother John, who shrewdly diversified her fortune in Fall River's burgeoning industrial infrastructure. She soon eclipsed all rivals as the richest person on the hill. After the death of Major Durfee, Colonel Borden continued his climb to the top of the heap. He invested in new mills, coal mining, railroads, and the beginnings of what became the famous Fall River Line in 1847. Along with Lizzie Borden the luxurious steamships of the Fall River Line would keep the city's name before the American public for generations. Originating in Fall River, the steamships shuttled well-to-do passengers — including Vanderbilts, Astors, and Belmonts — between Newport and New York City. Below deck the steamers transported finished cotton cloth to America's garment capital.

The Borden-Durfee enterprises suggest how the industrialization of Fall River embraced no grand communal plan, and certainly did not have the hundreds of thousands of dollars available to the Boston Associates. With limited capital Fall River's industrialists built small to midsized mills like their Rhode Island peers. On the banks of the Quequechan, self-made men presided over the birth of a potentially ruthless and destructive frontier industrial capitalism. Multiple corporations with their own typically modest-sized mills defined Fall River's industrial landscape. The mill town's small-time textile pioneers seized their main chance. They also found ways to bridle the self-destructive cutthroat competition of men on the make. Fall River's emerging industrial elites intermarried and formed interlocking directorates in the city's mill corporations. The Bordens, the Durfees, and then their Brayton in-laws astutely consolidated control over finance and transportation, including railroads. Over time, the Yankee elites would continue to fortify their economic stranglehold on Spindle City through an intricate latticework of family and corporate ties.

Unlike the Quequechan, the more expansive Taunton River was not a continual presence in my life. As the western boundary of the city, it was too far from where I lived in the East End. For a century the Taunton River had served as an industrial sewer like the smaller Quequechan. The fates of the two rivers were as linked as the economic fortunes of the Bordens, Braytons, and Durfees.

After World War II, Somerset, a farming town on the opposite bank of the Taunton River, slowly developed into a suburban escape from Fall River. Growing up I knew no one who lived in the raised ranches with shag carpeting and rumpus rooms, or the Capes and faux colonials that sprouted in what had been cornfields. I seldom crossed the river—except in the summer of 1963, before I left for college. My godfather and uncle by marriage, "Tippy" Carreiro, was the business agent for the local steam-fitters union. He managed to get me a good-paying job as an apprentice steamfitter constructing the Brayton Point Power plant in Somerset. There I earned money for college by making a bad show of acquiring the skills of a steamfitter. It took me a while to get with the manly program: sauntering out on twelve-inch-wide steel beams with nothing beneath me. If panic seized me, I heard whispers of "Chicken Boy." When I stood at least fifty feet off the ground, I received hazard pay—an extra fifty cents an hour, a penny per foot, a half a cent for a hundred feet, and so on.

As the Brayton Point Power plant rose that summer, I sometimes stepped outside on the fifth or sixth level and gazed across the Taunton River and the bay, taking in a prospect that was new to me. (Interstate 195's Braga Bridge, which soars over the Taunton River and offers a majestic view of the city, did not open until 1966.) I scanned the scope of Fall River's waterfront industrial development that stretched from the narrow north end of the Taunton River to where it widened into Mount Hope Bay. For the first time I saw the city as something of a whole—the smokestacks and church steeples competing for attention; the triple-deckers crawling up granite terraces from the river; and the grit mingled with the natural beauty of a city atop a promontory by the sea. Less than fifty years earlier, the Taunton River would have bustled with coal barges and the luxuriously appointed steamers of the Fall River Line.

The second act in Fall River's industrial revolution encompassed the Taunton River. The city incorporated in 1854 with a population of twelve thousand. By that time, the Bordens, Durfees, and their associates had harnessed all the waterpower of the Quequechan's eight falls. The advent of the steam engine in the 1850s altered the geography of industrialization in Fall River and opened its floodgates.

The new technology still required access to water for making steam and cooling engines. But the steam engine substantially expanded the water sites available for industrial development. Fall River's corporations were more nimble in converting to steam power than their large, inland competitors along the Merrimack. For one thing, it was cheaper to transport to Fall River the tons of coal required for steam-powered mills. As they made the transition to steam power, Fall River's mill corporations moved beyond the Quequechan's falls, blanketing its firm banks and mud flats with mills that stretched eastward toward the river's headwaters in the soon polluted South Watuppa Pond. And now the steam engine propelled rapid industrialization along the shores of the Taunton River and Mount Hope Bay. Indeed, the city's official seal, adopted in 1854, shows the Taunton River with smokestacks—one of Fall River's calling cards and a symbol of industrial progress—proudly, even boastfully, billowing soot over the skyline.

With the rise of steam power Fall River's old and newly formed textile corporations maximized the city's geographic advantages over its inland competitors to the north. Between 1870 and the turn of the century, upstart Fall River embarked on a journey that took it from modest textile town to Spindle City—the major manufacturer of cotton cloth for printing in the nation. Between 1871 and 1872 alone fifteen new textile corporations were organized and twenty-two mills constructed. By the end of the century, forty-three corporations with inbred interlocking directorates formed Spindle City's kinetic textile world. They controlled more than a hundred mills in one of the most heavily industrialized landscapes in New England; these mills were a manufacturing behemoth that had arrived in a jumble, without any communal vision or master plan—except the drive to corner the market on the production of coarse cotton cloth for printing.

I grew up with mills in my backyard, yet I didn't know as I passed the signposts from grade school to grad school that Fall River's granite industrial architecture reinforced its distinctiveness as a New England manufacturing city. From Connecticut to Maine, redbrick buildings defined the face of industrial New England. Even nearby New Bedford evolved as a redbrick city. From mills to boardinghouses, the Boston Associates constructed their planned communities redbrick by redbrick. In the main,

Fall River's industrialists spurned brick in favor of granite. A dense, gray granite, industrial landscape engulfed the city.

The corporations constructed their textile empire in granite because it was so readily available. Several granite mills were erected along the Taunton River. But here redbrick made a last stand against gray granite. It was costly and time consuming to haul blocks of granite from Fall River's hills to the waterfront. Corporations found it easier and cheaper to import bricks by water from kilns outside the city. "Above the hill," however, Fall River remained a cityscape created from a palette dominated by shades of gray. Durfee High School, city hall, the public library, and a large commercial block in the center of Fall River were all constructed of gray granite.

It was the granite mills, however, that commanded the skyline. The post–Civil War scramble to achieve market dominance in the production of coarse cotton cloth spawned dozens of mills, many of them from four to six and a half stories high. With labor cheap and granite plentiful, corporations often erected impressive architect-designed buildings. Among Fall River's most imposing mills were Italianate structures with church-like bell towers that rose above rooflines. Fine wooden features — brackets, cornices, eaves, and window frames — painted in stark white complemented the gray granite. Fall River's grandest mills, often emblazoned with a family name, took imaginative shape as granite odes to the profit margin and to the city's seemingly endless industrial horizon.

Though educated as an American studies historian with a focus on New England, I kept my intellectual distance from Fall River's past until recently. I became a specialist on colonial history, an era when New England seemed to me more New England, more the genuine article. Gradually I realized that growing up in Fall River had informed the choices I made about a career, the places where I went to study, and the time periods and subjects I decided to pursue as a student and teacher of American studies.

And yet I continued to resist examining the Fall River story that we were never told. There are a few scholarly studies of Fall River's past; they all focus on the city's tempestuous labor history. In preparation for writing this memoir, several years ago I finally decided to read them before turning to the works of local historians and numerous newspaper accounts. From historian Mary Blewett in particular, I learned how it required much more than elite intermarriage and interlocking directorates for Spindle City's Yankee overlords to ride herd on their multiple corporations operating sundry mills.

It was primarily the second generation of corporate cousins who fashioned what Blewett describes as a distinctive "Fall River Industrial System." Through institutions such as the Board of Trade and the Fall River Cotton Manufacturers' Association, mill owners crafted and enforced a set of flinty Yankee practices. All New England textile manufacturers benefited from a protective tariff on imports that stood at 40 percent in the 1880s. Within this protectionism, Fall River manufacturers specialized in the production of coarse, gray cotton cloth that needed to be bleached before it could be printed. Fall River's mills were constructed of gray granite, but Spindle City was built on gray cotton cloth. ✓

The city's numerous mills turned out far more cloth than local print works could handle. Possessing clear transportation advantages over rival cities, Fall River supplied both coarse, gray cloth and printed goods to markets throughout the Northeast. With a vast production capacity, Spindle City's multiple corporations dominated their corner of the textile market. Overproduction kept goods cheap, thereby discouraging potential competitors. The Fall River System also squeezed mill workers. The corporations exploited loopholes in a ten-hour workday law passed in Massachusetts in 1874. They also managed to evade child labor laws, often with the complicity of desperate immigrant families. But the principal way that the Fall River System affected textile workers was by keeping wages ✓ low. In other words, specialized overproduction, low prices, and slender wages formed the warp and woof of the Fall River System.

Still, there was more. The mills regularly relied on that hardy perennial of labor relations in Spindle City: the wage cut. When the economy slowed or profits did not meet projections, the mills uncorked wage reductions. If a strike ensued, as it often did, the corporations always had an inventory of cotton goods to help them withstand the strife. A rancorous strike that began in 1904 lasted six months. Among New England textile cities Fall River came to be known as a place of measly wages and chronic labor discord.

One headstrong man challenged the Fall River System, though he was unable to dethrone its kingpins: Matthew Chaloner Durfee Borden —

M. C. D. Borden to the public, "Matt" to his employees. Interestingly, growing up I never heard of M.C.D., the most powerful and accomplished of all the Fall River Bordens, even though I passed fleeting seasons of my youth in the Boys' Club he had built for the city. In the early twentieth century, the club's basketball teams had "M. C. D. Borden" inscribed on their uniforms. He became part of a history that Fall Riverites had forgotten, or perhaps more precisely, that they preferred to forget.

M.C.D. was the youngest son of Colonel Richard Borden and a distant cousin of Lizzie. He followed the custom of the country and married a Durfee in 1865. It is one of the ironies of Fall River's history that M.C.D. surpassed his ancestors and siblings as the most dynamic and distinguished Borden the city had ever seen, at the same time that Lizzie brought far-flung dishonor to the family name.

M.C.D. built and ran his Fall River textile empire from New York City, where he had started out as the sales agent for the old American Print Works, which he renamed the American Printing Company. Beginning in 1886 he acquired sole ownership of the company and then of the adjacent Fall River Iron Works. His father and Major Bradford Durfee had spearheaded both enterprises. Borden demolished the Fall River Iron Works buildings, opening up nearly twenty acres on the Taunton River waterfront for new industrial development. He was determined to wrest as much control of the coarse cotton cloth market as he could from the architects of the Fall River System, some of whom were his relatives. M.C.D. despised the system because local mills often drove hard bargains before they agreed to supply cotton cloth to his American Printing Company. Such tactics more than rankled; they inflamed the Borden competitive spirit. He resolved to create his own massive cotton mill complex on the banks of the Taunton River, using his financial and marketing connections in New York to advance his plans.

Between 1889 and 1904 Borden constructed seven large cotton mills on the Iron Works site and added buildings to the American Printing Company. By the time Matt Borden was done he had created by far the largest cotton mill plant in Fall River with perhaps an unrivalled capacity in the country to produce, bleach, and print cotton cloth. Once all of his mills were up and running, each week the Borden complex processed 1,500 bales of cotton, produced 100,000 pieces of printed cloth, and consumed 1,600 tons of coal. It also employed six thousand people, who were paid the highest textile mill wages in the city. Whenever he could, he avoided the sudden slashing of wages that was so common in the city. His expansive, planned industrialization of the Fall River waterfront and his paternalism resembled the earlier efforts of the Boston Associates. In 1895, he even donated $100,000 to Fall River for charitable purposes, including the Boys' Club.

For all the gauntlets that he hurled at the feet of Fall River's manufacturers, Borden still followed the local practice of concentrating on the production of coarse cotton cloth rather than diversifying his goods. The Fall River System depended on a steady supply of cheap, unskilled labor. Even though Borden paid higher wages, his mills also relied on unskilled hands. During the decades when the Fall River System coalesced and Borden was planning and executing his revenge, not only did the city's population soar, but also it was transformed from an English-Irish community to a predominantly French-Portuguese place.

Athletic trophies, not scholastic achievement, buttressed my adolescent sense of self-worth. Participation in local sports, along with a wintry stint in an Irish Catholic school from grades 6 through 8, exposed me to Fall River's historic ethnic tribalism. The summer of 1960 marked my last year of Babe Ruth League baseball in Fall River's Flint section, where Francos constituted the largest ethnic group. At the end-of-the-year banquet, my coach took me aside. "Joe, I'm sorry to have to tell you that you'll not receive the 'Most Valuable Player Trophy.'" The award was named for a local French Canadian standout athlete who was killed in World War II. "You see the coaches and league officials thought that the trophy should be given to a Franco youth," he went on. "But you're gonna receive an 'Achievement' trophy." He had obviously argued my case forcefully. Angered by the way ethnicity influenced what happened, he must have persuaded his peers to create another award, which he probably paid for out of his own pocket. "You clannish French bastards," I wanted to yell. "You think you own the Flint."

Three years earlier in the small Italian section of the Flint, I had received the "Pat Mauretti Trophy" sponsored by a local grocer and given by the

Columbus Little League to the most valuable player. Then, in 1962, I was awarded the "Donald Trevisano Trophy," named for a local Italian athlete who became a naval pilot and was killed in a crash in 1955. The award went to the outstanding lineman on Durfee High's football team. My coaches chose me, a five-foot-seven, 165-pound guard, who usually butted heads with much bigger linemen. I am sure that the coaches were swayed in part by the fact that the Italian American War Veterans presented the award and the ceremony would be held at the Sons of Italy Hall on my home turf in Flint Village.

At the time I did not fully understand, or I refused to believe, that anything beyond merit determined my awards. But no sentient mortal who grew up in Fall River during the 1950s and '60s could fail to see that ethnic loyalty flourished throughout the local civic ecosystem. In early September of 1970, I held a part-time morning job tending coffee, soda, and snack vending machines at two mills on the Quequechan River. Pope Paul VI announced that Bishop Humberto Medeiros of Brownsville, Texas, a teenage Portuguese immigrant to Fall River who had entered the priesthood in the city, was the new archbishop of the Irish-dominated Diocese of Boston. The Portuguese mill workers were ecstatic the next day. "The pope has finally stuck it to the Irish! The pope has finally stuck it to the Irish!" one gloated to me. The Franco mill hands were less enthused, pleased that the Irish chokehold on the diocesan hierarchy had been broken but disappointed that a Portuguese immigrant had vaulted over one of their own. The ethnic fracases, tribal grievances, and racial divisions that accompanied the rise of Spindle City remained etched into my Fall River's collective consciousness.

Explosive immigration accompanied the spurt of mill construction that followed the Civil War. In the decade after 1865, Fall River's population surged from less than eighteen thousand to more than forty-five thousand. During the 1890s alone, the city absorbed in excess of thirty thousand people to stand at a population of 104,863 at the turn of the century. The federal census of 1900 confirmed that among cities of one hundred thousand or more, Fall River had the highest percentage of immigrants in the country. The census conferred another distinction on Fall River. With more than twenty-six thousand textile workers, the city had far more mill hands in its workforce than its nearest competitor (Lowell). Fall River was a culturally diverse — and divided — place, and overwhelmingly a one-industry city.

Labor unrest wracked Fall River from the rapid industrial expansion of the 1870s through the convulsive six-month strike that erupted in 1904. Irish and English workers were the first large immigrant groups attracted to the city. Famine Irish labored at mostly unskilled textile jobs and helped build mills and lay out railroads. English immigrants from Lancashire were the most skilled and combative newcomers to Fall River. Operators of mule spinning machines, weavers, and loom fixers, for example, were jealous of their crafts. They were also schooled in labor militancy and coiled to contest the Fall River System. Craftsmen instigated resistance to a cotton cartel that rejected paternalism, wrung profits from workers in hard times by cutting wages, and tried to ride out labor insurgencies. Worker combativeness and class consciousness did trickle down in Fall River to an unskilled labor rank and file that was ethnically divided.

Though English and Irish immigrants continued to make their way to Fall River after 1870, the peopling of Spindle City shifted. As the granite mills multiplied and the corporations cobbled together their system of massive production of coarse cotton goods, the demand for unskilled workers swelled. Most textile jobs required no special skill. The Fall River System crystallized when the corporations found a steady supply of unskilled immigrants willing to work for low wages and to survive by bringing their children into the mills. At first French Canadians and then the Portuguese dominated the immigrant influx into Fall River. Though eighteen different nationalities were represented in the federal census of 1900, Spindle City's textile empire came to rest heavily on the backs of French and Portuguese men, women, and children. Circumstances compelled immigrant families to grind away long hours in muggy, lint-filled mills and to feel fortunate if textile work cost them only their youth.

When labor unrest roiled New England's textile centers in the 1870s, corporations looked northward to the distressed farming communities of Quebec for strikebreakers. In Fall River, and in other mill cities, a large permanent community of Franco immigrants began to take root. Franco workers came to be prized as more than strikebreakers. The unskilled, illiterate immigrants were willing to work hard at low wages. Most important, they had large families with many mouths to feed, but also with many hands to work. Agents for the mills recruited entire families, making adult work conditional on child labor. Not surprisingly, Francos in Fall River encountered ethnic hostility on the job. They also provoked antagonism within the Catholic Church.

One clash took place on a Sunday in March of 1887 at St. Joseph's Church in Fall River's North End. This recently industrialized stretch of flatland on the banks of the Taunton River stood directly below the rolling hills that plateaued at the so-called Highlands, where moneyed Yankees created their silk-stocking domestic refuge. The Francos arrived expecting a Mass in their native tongue. The Irish, who established St. Joseph's, showed up knowing that there would be only one service on this Sunday and their priest would lead it. When some Francos refused to leave, they were grabbed by their collars and dragged from the pews.

By 1900 Francos made up a third of Fall River's population. With the establishment of six French-speaking parishes in every corner of the city, Francos extricated themselves from the Irish and ethnic conflict at the parish level. However, they still feuded with the bishop when he failed to appoint French priests to their churches.

As the Francos had, the newly arrived Portuguese poured into the mills. The Portuguese, like Archbishop and then Cardinal Humberto Medeiros, were primarily immigrants from the Azores—the archipelago of nine volcanic eruptions, islands seemingly stranded in the middle of the Atlantic Ocean hundreds of miles from Portugal. New England whalers frequently stopped in the Azores on multiyear voyages during the first half of the nineteenth century. The Azoreans, "hardy peasants of those rocky shores," as Melville noted in Moby Dick, sustained themselves primarily through farming the limited cultivable land on their volcanic islands. Ship captains regularly recruited islanders into whaling. Many Azoreans were carried back to New England, especially New Bedford, where they formed the nucleus of Portuguese communities after abandoning the whale fishery. A century of ties between southern New England and the Azores fostered the mass migration of islanders to the thriving textile cities of Fall River and New Bedford, even as many of their compatriots sought opportunities in Brazil and California. A majority of Fall River's Portuguese came from St. Michael, the largest island in the Azores. The press of population against a finite acreage of good land dimmed islanders' economic prospects. The corruption and mismanagement of the Azores that emanated from Portugal further dampened the islanders' hopes, pushing tens of thousands off their ancestral land.

Portuguese immigration to southern New England increased during the last decades of the nineteenth century and then exploded between 1900 and America's entry into World War I in 1917. In 1905, there were seven thousand Portuguese in Fall River. Fifteen years later the city's Portuguese had more than tripled; they represented nearly 19 percent of Fall River's population. The Portuguese constituted Spindle City's largest immigrant group by 1920. (Many Irish and Francos were already second- or even third-generation native born.)

Mill agents funneled unskilled, often illiterate Azoreans into low-level textile jobs that Francos had dominated. In other words, the impoverished new immigrants threatened to undercut the Francos, just as the latter had seemed to imperil English and Irish workers a generation earlier. The mill yards and streets of Fall River became scenes where ethnic enmity boiled over into violence. "Portuguese and French Canadians Collided in French Town with Serious Results," a local newspaper announced in 1896 over a story that provided readers with bloody details. Pitched battles became common as the Portuguese population surged, and so did accounts of Fall River's "Race Wars" in which ethnic antagonists were armed with rocks, clubs, and knives. Four years earlier when Lizzie Borden's parents were butchered, initial suspicions focused on two Portuguese immigrants, one of whom was arrested and then released.

The Portuguese posed more than a new economic threat to worker solidarity in Spindle City. They also complicated Fall River's racial politics. Though the complexion of the new immigrants varied, on the whole the Portuguese formed the largest dark-skinned population in the city. Portugal had been the second-leading slave-trading nation, with the bulk of its human cargo deposited in Brazil. The Azores had long been a site where some racial mixing occurred, though African slavery never amounted to much on the islands. Azoreans, a colonial population, considered themselves Portuguese and therefore white. They knew that black Portuguese originated in former slave societies such as Angola, Brazil, and especially the Cape Verde Islands off the coast of West Africa. Cape Verdeans, like Azoreans, had been enticed into the New England whale fishery. Beginning in the late nineteenth century, Cape Verdeans were also recruited to work the cranberry bogs of southeastern Massachusetts. New Bedford had an established and growing black Cape Verdean community by the time immigration from the Azores spiked, and so did Providence.

The presence in southern New England of Portuguese-speaking Africans from Cape Verde only served to validate the self-image of Azorean immigrants as white. But others did not arrange the racial landscape that way. "Black Portagee" became Spindle City's equivalent of the "N word," a pervasive racial slur that endured into my youth, even in the Irish Catholic school I attended in the late 1950s.

In Fall River, the rising ranks of the so-called black Portagees gnawed at worker solidarity. Mill owners were interested in low-wage working families, not in playing a race card to undermine an already divided house of labor. Still, one local spokesman for Fall River's business community blamed the new immigrants for Fall River's high mortality rate, observing, "But the Portuguese are half Negroes anyway." Similarly a Columbia University doctoral dissertation on the Portuguese in southern New England, published in 1923, concluded that Azorean "immigration selects stock with a larger mixture of negro blood than is characteristic of their group as a whole." Azoreans toiled not only to earn a living in Fall River but also to win full membership in the white race.

Like the Francos who preceded them and the thousands of Poles who streamed into Fall River after 1900, low wages drove Portuguese families into the mills. To boost profits, corporations had long relied on child labor. Children and women were paid less than men for the same work. Mill agents and foremen became adept at evading ever-tightening child labor laws. Children often worked "off the books." Immigrant parents, dependent on multiple breadwinners, conspired in such evasions or devised their own. Parents commonly misrepresented their children's ages and pulled them out of school. When the Portuguese influx into Fall River began in 1900, probably more than 10 percent of textile workers in the city were under fourteen, the legal age for full-time work in Massachusetts. At fourteen, students decamped in droves from public schools, with many immigrant children, hampered by language and classified as slow-witted, having reached only the fourth or fifth grade. Consequently, the cotton cloth capital of America reached a new, though disreputable, milestone in 1917: it ranked as the city with the highest rate of illiteracy in the country.

Low wages, child labor, school dropouts, and illiteracy—as interlocking in the Fall River System as mill directorates—hobbled working-class social mobility across generations.

⅜

During my second year of teaching Portuguese kids within malodorous proximity of the Quequechan River, I was trying to decide where to attend graduate school to study American history and literature. Since my father had never learned to drive a car, there were plenty of nearby historical sites that attracted my interest but I hadn't visited growing up. Old Sturbridge Village in central Massachusetts was one. Assembled from buildings that originated in other locations, this living history museum represented pastoral life in New England circa 1840. Its Yankee village landscape was suspended in time—on the threshold of mass immigration and industrialization "when New England people were of our own blood," decried Harriet Beecher Stowe, the conscience of pre–Civil War America, "and the pauper population of Europe had not yet landed on our shores."

When Christmas vacation arrived I made the hour and half drive from Fall River to Old Sturbridge Village. A recent blanket of snow had perked up the landscape with its stark white village ensemble of churches, houses, businesses, and civic buildings. I had entered the imaginative terrain of Currier and Ives—the real New England preserved in a kind of giant snow globe, my face pressed against the glass. Though Fall River was only a short drive behind me, it seemed to belong to another country, not just another century.

The white village has been New England's iconic landscape. Its assemblage of Cape, colonial, Federal, and Greek Revival architecture seems to say, "Here abides the real New England." No wonder these building styles, revived and reinvented, have inspired residential development throughout the region for more than a century. The white village and its architectural spin-offs blinded me from seeing the "New Englandness" of the triple-decker landscape that encompassed my world.

In Fall River, triple-deckers far outstripped Capes and colonials. New England as a whole claimed the largest stock of triple-deckers in America, with most constructed during the decades of sustained immigration between 1890 and 1920. For at least two generations, extending from the late nineteenth century through World War II, a majority of New Englanders undoubtedly lived at least a part of their lives, as I did, in triple-deckers.

Fall River was not the triple-decker capital of New England. Worcester seemed to win that competition. But Spindle City did not lag far behind. Its mill corporations threw up cheap wooden structures when the demand for workers surged after the Civil War. In the 1870s and '80s, the mills deployed company housing to attract, control, and exploit families, especially French Canadian workers. Company tenements served as a condition of employment; mills deducted rent from pay; and labor contracts established eviction as the penalty for job actions.

By the 1890s, responding to a growing real estate market, speculators and private developers captured control of working-class housing from the clutches of mill corporations. Over the next three decades a new residential cityscape took shape — street after Fall River street crammed with triple-deckers that butted up against sidewalks and offered, at best, paltry patches of backyard grass. The triple-decker building boom endured over more than a generation for good reason. The multifamily structure offered a flexible form of housing to renters and owners in cities like Fall River with a mushrooming working class. Individual tenements were usually roomy enough to accommodate large immigrant families. The use of space could be adjusted as families expanded and contracted — newlyweds frequently moved into a spousal household, as my parents did, until they could strike out on their own. Boarders were often housed for extra income; my Azorean grandparents rented a room in their tenement to immigrants they knew from St. Michael. In Fall River's drawn-out strike of 1904, many tenements became vacant, in part because families combined households to survive. Family or ethnic ties often muted the tensions and conflicts of living in the bosom of dense triple-decker neighborhoods. Owners frequently occupied the first floor of triple-deckers, rented the other apartments to relatives or ethnic compatriots, and used the income to pay mortgages.

Spindle City came of age and persisted during my youth as a collection of inward-looking triple-decker mill villages with distinctive ethnic profiles. The expansive South End, which had originally belonged to Rhode Island, was heavily French with significant Irish and Polish communities. The East End, or Flint Village, was predominantly French with large Portuguese and

Irish populations and smaller groups of Lebanese, Russian Jews, Italians, and Greeks. The North End, or Border City, the last corner of Fall River to be industrialized, was home to Portuguese, French, and Irish neighborhoods. "Below the hill," in the center of the city, the Portuguese held sway.

Tribal markers appeared on civic space in Fall River's mill enclaves. My Flint Village contained public parks named for Lafayette and Columbus. The stigmatized Portuguese had to settle for a statue of Prince Henry the Navigator belatedly erected at a busy intersection "up the Flint," as it was called.

⸬

In September of 1953, Fall River celebrated its sesquicentennial. I was only eight years old, but I have vivid memories of the numerous festivities. After all, the city had few occasions for cheer in my youth. What I remember mostly is the colorful float-filled parade on a bright, warm Sunday in mid-September, a balmy display of how in southeastern Massachusetts summer surrenders slowly to fall. The parade route was thronged—two hundred thousand spectators lined the streets of the business district, reported the Fall River *Herald News*, by then the only local daily.

"The Fall River Story," a historical pageant staged nightly for nearly a week, was a centerpiece of the commemoration. A cast of 1,500 performers reenacted the city's history in Fall River Stadium—a tumbledown baseball park with a large, weathered, wooden grandstand. The stadium was wedged between a former granite quarry, called "Big Berry," and the Quequechan River. Any ball hit over the right field fence sailed into the river and sank to its grave in toxic muck. I attended the pageant and can recall musical scenes and dancers in old-fashioned costumes. But I was too young to grasp the interpretive arc of the historical performance, except for a vague sense that it was uplifting.

As part of the historic celebration, the Fall River *Herald News* published a special commemorative edition on September 19. I have since turned to the collectors' publication to understand the particulars of the "Fall River Story" that was told in 1953. It was an account of heroic men like Colonel Borden, of the glories of the Fall River Line, and of a time when the city's name meant much more than Lizzie Borden's hometown. The commemorative edition recited the history and contributions of the large and small immigrant groups whose descendants still defined the face of the city. Perhaps because the crackup of Fall River's textile empire was too recent, and therefore seared in collective memory, it needed no detailed retelling. I only grasped the enormity of what had happened to Spindle City when I immersed myself in its history.

Even as southern competition made inroads into New England's long-standing textile domain, Fall River's hard-shelled corporations failed to break old habits. They launched one final building boom to expand Spindle City's production capacity. Eight new mills were constructed between 1907 and 1910. Then in 1911, Fall River celebrated its Cotton Centennial, the anniversary of the city's first cotton mill. It had actually stood in the part of Rhode Island annexed to Spindle City only in 1862. The business district was festooned with decorations for a weeklong carnival that drew President William Howard Taft to the city. The president and others summoned visions of another century of steady industrial progress. But the Fall River System had already grown arthritic. Within two decades of the giddy centennial self-congratulation, Spindle City would be reduced to an economic ward of the state.

Fall River's industrialists had long shrugged off the threat posed by a South that had been decimated in the Civil War. Yet an emergent "New" industrial South began to attract capital and held some competitive advantages over places like Fall River, especially after 1880. States such as the Carolinas enticed investment with low wages, nonunionized workers, and especially meager taxes. Steady advances in technology reduced the skills gap between New England and southern textile workers. Inexperienced hands could be trained to operate machines like the Draper automatic loom, introduced in 1894. In the face of southern competition, Fall River's corporations resisted adequately diversifying their product line into finer fabrics.

They continued to concentrate on the manufacture of coarse, gray cotton print cloth. They also failed to adequately modernize their mills. Too often, the corporations cut wages and ramped up production in what became increasingly inadequate attempts to compete with the South. By 1905, the Carolinas and Georgia manufactured more cotton goods than Massachusetts. Five years later, the southern states, with newer plants and equipment than New England, produced more than a third of the nation's output of cotton textiles.

World War I enabled Spindle City to prosper on borrowed time. The war economy boosted production and employment. Then raw cotton shortages in the early 1920s inflated prices and earnings. Fall River's population surged to more than 130,000, a historic high, in 1922. Instead of investing profits from this era of prosperity in new machinery, the corporations paid handsome dividends to stockholders. These palmy times could not last. Spindle City was soon brought to its knees.

Beginning in the mid-1920s, Fall River's empire of gray cotton cloth imploded with jaw-dropping speed. The inflexible, shortsighted corporations were unable to fend off double-barreled competition from the South and from the growing popularity of imported silk and rayon, which increasingly left printed cotton dresses passé. Fashion taste shifted in the "Roaring Twenties," abetted by new mass advertising. The sophisticated, fashionable woman of the Roaring Twenties preferred clothing of silk and rayon. Confronted with southern competition and new fashions the American Printing Company, the once mighty enterprise of the now deceased Matt Borden, issued an ominous announcement in 1924. It was starting construction on a new plant, Borden Mills, in Kingsport, Tennessee.

The Great Depression arrived ahead of schedule in Fall River. Mills fell silent beginning in 1924. Eighteen mills folded in 1929 alone. A death rattle echoed through many others. Spindle City lost fourteen thousand people, nearly 11 percent of its population, between 1925 and 1930. Soon the city raised the white flag of insolvency.

The stock market crash and the onset of the Depression gave further momentum to the textile industry's collapse. Corporate taxes, assessed on the number of spindles in a mill, plunged. At the same time, unemployed homeowners could not pay their property taxes. Starved for revenue, Fall River declared bankruptcy in 1931. The state finance board took control of the city's fiscal affairs for the next decade.

Seventy-three mills ceased operations in Fall River between 1915 and 1940. Buildings fell into municipal hands in lieu of taxes. The city began advertising abundant, free mill space to prospective employers. Garment companies responded. Sewing machines gradually replaced cotton looms in Fall River mills. The Depression marked the beginning of the city's transition from cotton textiles to the "needle trades," the heavily female, low-wage manufacture of garments from dresses to raincoats and household items from curtains to bedspreads. The crucible of the Depression gave birth to Fall River's growth industry for the next generation—the "sweatshop," and its public face, the factory outlet store.

The city endured another setback during the Depression. The Fall River Line dissolved in 1937. Still, I would discover, its past glory remained preserved in literary references from Henry James to Henry Miller.

The most significant economic development in Depression-era Fall River also occurred in 1937. The Firestone Rubber Company purchased the vacant American Printing Company complex of buildings on the waterfront. Firestone created hundreds of jobs during good times. For more than a generation (before it too closed up shop), Firestone offered something almost as scarce in Fall River as unsullied waterways and millponds: good-paying, unionized jobs that enabled heads of households to support their families. Especially after production for World War II accelerated, Firestone and lesser companies that capitalized on Fall River's vast available industrial infrastructure helped stabilize the city's population temporarily at 115,000.

But the postwar economic slump, which again visited double-digit unemployment on Fall River, brought a return to the downward spiral of the 1920s and '30s. By 1960, the city's population had slipped below one hundred thousand for the first time since the 1890s. The cotton mills that had survived the textile meltdown of the Depression resumed the industry's flight to what would soon be labeled the Sun Belt. In 1961, there were only four cotton mills remaining in Fall River. No one that I can recall referred to it as Spindle City.

Many breadwinners who remained attached to the city's insular ethnic communities, like barnacles to a familiar rock, were forced to commute to places such as Boston, Providence, and Newport for jobs comparable to Firestone's. As the garment industry evolved into Fall River's dominant manufacturing sector, the city's workforce increased to nearly 50 percent female. The historic strategies that Fall River's families used for survival in a low-wage economy left a drag on the city as it was drop-kicked toward the postindustrial era. In 1960, Fall River's adult population averaged 8.6 years of education, among the lowest levels of schooling in the country.

History left its scars on Fall River's civic life, whose consequences I increasingly encountered as I matured. However, I failed to fully comprehend the cronyism that infected public life. The Yankee mill owners had controlled the reins of government for their own purposes. The Irish, who dominated city government and especially the school system, succeeded them. Cultural diversity remained a stable and durable thread in my Fall River's social fabric. Yet it often shaped the texture of a parochial political spoils system based on ethnic resentments and jockeying for advantage. In a postwar city plundered by Yankee lords of the loom and still listing, like a gale-tossed freighter, in the direction of the Great Depression, political influence and connections became the coin of the realm. A scramble ensued to get on the public payroll, particularly in the school system, which supplied one with steady employment without having to leave the city. I would aspire to become a local phys ed teacher and coach—a seemingly safe, attainable goal. Little did I understand how history, class, family, and Fall River itself framed that modest ambition.

The dissolution of King Cotton did not bring an end to generations-old abuse of the Quequechan River, the catalyst of Fall River's industrial odyssey. The Quequechan's picturesque falls in the heart of Fall River vanished in 1962. Instead of tossing burned-out mill residue into the tumbling river's foam, as I had for years, Fall River youth now fell back on another local rite of passage: defiantly hurling stones at the windows of abandoned and half-empty mills. Unable to reimagine the Great Falls as a natural asset for economic development and urban renewal, Massachusetts's highway planners decided that the Quequechan's most dramatic and historic feature stood in the way of Interstate 195. For the convenience of travelers to Cape Cod, engineers plotted a straight highway that drew a bead on the Great Falls. Water flowing toward the falls was diverted to underground conduits, burying a slice of Spindle City's history and a scrap of my youth.

❧ *Two* ☙

FAMILY MIGRATIONS

My immigrant forebears and their children have long ago completed their journeys from dust to dust. It is too late to make amends for blithely skating by my family's story for most of my life. Like Spindle City's history, I grew up with only patchy knowledge of my grandparents' ordeals: their flights from Italy and the Azores and their labors to survive before and after Spindle City's demise. I didn't fully comprehend my own parents' reverence for their parents. Nor did I appreciate what my parents endured to make their way in a one-industry city that had buckled under the weight of greed and southern competition.

Even after I became a professional historian of New England, I remained disengaged from my family's story—not to mention the larger drama of the mass immigration that transformed the region. I chose to specialize on early New England. Only much later did I realize that this decision partly represented a way of distancing myself from my family history, which always seemed inconsequential to the official pageant of America's past. Some mills grind slowly. I now see my choice as a denial of my roots—an attempt by an outsider from gritty Fall River to stride toward becoming something of an insider.

Fortunately, my oldest brother, John, interviewed my parents about our Italian and Portuguese family history and took helpful notes. We also discovered a few surviving family documents after my parents died. These pieces of evidence—fragments of multilayered lives—called on my skills as a historian to reconstruct as best I could another story that, like Spindle City's, I never knew or cared about. What follows is perhaps "burnt offerings" to my family.

The first member of my family who set foot in Fall River was a bastard. My grandfather, Salvatore Giuseppe Conforti, was the illegitimate son of a pharmacist in San Pietro, one of the rock-strewn hill towns in the province of Reggio, which is part of Calabria—mainland Italy's southernmost region. Beyond Reggio lay the Straits of Messina and Sicily, long a site of cultural crossings. As my grandfather entered his teenage years, he began to spend more time around his father's shop, much to the displeasure of the pharmacist's wife. In 1893, at the age of seventeen, Salvatore set out for America, his voyage perhaps financed by his father as a way of ridding a living irritant to his wife. The early 1890s marked an upsurge in southern Italian immigration to Massachusetts. Already *paesani* were staking a claim to Boston's North End. In the very year my grandfather left San Pietro and arrived in the Bay State, the popular New England writer Samuel Adams Drake seethed over what he observed at the Paul Revere House and its environs in the North End. "The atmosphere is actually thick with the vile odors of garlic and onions—of macaroni and lazzaroni," he erupted in a book titled *Our Colonial Homes*. "The dirty tenements swarm with greasy voluble Italians. One can scarce hear the sound of his own English mother-tongue from one end of the square to the other."

My grandfather bypassed Boston and made his way to Fall River because other immigrants from San Pietro, some of whom were related to him, had already settled in Spindle City. Historians call this chain migration—the human links that guide the destinations and destinies of people like Salvatore Conforti who dislodge themselves from their native soil and set their sights on a new world thousands of miles away. One earlier immigrant from San Pietro had moved to Fall River after living in New York, where he had been naturalized. He emerged as one of the first leaders of Fall River's small Italian community, meeting newcomers at the Fall River Line Pier and helping them find jobs and housing, usually in triple-decker tenements where groups of solitary male immigrants huddled together. My grandfather probably worked at a variety of jobs before he acquired the skills of a hatter, which would be his calling once he decided to put down roots in Fall River.

By the turn of the century, and now in his midtwenties, Salvatore was back in San Pietro, but he would not be one of the "birds of passage," the Italian immigrants who shuttled back and forth between the United States and the Old Country. Salvatore seems to have been on a personal mission: to secure a wife who would return with him and start a family in Fall River. He found his mate in Anna Juliano of San Pietro, a nineteen-year-old with striking features that would dominate the countenance of her nine children: an angular head and face, high cheekbones, and an earth-brown complexion that tanned easily and deeply. With Anna at his side, Salvatore returned to Fall River in 1901. They were married that year in Irish St. Mary's Church, the oldest Catholic parish in Fall River, which was located near the center of the city.

I know a good deal about the small Italian community that my grandparents joined in 1901 because my brother John wrote his master's thesis on its early history. Fall River's Italian population increased from less than a thousand in 1900 to a peak of 2,500 in 1910, after which it did not change significantly. Fully three-quarters of Fall River's Italians clustered in Fall River's East End—in and around Bedford Street, a major artery that extended two miles into downtown and formed one of the boundaries of heavily industrialized Flint Village. Fall River's Italians, however, were not first drawn to the East End for mill jobs. Instead, they came to work in the granite quarries operated by William Beattie and smaller competitors. "Quarry Street," which bisected Bedford, announced the kind of demanding and hazardous jobs that gave birth to a heavily southern Italian East End neighborhood.

Fall River's Italians tended to shun millwork, many preferring to labor outside. They were far less likely than the Francos and Portuguese to become mill hands. In 1900, for example, only 16 percent of Fall River's Italians labored in mills. The dominance of the textile industry discouraged large numbers of Italians from settling in Spindle City. Beyond the cotton mills, members of Fall River's small Italian community found work as laborers, masons, quarrymen, hatters, cobblers, barbers, and fruit dealers.

Though nearly all of his nine children, including my father, would dodge Fall River's textile mills and the sweatshops that supplanted them, Salvatore Conforti was not quite as fortunate. He did manage to steer clear of the cotton mills once he settled permanently in Fall River, but he ended up in a factory. He found a job at the James Marshall and Brothers Hat Factory, a four-story granite mill in the South End of the city, where an Italian was responsible for recruiting his compatriots. The hat manufacturer was one of Fall River's largest employers outside the textile industry, numbering more than 1,500 hundred workers by 1907. It produced twelve thousand felt hats each day. The company also made hats for women and children.

In 1903, shortly after my grandfather joined Marshall Brothers, a teenage Portuguese immigrant named Rose Silvia was the victim of the kind of horrific industrial accident that was all too common in turn-of-the-century Fall River. She was scalped down to one eyebrow. The revolving shaft of a machine snagged her hair and stripped the skin off her skull and most of her forehead. In what was undoubtedly considered a noble gesture for the time, the Marshall brothers hired four young men to give up skin from their arms and legs, and doctors attempted to graft the skin onto the young immigrant's head and face. But Rose Silvia was gruesomely disfigured for life. With no "worker's compensation," this immigrant daughter and sister slipped back into anonymity and undoubtedly to a life of family dependency.

My grandfather rose to be a foreman at the Marshall Hat Factory. He also supplemented his income by cleaning and restoring hats at home, since money was sorely, even desperately, needed for his growing family. My father, born in 1903, was Salvatore and Anna's first child to survive. They named him Orlando, but it was shortened to "Ollie" (pronounced Oh-lee) by his brothers and sisters. His unofficial name would become "Primo," the privileged first male in the patriarchal Italian family. My grandparents had eight more children over the next twenty years — three boys and five girls. They all looked up to my father as the oldest sibling who would become the second voice of patriarchy in the family. As my Aunt Natalie, the youngest of the nine children, told me, "I loved your father. He was like a second father to me." I would come to respect, fear, misunderstand, and sometimes feel embarrassed by him.

If gender and birth order defined my father's place in the family, he earned the respect of his brothers and sisters because he was the first Conforti to start a business — a barbershop — and he did so in the teeth of the Depression with Fall River still insolvent. Ollie would become godfather to many of his nephews and nieces, and as my grandparents passed into old age, he eased deeper into his role as the elder authority of the extended family. This deference provided compensations for his relationship with my mother, who cherished her own privileged position in her Azorean family. Their contest of birthrights, among other conflicts, would snare them in recurring marital strife that often drained affection from the household and put me on edge.

My father was a talker. He would carry on running conversations with customers in his barbershop over decades. He was not a writer. Even in the long years of retirement, he would scratch out only a few pages about his early life. They are the only family documentation of his formative years and of how he learned barbering.

My father was born on Orange Street, a working-class jumble of low-end triple-deckers, where he lived in a four-room apartment for thirteen years. As more sons and daughters arrived, my grandparents moved the family from tenement to tenement around the adjacent Bedford Street Italian colony. Then in 1922, after scrimping and saving for two decades, my grandparents purchased a small bungalow on Beattie Street, named for the owner of the large nearby granite quarry, which had seen its best days and would soon find new life as a public dump larger than a football field. The no-frills, laboring man's house was sited on a lot of nearly an acre. After two decades of tenement life, the Conforti family would now be able to live more like they believed Italians should. My grandfather laid out extensive vegetable gardens. He cultivated grape arbors and set up a wine press in an outlying shed. My grandmother raised chickens in addition to her brood of children. Salvatore and Anna acquired more land, purchasing an acre in an undeveloped section at Fall River's East End, about a half mile from their new home.

Growing up we were always told of my grandfather's capacity for work—and even his tolerance of pain—family folklore that was intended to cultivate our respect for his stooped, aged figure and Fall River fables to make us appreciate what we had. "Nonuzzo," as we affectionately called him, toiled in his vegetable gardens, including his distant field on some days, before he left for his day's work at the Marshall Hat Factory. Evening would find him back among his crops of zucchini, tomatoes, and cucumbers; cherry peppers, string beans, and kohlrabi; and sweet corn, basil, and romaine—to name some of the bounty I remember from my youth. "Once Nonuzzo had a really bad tooth but couldn't afford to go to a dentist," my father told us. "He loosened it with a knife and pulled the tooth out himself."

My father was nineteen when the family moved to Beattie Street. He recalled in his retirement jottings that two years after the property was purchased, my grandfather built an addition to the bungalow and installed a bathtub. "I was twenty-one years old, and I saw my first bathtub." To expand living space for the large family, the basement became a combination kitchen-dining-family room. A section of the basement was also partitioned into a bedroom. Family life for many Fall River Italians revolved around their basements, a link to the stone houses of places like Calabria. The basement of another bungalow, four blocks from my grandparents, would become the center of my family life beginning in 1955.

⊰⊱

My mother came from a fair-skinned, blue-eyed, propertied family with some claim to social status in the town of Pouvoacao on the island of St. Michael. But her immigrant family would live in a succession of Fall River triple-deckers and never achieve home ownership. My Azorean grand-mother, Alexandrina Faria, grew up on a farming estate with a comfortable, attractive house. Jose Bento, my maternal grandfather, lived on the same street with Alexandrina. Unlike her, misfortune fell his way, even though the Bentos also owned considerable farmland. His mother died when he was a boy. A stepmother who favored her own children mistreated Jose and his brother. My mother liked to tell a story that revealed her father's spunk at an early age and that suggested the source of her own feistiness when she went toe to toe with my father. When Jose was ten years old, "his stepmother was breast-feeding. One day she squeezed breast milk into a bowl, broke some bread in it, and handed it to him. He took the bowl and threw it at her." On his father's deathbed, the stepmother, urged on by her own children, bribed a lawyer to change an existing will so that Jose and his brother inherited land that amounted to little more than a pile of rocks.

After service in the Portuguese army on St. Michael, Jose married Alexandrina in 1889. He was twenty-five, she eighteen. Jose moved into his mother-in-law's house and managed her property. During the next eight years, Alexandrina gave birth to three children, including a son named for his father who died of pneumonia at eighteen months. More setbacks followed. Jose grew restive living under the thumb of his appar-ently overbearing mother-in-law. Among other things, she was stricter than he liked toward his son Manuel and daughter Maria. Jose resolved to strike out on his own.

In 1899, at the age of thirty-six, he joined the exodus of Azoreans who were departing for Fall River, leaving behind his wife, seven-year-old son, and one-year-old daughter. His goal was to earn money, return to St. Michael, purchase his own land, and free his family from his mother-in-law's imperium. But Jose's future would jump the tracks of his imagination.

He would never return to St. Michael permanently. He would trade an overbearing mother-in-law for an overruling cotton mill foreman.

On his first sojourn to Fall River, Jose stayed for three years. He boarded with a cousin on Columbia Street, which descended from Main Street below all of Fall River's hills to the industrial waterfront. Columbia Street was one of Fall River's first Azorean enclaves, as the new immigrants increasingly displaced Irish and French residents from the standard-issue, low-rent triple-deckers that marched down the hill to the American Print Works complex. Santo Christo, Spindle City's first Portuguese Catholic Church, was established on Columbia Street. Like Salvatore Conforti, Jose Bento found work at the Marshall Hat Factory for at least part of his first stay in Fall River. In the course of those three years, he changed his plans to return permanently to St. Michael, most likely influenced by the testimony to worsening conditions on the island from the rising tide of Azoreans arriving in Fall River. His change of heart was perhaps fired by the dream of buying his own house and land in a rapidly growing city where work was abundantly available, even for Portuguese adults and their children who spoke no English. Little did he know that he would never own an inch of soil in America, a double wound for a proud man who had already been cheated out of his father's land on St. Michael.

After three years in Spindle City, Jose sailed back to the Azores in 1902. He tried unsuccessfully to persuade my grandmother to return with him to Fall River, where island friends and relatives continued to settle. She did not want to abandon her mother, leaving the elderly woman dependent on a couple of hired servants. Once again, my grandfather displayed his gumption. I have his passport, which shows that he left St. Michael in 1905. He was forty-two years old and would spend the next four years exiled from his wife and children and from his native island, where the temperature hovered in the seventies during the summer and seldom fell below fifty degrees in winter.

Upon his return to Fall River, Jose found work with a man who held the contract to collect garbage in the city. Azorean immigrants had come to dominate this sordid line of work—but not without controversy. The contract with the city specified that only "resident citizens" were to be employed. At one point a headline in a local paper reported, "Board of Aldermen Desire American Citizens to Man Swill Carts." The image of the alien black Portagee inflamed the dispute over why resident citizens,

"Americans," were not hired for jobs paid for with public money. The local contractor insisted that he could not find American citizens willing to take the jobs. Some would work for a day or two and then quit, he claimed. The despised Portuguese, in contrast, were eager, dependable workers. The ethnically and racially charged wrangling subsided only after it was determined that Portuguese immigrants living in the city qualified under the resident citizens language of the contract. My grandfather was apparently spared the indignity of actually collecting swill—at least my proud mother did not reveal otherwise to my brother John. Instead, Jose labored on the contractor's farm in the North End, where there was a boardinghouse for workers. He tended the horses that pulled the swill wagons, mucking the stalls, barely tolerating the summer stench of garbage fed to pigs, and perhaps thinking that at least it beat collecting human slop all day long during Fall River's hot, humid summers and sometimes snowy winters.

Jose worked for the garbage contractor for four years. Then, in 1909, he received a letter from Alexandrina informing him that her mother had died. My grandmother was now willing to join her husband in Fall River. He returned to St. Michael, gathered up his thirty-nine-year-old wife, seventeen-year-old son, and eleven-year-old daughter, and crossed the Atlantic for the last time. The family moved into a tenement on Orange Street, two houses from where the Confortis lived—though the families only knew one another from a distance. Jose found work in the Durfee Mills, a short walk from Orange Street. This cotton cloth plant had expanded over the decades to a cluster of large granite buildings. A six-foot-high wrought-iron fence—the barbed wire of class conflict in Fall River—encircled the mill property; it even protected some textile barons' homes in the Highlands against labor unrest. The Durfee Mills stretched from the northern bank of the Quequechan River to Pleasant Street, which paralleled Bedford Street. The two major east-west thoroughfares helped define the boundaries of Flint Village. My grandfather would spend the next twenty-five years mired near the bottom rung of the textile mill hierarchy along with scores of other oft-despised Azoreans. He labored in the spool room, doling out yarn to machine operators and most likely nursing his disappointment with how his life had turned out.

Pleasant Street, where my grandfather spent the bulk of his working life in Fall River, was the city's oldest manufacturing district. The street was misnamed, and not only because of its industrial grit. During his two and a half decades in the Durfee Mills, Jose undoubtedly witnessed and heard about industrial accidents like the one that victimized a recent Portuguese immigrant in 1903. In the Crescent Mill, just down Pleasant Street from the Durfee complex, a twenty-four-year-old Azorean by the name of Jose Pacheco, who had been in Fall River only four months, was strangled to death. His shirt became caught in the shaft of a machine, which twisted it around his neck like a noose. When his mother was informed, she raced from her tenement in Flint Village a mile and a half away to the death scene. In desperation she took to the middle of Pleasant Street because the sidewalks were too crowded, dodging horse-drawn wagons and cars and wailing in her grief. She arrived at the Crescent Mill, and "her agonizing shrieks and cries resounded high above the machinery," a local paper reported in matter-of-fact newsprint. Jose Pacheco represented just another Portagee industrial casualty—an expendable immigrant cog in the Fall River System.

The Bentos weathered adversity but nothing like the anguish of Jose Pacheco's mother. A year after my grandparents settled in Fall River, they were buoyed by the arrival of my mother, their only American-born child, whom they named Agnes. She would never work in the mills; my mother occupied a privileged place in the family, and not just because she entered the world on American soil. The youngest child born to parents in their forties, she grew up to be pretty and smart, unlike her homely older sister who was of borderline intelligence and whose name was bleached of its immigrant blush. Maria gave way to "May" in Fall River.

Jack London described the Portuguese in 1913 as "these small brown skinned immigrants." I never fully appreciated how, from the Azores to America, the Portuguese became a marked people whose unstable racial identity apparently spurred the Bentos' overinvestment in their light skin and blue eyes. I have a revealing studio portrait of the reunited family taken in 1912, two years after my mother was born. With their fair skin, formal attire, and confidently cultivated pose, the Bentos hardly resemble penurious, recently arrived Azoreans. My grandmother and Aunt May are outfitted in formal gowns. Jose and his son Manuel are stylishly dressed in three-piece suits with the chains of fob watches showing. My mother, the Portuguese-American princess of the family, also sports a child's gown. She stands in the center of the photograph leaning for support on her parents.

The deluxe Bento studio portrait serves as a foil for an early Conforti family photograph that I also possess. (Both are included in this book's photograph section.) It is a posed but much more informal, spontaneous snapshot, with Salvatore and Anna's younger children unable to freeze themselves in place. They are photographed outside, in the backyard at Beattie Street, and their best off-the-rack clothes cannot compete with the sumptuously dressed Bentos. The photographs serve as visual shorthand for the social distinctions between the families — distinctions that would run like a tripwire through my parents' often volatile marriage. The studio portrait speaks to me of the Bentos' social and perhaps racial aspirations, their stake in respectability, even refinement, and their confidence that they would regain in Fall River the class standing they once claimed on St. Michael. Even as my grandparents failed to recover their lost world, my mother inherited their social quest in America. My fair-complexioned mother also confronted the second-generation dilemma of coming to terms with her ethnic heritage while proving to others that she was not just another Fall River "Portagee." This common ethnic slur, a kind of Portuguese equivalent of "Wop" or "Dago," usually referred to lower-class, poorly educated immigrants and their children. For some it served as an alternative to the more cutting "black Portagee."

After the reunited family settled on Orange Street, eleven-year-old May attended school for a few of years and reached the fifth grade. She never learned to write English. Years later, when I was away at college, she would occasionally scribble a few lines in badly mangled English at the end of letters from my mother. May's woeful efforts would reduce me to tears. She didn't have a chance in America. She was quickly dispatched to the mill, where she labored at low-skill tasks for six dollars a week. Eventually her full-time job became caring for her aged parents, while she began a lifelong dependency on my mother. By then their brother Manuel had left Fall River to start his own family in Pawtucket, Rhode Island, another former textile giant that was on the skids.

My mother attended Durfee High School for two years. She spoke perfect eastern Massachusetts–accented English and fluent Portuguese. In 1926, when she was sixteen, she took the only extended trip of her entire life. She sailed with her mother to St. Michael. My grandmother continued to own land on the island that yielded a little money for the family in America. She returned to settle problems that had arisen with the management of her property. Once back in Fall River, my mother increasingly served as a lifeline between her immigrant family and the larger non-Portuguese world. In her twenties, she found steady work in women's apparel stores on Main Street, where she conversed easily with customers in English and Portuguese. On summer evenings she served patrons across the concession stands at Fall River Stadium. During the Depression her modest earnings proved critical to the Bentos' survival, especially after the Durfee Mills succumbed to Fall River's textile meltdown in the mid-1930s and her seventy-one-year-old father never worked again.

From her late teens through her twenties my mother's good looks attracted numerous suitors. She was a petite five foot two with reddish brown hair, blue eyes, and light skin. One young man who pursued my mother, probably when she was in her early twenties, wrote her a long poem, "My Gal," which she must have cherished because we would find it among her few personal keepsakes when she died seven decades later. The author, named M. J. Boise, announces,

> Now I'll tell you all about my gal,
> the nicest in the town.
> She has eyes of azure blue, tho' she'd rather
> have them brown.
> She has beauty and is charming, of her clan
> like her there's none —
> She's a daughter of the Islands,
> while I'm a son of a gun.

For over a year Boise and my mother dated after a fashion. The poem records that she often turned down his invitations, citing family responsibilities as an excuse.

> My sister is an ailing girl — we must not keep her up.
> My father cannot do a thing, our boarder is at work —
> From head to heel it makes me feel like an old dejected Turk.

Boise describes his competition for her affections, and I wonder how many times she read his verse after she married my father and disappointment took up residence in her heart.

Now there are three and forty males
her beau would like to be:
They range in age from eighty-five
to boys in infancy.
Everyone that takes her home,
she tells them where they stand.
It was all right to take her arm,
but they could not have her hand.

"My Gal" offers a sentimental but revealing glimpse of my mother as a young woman that rings true: a pious daughter of immigrants, choosy and standoffish when it came to the opposite sex, devoted to her parents, and protective of her older, hapless sister. Then, approaching the age of thirty, she began a courtship with my father, who was seven years older and still living on Beattie Street.

When the Conforti family moved to Beattie Street in 1922, my father had been barbering full time for three years, and his earnings, however meager, undoubtedly assisted my grandparents' entry into the property-owning class. The family economy that prevailed among immigrant groups in Fall River operated on an ironclad custom: regardless of age, sons and daughters living at home turned their pay over to the household head. (I would learn this lesson when my father confiscated everything from newspaper route earnings to my summer pay when I was in college.)

Growing up, we were offered a steady diet of tales and advice from his school of hard knocks. He loved to remind us when we were in grade school, "I was cleaning out spittoons when I was your age." At the time, I did not fully appreciate that he was paid nothing for his first job, except the chance to learn barbering. Nor did I recognize the audacity, determination, and industry that he summoned to venture out on his own during the Depression, and to succeed in the highly competitive barbering world of downtown Fall River, whose vital signs were continually monitored by the state finance board.

For Fall River's Italians, the barbershop—like the cobbler shop, tailor shop, and fruit stand—offered an alternative to the mills, construction work, or quarrying granite and held out the promise of gaining a toehold in the middle class. My father learned barbering the old-fashioned way: through a kind of unpaid apprenticeship that began in 1914 when he was eleven years old. After school he would go to the shop of a low-end barber known as "Scabie Mike." For rock bottom prices customers received haircuts and shaves—and sometimes little itch-producing critters that hitchhiked under the skin. Not hygiene but tobacco chewing and spitting were Scabie Mike's strong suit. He positioned a spittoon right by his chair and reserved others for his waiting customers.

In this tonsorial hovel, young Ollie shouldered menial, even disgusting chores. "I would sweep the floor and clean spittoons," he recalled in his retirement scribbles. "I would take them to the toilet, empty them [and] put water in them with some barbanol[,] which was a disinfectant." My father also cut newspapers into squares that barbers used to hold their lather. The squares also served as toilet paper for customers. Along the way, my father learned the rudiments of barbering from Scabie Mike. Young Ollie also absorbed another lesson. He vowed, "If I ever own a shop, no spittoons."

My father, like so many children of Fall River's immigrants, left school at the age of fourteen having completed the eighth grade. By sixteen he was barbering full time, the junior member of a shop on Bedford Street, a few blocks from Main, run by a Franco-American who spoke Canuck English that my father quoted to us repeatedly years later. "Throw the horse over the fence some hay," was one of my father's favorites. Ed Grenier, the owner of the shop, would tell customers to "sit down a little higher." Or he would ask, in a convoluted way that commented on Fall River's hilly urban terrain, "How'd you come down, walk up?" My father mastered his trade under Grenier and grew into young manhood. Through the bleak years of the 1920s and the official onset of the Depression, my father clung to the hope of one day owning his own barbershop.

He took the plunge in 1936, when he was thirty-three and still living at home. For years his earnings had helped support his large family; he was also apparently able to lay up some money toward fulfilling his dream. My father was always a saver, a habit originating in the self-denial of immigrant life and forged during young manhood in the blast furnace of Spindle City's economic grind to survive. But he did not have anywhere near the money needed to open the kind of shop he wanted. The pastor of Holy Rosary, the church of the Bedford Street Italian community, came to his aid. Father John J. Sullivan encouraged my father to buck the Depression-era odds stacked against a new small business — another barbershop — in beleaguered Fall River. He also loaned my father money to open his three-chair shop in the center of the city in 1936.

Two decades later I would simply take my father's barbershop for granted. It was always there, and more or less successful I would assume. He was a different person in the shop from the man I knew at home — more self-assured, seemingly content, and certainly better dressed than the threadbare clothes he preferred away from work. He always wore a tie and a crisp, white shirt under a clean, white waistcoat. He engaged his customers in animated discussions of politics, baseball, and the state of the economy. He held sway in his barbershop. Small wonder he would only close the place after he turned seventy-six.

Until recently I had no idea of the sacrifice he made to establish his business during an unsettled era in a city still reeling from a decade of seismic economic upheaval. For the first time I read the only remaining records of the shop: his account book for the first five years, 1936–1941. The fourth-grade arithmetic and occasional simple declarative sentence reveal a story that humbles me. I wish I had known while he was still alive, while I was growing up. He avoided Fall River's sweatshops only to put in more hours each week than mill workers, and to forgo not only vacations but also single days off during the first years of his business.

It cost him the princely Depression-era sum of $1,900 to open his shop. The major expenditure — $1000 — went for three barber chairs, six waiting chairs, a barber pole, and a cash register. He itemized his expenses down to "Bon Ami, Polish, Feather duster, Thum tacks [and] Nails." The list shows an attention to cleanliness and comfort that positioned the new shop at the high end of barbering in Fall River. The inventory did not include spittoons.

My father opened for business on August 27, 1936, at 18 Granite Street, one block from Main Street and two blocks from the Quequechan's scenic falls. He rented space on the ground floor of the Eagle Building, which was owned by Chinese immigrants who operated a popular restaurant with an annex adjoining my father's shop and a more formal dining room on the second floor. He sent printed letters of announcement to the largely Catholic, professional workers in downtown Fall River whom he hoped to attract to his well-appointed shop.

I hereby formally announce that on next Thursday August 27 I am opening my own barbershop at the convenient location of 18 Granite St., where I shall be pleased to meet my friends and acquaintances.

For seventeen years I worked with Ed Grenier, 122 Bedford Street, and with this experience behind me I feel that I am qualified to offer efficient service in all lines connected with my trade.

Frank Miozza, who formerly owned and operated a barbershop on New Boston Road, will be with me as an assistant.

I hope I may have the pleasure of welcoming you at my new place of business.

These are not my father's words, a man who could write cursively but preferred to print, who could string sentences together but not form a coherent paragraph, and who was bilingual and spoke without an accent but had difficulty pronouncing many words and names. (A rabid Red Sox fan he unfailingly butchered Carl Yastrzemski's last name and to our amusement called journeyman Faye Throneberry "Troneberry.") My father's pastor and patron, Father Sullivan, most likely crafted the announcement of the opening of the Eagle Barbershop, as it was named.

The business started slowly according to the detailed figures in my father's account book. He charged 25 cents for a haircut and 10 cents for a shave. The worst early week ended on September 19 with a balance of 47 cents, what my father took home after paying expenses that included $11 to Frank Miozza.

I don't know if fear of failure haunted my father and tracked him down even when he was surrounded by his affectionate extended family. His account book is a chronicle of tenacity and industry that is impressive even for unforgiving Fall River, where many, like Salvatore Conforti and Jose Bento, exhausted themselves just to stay afloat. I never appreciated what he endured to create a business that provided us with an economy-class but mostly stable standard of living. He worked Monday through Saturday from 8 a.m. to 6 p.m., with an hour off for lunch—a fifty-four-hour workweek that had long been a relic in industrial New England by the 1930s. He and his assistant even worked on holidays such as Washington's Birthday, Memorial Day, and the Fourth of July. Incredibly, my father kept his shop open on Columbus Day, which had been a holiday in Massachusetts since

1910, and an occasion of great pride and festivity for the Bedford Street Italian community.

Near the first anniversary of the opening of his business, my father recorded what all his labor had won him. He scribbled, "My average pay for 51 weeks of my first year [was] $15.30." This apparently excluded tips, which were most likely modest. My father also had a large display case facing the waiting customers. It was stocked with items for sale: cigarettes, cigars, candy, gum, razor blades, styptic pencils, hairbrushes, combs, Vitalis, Bay Rum, Wild Root, Jeris Hair Tonic, and other products. My father soaked up the sweet aromas of the barbershop and carried them home with him. The incense of his calling lodged in my father's clothing and suffused his hands and skin, constantly reminding family and friends who he was nine hours a day. In the back of his account book, he kept meticulous records of the fragrant hair and facial products and other items that he sold from the showcase. They generated a small additional profit.

My father's first days off came in March of 1938. His shop had been open for nineteen months. He simply recorded, "I was out 3 days sick," an understatement for whatever kept him from his beloved business.

He continued the grueling work schedule for two more years before illness struck again. "Out sick in hospital one week," he noted in late January of 1940. He also missed two days the following week. This must have been when he had surgery for a severe case of hemorrhoids, most likely brought on by the punishing stress of building his business. When I was young he referred to it as his painful bout of "piles."

My father's account book does record how, drawing on his previous barbering experience and through unremitting toil, he quickly became a successful, respected small businessman in downtown Fall River. The average number of customers each week grew steadily between 1936 and 1941, from the low 100s, to 150, then to 175, and finally to near 200. Usually for the week before Easter or Christmas he would make a note of reaching a "New High": 196 customers in December of 1938 and 219 in April of 1941, when he earned $36.77 for haircuts and shaves.

Well before then, Arthur Seneca, an Italian from the Bedford Street community, had replaced my father's original second barber. He was highly skilled, attracted his own following, and thereby boosted my father's business. Arthur, a mild-tempered, unassuming man, never chanced that he might succeed on his own, despite impressive barbering skills. He was content to pocket his weekly pay from my father. He lived in a triple-decker that he owned and collected rent from two tenants. It was enough for a man with simple wants who never forgot the Fall River body count of the 1920s and '30s, when, like my father, he mastered his trade. They would work together for four decades. A cast of young and old barbers would eventually serve as the caretakers of the shop's third chair, reserved for those customers who were not fussy, often because a hairpiece rather than a haircut might have served them better.

As my father's business won a growing loyal clientele in the late 1930s, he began occasionally to indulge in a day or two off from work. And then at the end of August 1939, he notes in his account book, "I was on vacation this week and the next one." This was the longest vacation he took during his six decades of barbering. It also involved the farthest he ever traveled from Fall River. He rode the train to Tucson, Arizona, to visit his revered patron, Father Sullivan, who was trying to recover his health in the dry desert air. This expedition was a touchstone of Ollie's simple life that he often returned to in conversation. It was an epic event against the backdrop of an existence tethered to a few corners of Fall River: the unceasing shuttle between Beattie and Granite streets, with our house later added to the circumscribed circuit of his life where he found contentment.

The excursion to Arizona represented his only encounter with the continental expanse that constitutes America. He loved to describe the exhausting trip by rail before the era of air-conditioning; the majesty of the Grand Canyon; the withering heat of Arizona in August; and the reunion with Father Sullivan captured in photographs with cactuses in the background. My father also brought back a cheap souvenir, which he hung in his barbershop until he oiled his hair clippers and sharpened his scissors for the last time. It was a reminder of the only venturesome journey of his nine decades of life in Fall River. I inherited the memento—a colorful woodcut with stereotypical Mexican figures like those seen in John Ford Westerns or on *The Mark of Zorro*, the popular 1950s television show. In the woodcut, a swarthy man in a sombrero and poncho extends a pitcher to a dark-skinned brunette holding a basket of vegetables. An adobe mission church occupies the background with a Franciscan in his brown cloak reading his breviary. The Arizona woodcut and his account book are the only artifacts I have from my father's barbershop—tokens of a place that I never appreciated and of his early years, when he worked harder than I ever had to.

After my father's trip to Arizona and my mother's visit to the Azores, they would leave Fall River on vacation only two more times during the course of their lives. On both occasions they traveled together as husband and wife. In September of 1941, they spent their honeymoon in New York City. My mother saved the ticket stub of their visit to Radio City Music Hall, an indication that she thought she had won the marriage lottery after spurning many suitors. The ticket stub records the purchaser's weight, 144 pounds. That would be my father when his spare, sinewy, five-foot-seven-inch frame was trimmed with a three-piece suit and a businessman's felt hat. Ten years later they returned to the Big Apple to celebrate their anniversary. They never left Fall River for an overnight trip again.

My father was thirty-eight, single, and still living at home when he married my mother. With his business established and forty staring him down, he decided it was time to marry and raise a family; most of his younger siblings had a head start on him. As my choosy mother passed the age of thirty-one, she too became eager to find the right man and leave the care of her aged parents to her older sister. Ollie and Agnes took the measure of one another along Bedford Street and Main Street. My mother would later tell us how she was taken with my father's neat, handsome figure in his trademark three-piece suits, his energetic stride, and his air of self-confidence. She would recount this perhaps only to underscore how my father never met her expectations, how marriage exposed his unseen flaws that competed with and often defeated his virtues in her eyes.

My father was not the type to pen love letters. My mother certainly would have saved them. What she did save was a kind of memorandum of agreement that my father wrote to her as he inched closer to proposing marriage. It was scrawled in fractured spelling, grammar, and punctuation on the back of a leftover announcement of his barbershop's opening. His declaration begins, "I like you and am growing founder of you more and more but you know theres certain things you have to think of if you are going to live with a person the rest of your life." He goes on to explain how he had to go to work at the age of fourteen to help support his large family. "My mother got up at six o'clock every morning preparing meals for everybody and having my breakfast ready and waking me up two or three times to go to work." For all of her burdens, he claimed, "my mother wouldn't trade places" with women who "pittyed" her and said she was not happy. "You know everybody is searching for happiness and their looking for an easy way to it, but the best and easy way is hard work and keeping your mind occupied[;] when you have to get up at a regular time every day and have regular meals their isn't much danger of your health breaking down."

My mother was astute enough to read the warning signs, but her heart prevailed. Then, again, she readily accepted a woman's domestic role, and she didn't shrink from hard work. It served as an outlet for the energy generated by her high-strung personality. My mother had rebuffed wooers not only because she was a bit old-maidish but also because she remained responsible for her aged parents' and her older sister's welfare. At thirty-eight my father was set in his ways and didn't expect marriage to change the basic contour of his life, except to give him kids to round out his sense of Italian manhood. In fact, once my mother and father were engaged, he revealed his expectation that after marriage she would come to live with him and his parents on Beattie Street. My mother had envisioned him providing a tenement of their own that would be close to her parents. She refused to join the household on Beattie Street. "All right," he said, "we'll move in with your parents," a practice that was common for newlyweds in a city staggering from King Cotton's disintegration and the Depression. Little did she know that much of his weekly routine would continue to revolve around Beattie Street.

From his nearly four decades of living at home, my father had formed a close bond with his mother Anna, or "Nonna." My mother used to tell us that when she and my father were about to leave on their honeymoon after a reception on Beattie Street, "Nonna became hysterical, crying and screaming, 'Orland, don't leave me. Orland, don't leave me.'" My mother may have exaggerated. When it came to her in-laws, she stitched into the tangled skein of her memory the slightest incidents that cast the Confortis and my father in an undignified light. But I believe her retelling of the episode, whose details never deviated. In 1953, when my grandmother's third oldest son, my uncle Chippy (who was also a barber), died of lung cancer, my eight-year-old eyes would witness Nonna's inconsolable grief at St. Patrick's Cemetery on a sunny early November day after all the trees had shed their leaves. She wept and shouted to her dead son as the priest tried unsuccessfully to comfort her. She had to be pried from the casket as it rested next to the open grave ready to be lowered as soon as we left. My grandmother with her one leg (the other had been lost to diabetes) and her cane as her constant companion was a tower of strength and emotion — a volcano of love for everyone in her family, especially the children of her Orland.

My father became the third Conforti to take a Portuguese spouse, coupling two ethnic traditions in the extended family. The newlyweds returned from their honeymoon and moved into 61 Bowler Street with Jose, Alexandrina, and May Bento. The tenement, located off Quarry Street, was a first-floor, cold-water flat with no central heating. The building housed six families; it closely resembled two triple-deckers that had been merged into a boardinghouse-like, wooden structure. My grandparents occupied a bedroom at one end of the tenement. My parents' bedroom was at the opposite end with May in the middle. These arrangements did not last very long, however. Within the first nine years of marriage my mother gave birth to five children and lost her parents. She also became permanently estranged from her brother and his family and assumed responsibility for her slow-witted sister. At the same time she grew resentful of the large amounts of time my father spent on Beattie Street. Already feisty and tightly wound before marriage, she now often operated with a revved-up nervous system. In those moments her disposition seemed awash in adrenalin, cortisol, and all those overworked hormones that generate edginess at best and anxiety at worse.

When my mother was planning her wedding, she passed over her loyal but pudgy, plain-looking sister as her maid of honor. Poor Aunt May probably accepted the decision. She always felt, or was made to feel, subservient to or dependent on her younger, smarter, more attractive American-born sister. My mother chose her niece, Lydia Bento of Pawtucket, her brother's daughter, as her maid of honor. She was close to her brother Manuel and his family then, even though they lived twenty-five miles away. Sometime after the wedding — the details were always hazy — my mother learned that her niece Lydia and my father were seen walking arm in arm down Main Street in Fall River. My mother apparently assumed the worst; she often did so about my father. A family tempest erupted. My mother severed ties with my uncle and his family. I would never know him. All I would hear growing up were occasional hushed references between my mother and aunt to "brother." My mother and her steadfast sister never mentioned him by name and apparently never saw him again, not even when he was stretched out in a casket.

The Bentos had survived my grandfather's solitary sojourns from St. Michael. The family endured their uprooting from the island and permanent transplanting to the gray world of Spindle City, the oldest son's new start in Pawtucket, and the Depression's nadir. Then they foundered on what seems in retrospect a pique of jealousy and mistrust. My father's vices were mostly small change: he smoked too much; he occasionally drank too much at family gatherings; he was a petty gambler; he kept my mother in the dark about his finances; he made her ask, sometimes plead, for money to buy things for her kids (Keds for the summer and Thom McCans for the new school year); and he often spent as much time on Beattie Street as on Bowler. But he was not a womanizer as far as I can tell. The wine press he inherited from my grandfather; a summer evening in his vegetable garden; a televised Red Sox game; and the extended Conforti clan were my father's mistresses.

How my aged Portuguese grandparents handled the Manuel crisis in their family remains a mystery to me. But they were not long for life after my mother married. On January 3, 1944, thirteen months before I was born, Jose Bento collapsed to the ground on Pleasant Street, two blocks from the Durfee Mills where he had worked for twenty-five years into his early seventies. He was dead of a heart attack two months short of his eighty-first birthday. I remember my frail Portuguese grandmother, who became bedridden from a stroke shortly after my grandfather died. I recall helping my Aunt May support my grandmother as she made her way to the bathroom. I learned to say in Portuguese, "Vovo, mija aqui," once we had positioned her over the toilet. I must have been four years old because she died in January of 1950. She was laid out for two nights in the parlor of Bowler Street right across from the bedroom where my brothers and I slept. Mourners, many of them immigrant family friends from the Azores, came to pay their respects. My mother's birth family, except for Aunt May, who was now totally dependent on her, dissolved before she celebrated her tenth wedding anniversary. She was only thirty-nine and bereft of an extended family. My mother would speak reverentially of "father" and "mother" and contrast their devotion to each other with Ollie, who divided his time and loyalty between Beattie and Bowler Streets.

Throughout the tribulations of the 1940s, sons kept arriving while my mother prayed for a daughter. She gave birth to the first son in July of 1942; he was named for Father John Sullivan. Bill arrived in September 1943. I was the middle child born in February 1945, and named for my Portuguese grandfather. Still, my mother kept supplicating the saints and the Blessed Mother for a daughter. She gave birth to a fourth son, Orlando Jr., in February 1947. There was a battle over this name. My father wanted to name my brother Salvatore in honor of his father. My mother always preferred more "American" names, a sign of her conflicted ethnic identity and longing for assimilation. (In her marriage notice and in his obituary, Jose Bento is identified as "Joseph.") They compromised on Orlando Jr., but he would never be called by that name. He was, more accommodatingly for my mother, known as Junior. Then around the age of eight he acquired a lifelong alternative to his Old World baptismal name. After my father cut his finger on a hike in the woods at Fall River's East End, my brother wrapped the wound in leaves. My father said offhandedly, "Thanks, Doc." By some alchemy, Junior emerged from the woods permanently rechristened "Doc."

Finally, pregnant for the fifth time in 1948, my mother made a wager with St. Anne. In return for a daughter, my mother promised to devote a yearly novena to Anne at the magnificent French church in the South End named for the saint, where evidence of miracles abounded: the crutches and braces, for example, of people whose injuries and infirmities had apparently been cured. My sister, baptized Elizabeth Anne and called Betts by us, was born in July 1949.

Dedication to her children replaced devotion to her now deceased parents as the axis of my mother's life. Aunt May, who would live the rest of her days in our family, assisted my mother with the care of her children and contributed a measly disability check from the city to the household. A simple, devout, hardworking immigrant, Aunt May gave her life to us as if we were her own children. For good and for ill, we grew up with two mothers, both hypervigilant over our lives and often conscientious and protective to a fault when it came to what passed for our welfare. They nurtured bonds of love but also cultivated cords of dependency—a sometimes disabling aversion to risk and change that would remain my consort even in adulthood.

My mother's birth family now depleted, she competed with my father for our affections and with the lure for us of his vital, affectionate, expansive clan. In her mind, by the standards of immigrant-ethnic Fall River, she had married a respectable businessman. But my mother found herself caught in the vortex of an earthy, expressive, largely working-class Italian family. Unlike my Portuguese uncles who blended seamlessly into the family, she resisted the Confortis' embrace throughout her life and tried to shield us from their influence. They resembled the insufficiently scrubbed, often darker Azoreans from whom she remained aloof, even as she cherished her Portuguese heritage and identity.

In my Fall River of the 1950s, the Confortis and their Portuguese in-laws embodied the ethnic vitality that enlivened a city whose coat of arms might have been a sweatshop with a factory store in a half-empty granite mill. Both sides of my family made their own history. My Italian and Portuguese grandparents and their offspring helped transform the homeland of Pilgrims, Puritans, and Yankees. In 1950, 49.5 percent of Massachusetts' population, twice the national average, consisted of immigrants and their children. Only nearby Rhode Island had a slightly higher average. I would only discover this fact decades later. Had I possessed such knowledge earlier, it might have eased my feelings of being an outsider and perhaps altered some decisions that shaped the trajectory of my life.

Three

STREET AND TENEMENT

I spent the first ten years of my childhood at 61 Bowler Street in what had been my Portuguese grandparents' final cold-water tenement after their nearly four decades of life together in Fall River. We could walk to the neighborhood Brown School in five minutes. This generations-old, three-story, redbrick building was located on Bedford Street between vibrant Portuguese and Italian parishes. The Macaroni Shop, which was run by immigrants who lived over their store, stood next to the school. The shop was filled with the salty scent of imported Italian cheeses, which the owners grated and sold in little plastic bags. Three short blocks down Bedford Street from the opposite side of the school, a family from the Azores operated the Chourico Shop, with enticing samples dangling in the window. The peppery smell of the baking Portuguese sausage greeted you from a block away.

Other ethnic aromas enveloped Bedford Street on both sides of the Brown School. Marzilli's brick-oven bakery produced crusty Italian bread and tomato pizza, which was sold in small, rectangular strips. The bakery's seductive daily fragrances became as familiar as home. They overspread Columbus Park and anchored the Italian community perhaps as much as nearby Holy Rosary Church. The Portuguese flocked to Moonlight Bakery, which was around the corner from St. Anthony's Church. The aroma of baking round loaves of massa, or soft sweet bread, clashed with chourico as staples in the air over bustling Portuguese life on Bedford Street.

The Brown School sometimes produced its own distinctive smells. From kindergarten through fifth grade, the school's teachers were almost ex-clusively single Irish women—dedicated, caring, and, I am sure, poorly paid. Mr. Kozak, the Polish janitor, was the only man in the building. He kept the capacious coal furnace roaring in winter, maintained the lavato-ries and classrooms, and stood on call to sprinkle a sawdust-like material on the all-too-regular vomit of sick students. He mopped up the mess, yet the pungent odor of puke lingered, like the trail of the swill truck on collection day.

I remember only one dispiriting experience during my six years at the Brown School. It also disrupted the school's routine tranquility. Our fifth-grade teacher fell ill. The principal searched for a long-term substitute. The first person self-destructed, but not before she lashed out at what we Bedford Street ethnics represented in her eyes.

Mrs. McCready was a silver-haired lady who may have been a retired teacher, or a former lingerie saleswoman in the popular McWhirr's Department Store on Main Street. It was difficult to tell. She had trouble controlling a mostly decent and largely Portuguese-Italian class. Only one of us—little reticent Richie Cardoza—ended up a convicted murderer as far as I know. One afternoon, as if to placate her sometimes restive, ten-year-old charges, Mrs. McCready invited the class to tell jokes. Loudmouth Judy Tacovelli shot up her hand. "Why did the man cut his toilet in half?" she asked. The class responded with the requisite "Why?" "Because he saw his half-assed brother coming down the street." Judy's boldness stunned me, but many in the class laughed. Not Mrs. McCready. She curled her lip and sneered, "Well, I'm just not used to this part of Bedford Street!" Some of the students hissed. She had impaled us with her contempt.

Now in open rebellion my classmates soon escalated the hijinks that drove poor, old Mrs. McCready from the Brown School and the stretch of Bedford Street that she disdained. Anthony Ferry and Rocco Mazzarella, self-appointed classroom jesters representing, respectively, the Portuguese and Italian factions, conspired to feign uncontrollable loud hiccupping. Ferry would start, and Mazzarella would respond like a mating ritual of frogs in a swamp. A shy, obedient middle child, I simply observed how discipline dissolved. I was glad to see that Mrs. McCready cut and ran, or was sent packing, but her words continued to sting. Bedford Street seemed to fail some all-important American civic test.

My mother showed up at recess every morning before a milk program was established by the time I reached third grade. She brought my brothers and me coffee-flavored milk and a snack, one of the few mothers on the playground, hovering over her kids instead of setting them free to play for a few minutes. My mother's often overattentive parenting was mostly well intentioned. Ultimately, she dreaded that we would not turn out "right," that we might become Anthony Ferrys or Rocco Mazzarellas, and it would reflect on her, frustrating the abiding Bento family quest for American social respectability.

Near the end of my last year at the Brown School, I was summoned to the principal's office. Miss Connors was there with another well-dressed woman whose name escaped me. I was introduced as the captain of the patrol monitors, the special students who wore white belts across their chests and helped their classmates march in orderly lines into and from school, including across busy Bedford Street. It was news to me that I captained the monitors. I felt as if I was on display as a model Bedford Street ethnic — a diligent, docile, cleanly dressed, and well-groomed student. In retrospect I see myself reflected in Miss Connors's eyes as the son my mother labored to mold: an exemplary third-generation ethnic who was not just another Bedford Street Portagee or Wop.

The Bowler Street of my childhood was mostly a tired, tattered nook of Fall River's East End. The street had less than a hundred yards of pavement before it tapered into a dirt lane, rutted and gullied by rainstorms for its remaining five hundred feet or so. Many roads in our neighborhood — Doyle, Crane, and St. Germain, to name a few — were dirt lanes or only partially paved. The city was always strapped for money, and our ward had neither the clout nor the connections downtown to bring about improvements. We felt fortunate when the city got around to plowing our street in winter.

Bowler Street consisted of only eight dwellings, three of which were nondescript, small, single-family, working-class houses. No ethnic group dominated the street, though the French outnumbered the Portuguese, Italians, Jews, Irish, a few Yankees, and one Syrian who made up its residents. Our six-family tenement was the largest home on the street. A narrow backyard ended at the six-foot fence of the junkyard owned by our coarse landlords, the Sanfts. The imposing Stafford Mills, a five-story, granite complex initiated during the building boom of the 1870s, shaded the Sanfts' junkyard and loomed over our lives.

With five children and three adults we were the largest family by far living at 61 Bowler Street. Not surprisingly, the Sanfts policed our movements; they feared the wear and tear we would inflict on their precious property. The ever-vigilant Rose Sanft served as the eyes of the family. She kept tabs on us from the bottom tenement of her triple-decker directly across the junkyard entrance from our flat. We called this diminutive gray-haired woman "Old Rosey." When my brothers and I gathered on our back porch, she often called my mother with an ultimatum: "The boys are jumping on the porch. They have to stop," she commanded. My mother complied, worrying that if we accumulated enough demerits the Sanfts would raise our rent or maybe even evict us.

Moments of excitement sometimes punctuated our daily routine. One evening the adult daughter of the elderly Mrs. Dussault, who lived on the second floor directly above us, knocked on our door. "Can I use your phone," she asked my mother. "My brother and his girlfriend are drinking heavily upstairs, and they refuse to leave my mother's place. I need to call the police." Within minutes the paddy wagon arrived. The police escorted the drunken son and his painted moll down from the second floor and past our open door. Dussault's companion reminded me of the women I saw coming out of Pier 14, a notorious bar on lower Bedford Street named for the berth where ships of the Fall River Line once docked in New York Harbor.

Occasionally, we were awakened in the middle of the night by shouts and the sound of fire trucks when flames broke out in one of the detached small buildings of the Stafford Mills. No one grew up in Fall River without hearing stories about and seeing the remnants of earlier mill conflagrations. In fact, a large building, part of the original Stafford Mills, had burned decades earlier. The rubble had been removed, creating a parking lot that was never filled with cars because it was the size of two football fields. Stray fragments of burned-out mill remained, as did a gap-toothed, six-foot, gray, wooden fence. We could see the lines where the walls of the building stood. With evidence of a major mill blaze so near at hand, we feared that the Stafford complex would go up in smoke taking our tenement along with it.

One night when I was in the third grade, there was a mill fire in another part of Fall River. Workers salvaged more than a hundred bales of cotton, which they scattered across the Stafford mill yard. I had never seen a single bale of cotton, let alone dozens strewn throughout the mill parking lot like CARE bundles that had fallen from the sky. My friends and I played hide and seek, running through and under the burlap-wrapped bales and jumping on and off them with abandon. My legs ached for two days after that.

The six families in our tenement building seemed to be just scraping by. Some owned old cars while others, like my father, relied on their feet or public transportation to navigate the city. Freddy Robillard, a husky, tobacco-chewing Franco who was my father's age, lived in the first-floor tenement that adjoined ours. He didn't drive. He worked at an unskilled job in the Arkwright Mill along the Quequechan River. His son Alan was my age and we were best of friends.

I was also fortunate to have three brothers to play with. We got along in part because we accepted our place in the birth order. John was something of the Primo of the family, the favored son and stellar student. From my earliest memories he was destined for the priesthood, the only one of us who served as an altar boy at St. Anthony of Padua Church. Bill was also an excellent student and more easygoing than John. As a middle child I followed in the tracks of my older brothers, until I would stop competing with them in school when I discovered between the sixth and seventh grade that I had more athletic ability than they possessed. As the youngest brother, good-natured Doc frequently did not tag along with us, and when he did he fell into lockstep.

I regularly inherited ill-fitting hand-me-downs from John and Bill as well as from others who took pity on my mother. My only pair of blue jeans on Bowler Street had to be folded into six-inch cuffs. They were worn out long before I grew into them. My mother had a hard time keeping us well clothed, and she welcomed shirts and pants that were passed along to her by friends and a Conforti cousin. None of us joined the Boy Scout Troop at St. Anthony's Church because we couldn't afford the uniform. Bill and I went to a few meetings and participated in games in the church hall. But everyone else wore uniforms that sparkled in my ten-year-old eyes. I quickly stopped attending meetings, knowing that I could never become a member of the troop. It made me feel like a Bedford Street Portagee.

My brothers and I were part of a gang of ethnically mixed neighborhood kids who played together, mostly peacefully and mostly in the street: Bobby Potvin, Bobby Johnson (the only Protestant), Gerry Paiva, Butchy Barboza, Alan Robillard, and Freddy ("Fat") Duclos, who must have scaled two hundred and fifty pounds as a young teenager on his march toward another hundred and a lethal heart attack before he reached forty. We played basketball with a bottomless bushel basket that someone nailed to a tree in front of Bobby Potvin's house.

Throughout the summer we formed teams for "pinky ball." This game required only an inexpensive rubber ball. Striking the ball against the curb, we attempted to hit a line drive over the heads of the opposing team for a home run, or get a lesser hit while trying to avoid a groundout or pop-out. Our pinky ball games regularly became too boisterous for some neighbor, usually Old Rosey, who called the police. We were forced to take a short break from the game until the heat was off. Our fear was that the police would write our names in their little notebooks. The street gospel in Fall River had its own version of three strikes and you're out. We were constantly reminded by some older member of the Bowler Street gang, "If the cops take your name down three times, you go straight to reform school." This was the era of *Rebel without a Cause* and *Blackboard Jungle*. Juvenile delinquency was in the air. I inhaled it the way I took in the fumes from the Stafford Mills' two smokestacks.

In the fall we organized tackle football games wearing primitive equipment—cheap plastic helmets, for example, that had no faceguards. We played our games one small block over from Bowler Street, on a strip of grass between the Sanfts' junkyard and the Stafford Mills that almost miraculously turned green each spring in the midst of grit and gray. I took a knee to the mouth on that makeshift gridiron when I was nine years old. A lower tooth broke in half, and a top one was badly chipped. I clutched my mouth in pain and ran home crying. The mirror continually reminded me of this childhood humiliation. There would be opportunities on other football fields never to let it happen again.

Of course, we played cowboys and Indians. One of our favorite places was a former granite quarry that we fancifully called "the Rocky Mountains." The site was on Quarry Street next to the mysterious Orthodox Jewish synagogue. The quarry had been filled in haphazardly like so much else in Fall River. Boulders protruded from the surface at different angles and heights, an ideal setting for us to stage our childhood Western fantasies.

Fall River's abandoned quarries were concentrated in corners of the East End within easy walking distance of Bowler Street. Like our Rocky Mountains, they found new uses. The city's winos sought shelter in the granite "caves" of one former quarry off nearby Pleasant Street. They created a hobo haven paved with broken liquor bottles. Another quarry, located in the East End woods near the acre of land my grandfather owned and planted, served as a swimming hole for adventurous kids. The brown water was said to be fifty feet deep. It occasionally claimed the life of a local youth. We visited the former quarry whenever we helped my father work in my grandfather's distant garden. I stood at the murky water's edge, terrified that I would make a fatal slip and sink fifty feet below before my lifeless body resurfaced.

Fall River's largest abandoned quarry was also its most toxic. William Beattie's once thriving ten-acre site became a convenient place for Fall River to dump the garbage collected from the East End. At least the trash filled in another swimming hole where kids sometimes drowned. Beattie's former operation was located on North Quarry Street, less than a ten-minute walk across Bedford Street from our tenement. I passed the dump often, taking in the singular smell of layers of reeking human refuse. On sweltering summer days one could almost see a cloud of gas rising over the decaying waste. Scavengers picked through heaps of rubbish while sidestepping the scores of city rats that colonized the site.

We lived just far enough away so that we did not have to endure daily the toxic by-products of Beattie's dump. One of my Conforti aunts was less fortunate, however. After World War II, the city chose a site adjacent to the dump for a public housing project called Hillside Manor. The message was clear: people like my Aunt Virginia should be grateful to live in publicly subsidized housing, even if it was located next to a noxious, rat-infested dump.

Between fifty and sixty Fall Riverites called Bowler Street home. Most were hardworking, churchgoing ethnic Catholics like the Potvins, whose various family members occupied a triple-decker across from the Sanfts. Yet in retrospect Bowler Street seems to have harbored more than its share of uncommon residents and individuals lamed by life.

Our landlords headed the procession of Bowler Street eccentrics. There were five Sanfts, American-born, secular Jews who dressed in rags and never came within hailing distance of the synagogue on Quarry Street. Jack was the oldest brother: a man in his sixties who sometimes left the Sanfts' first-floor tenement in a suit but didn't seem to work and never spoke to anyone that I can recall. "Click" ran the junkyard with another brother, whom my mother and aunt referred to in Portuguese with something that sounded like "Zhawn-Zhawn." Six long days a week, they bought and sold scrap, occasionally grunting at us when we came face-to-face with them. Old Rosey was their bossy sister. Comfortable in her threadbare clothes and trademark moth-eaten, gray coat sweater, she only left the house to shop for groceries. "Young Rosey" was her niece. She flitted around the neighborhood with a simpleton's smirk on her face and was later arrested for prostitution.

Every Friday my brothers and I took turns carrying our rent to Old Rosey. The Sanfts' windows were sealed shut year round, blocking out the world beyond their crass circle and locking in the accumulated fetidness of their wretched lives. I remember the first time I delivered the rent. I knocked and Old Rosey opened the door. A wave of hoarded cooking odors, unwashed bodies, and mustiness assaulted me. Rosey said, "Wait a minute. I have something for you." I stood in the doorway wanting to run from the reeking place while Jack sat at the kitchen table reading the paper and not batting an eye. Rosey returned with a graham cracker. I took a bite of it after I left the house and immediately spit it out. The cracker was as stale as the Sanfts' lives. We all learned to say "No thank you" on those occasions when the Sanfts offered us some throwaway piece of their piddling lives.

Through their money-grubbing industry, the Sanfts had forged a little empire on Bowler Street. They owned our six-family tenement, the triple-decker they lived in, and another triple-decker adjacent to them whose address was actually on the next street over, Doyle, which ran along the Stafford Mills. All of these multifamily houses were painted gray as if they had surrendered to the aesthetics of the nearby mills. The Sanfts also owned their junkyard and its buildings, a property that extended almost the entire length of Bowler Street on our side. Across from our house, there was a large overflow lot—a kind of annex to their junkyard. The Sanfts fenced all of their junkyard property with six-foot vertical boards that were spaced so tightly you could not see into their working sanctum. Then they saturated the fences on each side with used motor oil, both as a preservative and a deterrent to anyone tempted to scale the barrier. They stashed their money, never went anywhere, and kept their distance from tenants and neighbors alike.

Millie Taylor, who lived almost directly across from the Sanfts, would have been a misfit on any Fall River street. She occupied the first floor of her aged grandmother's triple-decker and turned it into a hovel. The slatternly "welfare queen" of Bowler Street, Millie was at best of borderline intelligence. She was about forty years old with a pear-shaped body and a well-developed belly. She had a small, round head with whiskers on her chin and above her lip. Millie bore three children, one of whom was biracial, by different men. Childrearing, especially toilet training, presented a challenge to her. When her kids were small, they were accustomed to shitting on the floor in a corner of her tenement. As the boys grew older, they wandered the neighborhood at will, carrying their impetigo and head lice with them.

Millie would sit in the window year round, staring into the street and hoping that something more than a one-night stand would come into her life. We sometimes peered into the tenement when she was not on watch. The rooms were almost bare of furniture with clothes strewn about. The fetid tenement repelled me. But had I been blindfolded, I could have easily got wind of the difference between the stench of Millie's first-floor flat and the Sanfts'. At least Millie opened her windows in summer, as if she was reaching out to the world. Millie followed our street games day after day. All summer long, she proved to be as predictable a presence in our lives as Fall River's humidity. No one played any tricks on Millie or was disrespectful to her that I can recall, but we did keep our distance. We all realized that she was slow-witted, and in her own way she loved her kids. She could barely take care of herself, let alone three boys.

Manny Cabral, the owner of the neighborhood variety store, was another forlorn fixture in our lives. He bought the business in the early 1950s, when decent jobs were hard to come by in Fall River—especially for an unskilled son of Portuguese immigrants who had stumbled into middle age. He ran the kind of place that convenience store chains like Cumberland Farms and Seven Eleven have laid waste to. Cabral's Variety was wedged into the first floor of a small house. Manny's store was where we bought our penny candy and popsicles, Creamsicles, and Fudgsicles during the summer. Manny had a cooler for Royal Crown and Coca Cola, Hires Root Beer, and Nehi Orange, grape, crème, and sarsaparilla soda. He also sold milk, American cheese, and packaged cold cuts from a refrigerator. He carried Wonder and Sunbeam bread and pastries such as Hostess Cup Cakes and Table Talk Pies, as well as cigarettes, cigars, and sundry other items.

The years rolled by, and Manny remained behind the counter ringing up mostly petty sales on his beat-up register six and a half days a week. He opened at noon on Sunday. As far as I could tell, Manny never took a vacation. He had olive skin that looked slightly sallow at summer's end from lack of exposure to the sun. He seldom broke a smile, but he did show admirable, or rather helpless, patience with us as we carefully chose our penny candy and frequently changed our minds. "I'll have the root beer barrel instead of the jaw breaker." "Give me a malted ball, not the wax bottle."

Manny lived in a triple-decker on Quarry Street, directly across from Bowler. He carried his lunch in a brown bag the twenty-five yards from his rented tenement to his store. Sometimes he gave one of us a free ice cream if we hurried down Quarry Street past the Rocky Mountains to the always-bustling railroad-car Stafford Square Diner and picked up his lunch. He remained behind his counter with the television for companionship until his wife came home from her secretarial job. She made supper and either delivered it to him or took his place while he ate at home.

Mrs. Cabral was a fiery Irish redhead married to a Portagee, another name for a Fall River nobody. As she aged she began to lose her teeth along with her temper. She snarled at Manny, only stopping before she left bite marks. She took to contemptuously referring to her husband as "Cabral." She spit out her scorn: "Cabral, when are you gonna sell this dump and get a job that pays?" She seemed to especially enjoy belittling him when customers were around, even youngsters like me. "Cabral," she badgered him, "when are we gonna move out of our lousy tenement across the street?" Manny usually failed to respond to such verbal goading, except to retaliate feebly by referring to his wife as "Murphy." I wish I knew what happened to Manny—a man whose silence betrayed his powerlessness, even before a ten-year-old kid with only a nickel to spend. For poor Manny, life in Fall River seemed a steady drip of disappointment.

There were no murders on Bowler Street, at least during the twenty-five years I lived in Fall River. But there was a double suicide before we moved in 1955. It took place on the third floor of the Sanfts' triple-decker that was adjacent to their tenement. The victims were an elderly Portuguese immigrant couple, the parents of Manny Santos Jr., who lived on the third floor above us. Manny Sr. began acting oddly in public, especially in church. I remember him standing up during Mass at St. Anthony's when everyone was sitting down. His deepening senility culminated in tragedy for him and his compliant wife. I awoke one morning to learn that he had mixed a concoction of Mercurochrome and rubbing alcohol, apparently with the idea that it would heal whatever physical ailments he and his wife endured or conjured. They both drank this witches' brew and were found dead the next day.

Other characters who staggered down bedraggled Bowler Street added to its human drama. Alphonse Gagnon was a skilled carpenter who built one of the single-family houses on the street. It was a small ranch house where he lived with his wife and sister-in-law and his beloved pugs, Buddy and Buster, world-class yappers. The Gagnons never went anywhere. The sisters spent long winter nights putting together picture puzzles, not brooding over the pattern of their lives. When they tired of some puzzles they kindly passed them along to us before they attacked a new set. Alphonse put things together for a living. He had no interest in puzzles, except perhaps the riddle of his life. Alphonse was a Canuck who spoke with an accent, though he was a man, like Cabral, who kept his own counsel. He tried to drown in drink whatever furies tormented him. At the end of the workweek he sometimes hobbled home, swaying from one side of the street to the other. We gave the silent, besotted carpenter a wide berth, as we did for another menacing-looking figure.

Seraphim, an untalkative Portuguese immigrant who belonged to St. Anthony's, marched down Bowler Street a few times a week, especially in summer. He owned a slice of land on the opposite side of the street from our tenement house, perhaps a hundred feet away. A six-foot chain-link fence protected the lot where he planted vegetables. But Seraphim wanted more security for his garden, fruit trees, grape arbor, and lean-to sheds. He chained two dogs on both sides at the back of his property. Every few days he arrived to make sure the dogs were barely alive: he tossed "Rex" and "Tiny" moldy Portuguese bread, the only food I saw them eat. He never released them from their chains; they were shackled for life. Occasionally, we were tempted to scale Seraphim's fence and gather some apples or grapes. Tiny, a little mongrel, didn't scare us off. Rex, however, was a German shepherd who growled and barked whenever we approached the fence. "If Rex breaks his chain and bites you," one of our gang usually warned, "you'll get the rabies. He has a blue tongue. You could die!" Then, too, the tight-lipped, unsmiling Seraphim might collar you; his visits were so unpredictable.

Still other regulars added distinctive dashes of local color to my rich prepubescent years on Bowler Street. Stella (I never knew her last name) was my most memorable female. She lived with her mother on the third floor of the Sanfts' triple-decker. She was seven or eight years older than me. Plumpish with well-developed breasts, Stella must have purchased her ruby-red lipstick by the pound. Her boyfriends always combed their hair in the "duck's ass" style so popular with many working-class teenagers in the 1950s. One of her beaus had a convertible, and they would park in front of her house with the top down in the summer, talking and laughing and touching one another. They would return from the beach with their swimsuits lying on top of each other attached to the car's antenna to dry. It stirred feelings in me that I couldn't name, seeing suits that had covered their naked flesh positioned in such intimacy on a car antenna. I gradually absorbed the lesson that expressive working-class girls were off limits; eventually, I would acquire a common lingo that stigmatized many of them as sluts, tramps, and whores.

In the regimentation of tenement life I atoned for the freedom I experienced with my brothers and friends on Bowler Street and its treasured nearby ribbons of grass. My mother and her second in command, Aunt May, whom we called Titia, Portuguese for aunt, controlled us during our preteen years. They ran the household smoothly and efficiently, not unlike the Stafford Mills — minus the bells and whistles. They leaned on their Portuguese when they wanted to speak in code, but our consistent exposure to the language defeated their secrecy. We ate at the same time everyday with an unvarying menu, a blend of Portuguese and "American" food. Hot dogs and hamburgers on Thursday; Portuguese kale soup and spicy Portuguese blood pudding on Friday; roast beef, chourico, and potatoes on Sunday. If we made too much of a fuss at the table or in other ways threatened the steady operation of the assembled household, my mother trotted out a three-foot leather strap that was cut into strands. When she really meant business, she went for a more intimidating means of punishment — my father's shaving strop, which hung in the bathroom. In most cases, the mere appearance of these disciplinary aids was enough to stop us in our tracks. One time while we were eating, however, she drew blood. It happened at the supper when she served her tasty homemade pizza. John was acting up. "Stop it!" my mother commanded across the table. He continued, seemingly trading on his privileged position in our family. "John, eat your pizza and shut up." He ignored her. "Shut up," she yelled as she hurled a plate at him. It hit his arm, broke, and opened a small gash. I froze in my chair. Stunned for a moment, John jumped from the table and went in search of a large Band-Aid. For all of her edginess, this was the only time I can recall that my mother lost self-control with us.

My father's simple presence at home deterred misbehavior. He only laid hands on me once that I remember. We knew that we were to finish uncomplainingly any food placed before us. One night my father was home for supper on his Wednesday day off. I must have been nine or ten. I refused to finish string beans, which he had grown. "You're gonna sit there until your plate is clean," he ordered. An hour passed and I hadn't even lifted my fork. He firmly grabbed me by the neck and shoved my nose within an inch of the beans, like I was a puppy who had just shit on the carpet. "Finish eating those beans!" he shouted. I broke free from his grasp and rushed from the table in tears. I guess this battle of wills ended in something of a standoff.

While we lived on Bowler Street, my mother bought her Portuguese provisions and other groceries at Manny Camara's Red and White, part of a chain of independently owned neighborhood markets. Manny extended credit and delivered his goods, which could be ordered by telephone. My mother always carried a debit. Manny's store was located in the heart of the Portuguese community. He billed it "Your Meating Place." This good-hearted grocer had thick unbroken eyebrows that extended like an untrimmed hedgerow across his face. We cruelly joked that this was his real "meeting" place. (Years later, after large supermarket chains drove him out of business, generous Manny would become a deacon in the Catholic Church. About that time the local paper ran a front-page story on an academic book I had published. Manny sent me a note of congratulations that ended, "God bless you and your family unit." Manny had not lost his way with words.)

Saturday was bath night in our cold-water tenement. With five kids, it required a quickened, crisp regimen. We ate supper earlier than usual—4:30 in winter—and Titia began heating large pots of water on the gas stove. Once there was enough warm water in the tub, we bathed in birth order or sometimes together. Fresh hot water was added for each of us as the assembly line continued. By six-thirty we were all in pajamas and it was time for my mother to bathe followed by Titia.

Since there was still no central heat, we huddled by the kerosene stove in the kitchen that we filled by hand from a fifty-gallon drum in the basement. I slept in the same bed with my brother Doc, buried under blankets and quilts against the winter's cold. When the outside temperature dropped near or below zero, my mother broke out an ancient kerosene heater and placed it in our room. The glowing glass contraption with a metal base frightened me. This timeworn space heater, which my Portuguese grand-parents must have carted from Orange Street to Bowler with cold-water flat stops in between, probably would have been banned by the fire de-partment, or the Sanfts, had they known about it.

The year 1952 was momentous in our lives because my father bought a fourteen-inch Admiral television, which we placed next to the kerosene heater. We joined an entertainment revolution. The number of television sets in the United States exploded from four million at the start of 1950 to more than twenty-five million three years later, when we were among the 50 percent of American homes with TV's.

I still remember my first TV images. I was introduced to this new inven-tion in a Conforti aunt's tenement in 1951 before we bought our Admiral. There was a college football game on the screen—Utah playing some school named Brigham Young. One could see the stadium nestled against the majestic peaks that belonged to the real Rocky Mountains.

The Rockies formed part of the magical landscape of the Western mov-ies that my father had begun taking us to. We saw "Shane," dressed in his buckskins, ride out of and back into the snowcapped mountains that I would much later learn were the Grand Tetons of Wyoming. They di-minished Fall River's hills to stunted urban mounds. John Ford's Westerns such as *She Wore a Yellow Ribbon* introduced us to a splendidly austere desert with stark rock formations, a panoramic landscape that seemed to belong to another country from my world of triple-deckers, granite mills, and oil-smeared six-foot fences. The visual one-two punch of the Rockies and Monument Valley pressed home Fall River's physical drabness and its location at the tail end of a nation with overpowering physical beauty and a dramatic history that, along with the Pilgrim-Puritan epic, seemed to distill the essence of the real America.

Western movies were a rare treat. Television offered Westerns as daily fare. Shows starring Gene Autry, Hopalong Cassidy, Wild Bill Hickok, and the "Range Rider" were early Westerns that would be followed by a marathon of others. My mother allowed us to watch as much television as we wanted. It kept us occupied and temporarily relieved her of the role of household ringmaster when my father was at Beattie Street or in his barbershop. We sometimes fought over TV. Our arguments over what station to watch progressed from shoving to wrestling on the floor (I don't recall throwing real punches at one of my brothers until I was well into high school). My mother usually restored order quickly by waving her strap over our roughhousing.

Of course, I soaked up the images that multiplied on television of ideal American family life in sun-kissed suburban California. It never rained in the Hillsdale of *The Adventures of Ozzie and Harriet*. And the same might be said for the Mayfield of *Leave It to Beaver* and the Springfield of *Father Knows Best*. Even working-class stiffs like Chester A. Riley in *The Life of Riley* could enjoy the comforts of California living and on the weekend tackle the suburban art of outdoor grilling on his patio, a word that was as foreign to me as filet mignon. In between these episodes Dinah Shore crooned, "Drive your Chev-ro-lay, through the USA! America's the greatest land of all!" We could not even explore the outlying precincts of Fall River. My brother John would not earn his driver's license until 1959, when he was approaching seventeen, and we would finally acquire a car. My father would shun a Chevy for a rattletrap 1950 Ford that he bought for a hundred bucks.

My parents had friends who joined the postwar exodus to California. They sent Christmas cards with return addresses that stirred my imagination. And then there was the Rose Parade with all those bands from exotic-sounding places—Santa Ana, San Bernardino, and Sacramento. The Rose Bowl game kicked off in sun-drenched Pasadena around 4:30, just as darkness settled over Fall River and veiled a landscape often sheathed in snow and ice.

At the age of nine or ten, my imagination flushed with TV images of lotusland, I dreamed of moving to California. I would never make it. Yet my Western longing would have consequences. TV images of an American promised land and the silver screen's depictions of overpowering Western landscapes would eventually help me gravitate toward the field of American studies. My academic preoccupation with the seemingly elusive meaning of this sprawling continental nation would parallel my quest for the real New England. Both would be the long-delayed fruit of early life on and in 61 Bowler Street and the popular culture that introduced me to other

Americas, countries of the imagination seemingly out of my reach. I know from my bone marrow to my nerve endings that once I belatedly awakened to the life of learning, I would pursue long-incubating identity questions born of an outsider's experience in Fall River.

On Bowler Street and for many years after, I felt conflicted over my ethnic identity in a city where nationality mattered. My father worked on Saturday, usually the busiest day in the barbershop; even during the week he never arrived home before 6:30, well after we had finished supper. My mother and titia had plenty of opportunities to talk in Portuguese and to serve us food that they had eaten all their lives. Beyond the weekly menu there were special occasions such as Easter, when my mother made Portuguese sweet bread that was moister and tastier than the Moonlight Bakery's.

Then, too, we followed the Catholic custom of the time and belonged to my mother's church. St. Anthony of Padua was established in 1911 for the Portuguese immigrants who clustered in the triple-deckers around Bedford Street. My mother had been very prominent in the women's societies of the church before she married and gave birth to five kids. Every Sunday morning she took us to the 9:30 Mass, which was said in Portuguese. My mother did not have to instruct us that we were Portuguese—not Portagee. We marched off to church the way we were dispatched to school: scrubbed up, dressed neatly, and expected to behave obediently and speak politely, in proper English.

My father never set foot in St. Anthony's, except when we were baptized, made our First Communion, and participated in the Sacrament of Confirmation. For him, the church was too Portagee, filled with immigrants and their working-class offspring, women who always dressed in black mingled among men in shiny green and blue suits—a giveaway that they were bargains from a factory outlet. The pastor and curates, one of whom could barely speak English, were also Azorean immigrants. My father continued to meet his Sunday obligation at his home Italian church and then shifted to an Irish church in the neighborhood. (In the end it wouldn't matter, except to my mother. She would have his casket rolled into St. Anthony's; he would be buried from her church with the Requiem Mass said by the Azorean immigrant pastor.)

My youthful identity was predominately Portuguese. But I was also a member of my father's large, extended, and spirited Italian family. After his marriage and for the next twenty-five years, until Nonnuzzo (my grandfather) and then Nonna died, my father looked at Beattie Street as a second home. He ate supper there on Sunday, Wednesday, and Friday nights. He also visited every Sunday morning while my grandparents were alive. We accompanied him when we were young. We ate garlicky Calabrian-style fried meatballs and sipped my grandfather's homemade wine starting at the age of five or six. We kissed our grandparents' soft sunken cheeks when we arrived and left.

My Aunt Edith presided over the household, caring and cooking for my grandparents. She was the homely oldest daughter destined never to marry. I am not sure who wrote the script that gave her the role of permanent caretaker for her parents. I suspect it was just a fateful confluence of circumstances: her place in the birth order, her homeliness, and her sense of duty that was half imposed and half conscience based. Her whiny voice and glass eye (the consequence of a childhood accident) added to her unattractiveness. She was kind, even loving to us as she slaved over a frying pan in the basement of Beattie Street producing meatballs that we devoured. Yet we took to calling her "Cyclops." We heard that she had a low boiling point, probably from my mother, who had little use for her. She once chased a brother-in-law, my Uncle George, around the yard at Beattie Street with an axe in her hand, threatening to break open his skull. Uncle George dashed to our house because my father was the only one she would listen to. "She's crazy. She's a witch," he exploded, still out of breath. I could only think the Conforti family was a little too colorful. Perhaps we sheltered a potential Lizzie Borden.

The incident with Uncle George suggests something about the easy relations between my father and his Portuguese brothers-in-law. He grew close to my Uncles George Grillo and Tippy Carreiro. They respected his role as the Primo of the family.

When we lived on Bowler Street my father had a large garden plot on Beattie Street. As my grandfather aged and became more infirm, he reduced the land that he tilled. Some of his sons who lived in tenements laid out their own gardens and shared the bounty with my grandparents. Once or twice a week during late spring and on summer evenings, we followed my father to Beattie Street where we helped him plant, water, and weed his section of the garden. We walked home in the dark to the dance of fireflies. On particularly warm nights my father would stop to talk about his beloved Red Sox with men he knew who congregated on a Bedford Street stoop.

While my grandparents were alive, most of the Confortis gathered for holiday celebrations. On the night before the Fourth of July, a cookout of hotdogs and hamburgers, along with my grandmother's delicious, thick Calabrian-style pizza, was an annual event. We spent our Christmas Eves through the 1950s on Beattie Street. I have on videotape the grainy home movies my father took on this festive night. Aunts, uncles, and cousins are wedged into the basement, though I never felt a forced physical intimacy. The adults encircle a large table laden with Italian food, including special honey-glazed and anisette-flavored Old Country desserts. The aunts and uncles are talking, laughing, puffing on cigarette after cigarette, and drinking wine and beer. My grandparents are quiet with the unmistakable look of contentment on their faces.

I loved all the time I spent on Beattie Street, especially Christmas Eve. Unfortunately, we were always the first to leave the party. My Portuguese uncles and the Confortis engaged in a mutual embrace, despite an occasional outburst from Aunt Edith. After all, the Confortis closely resembled many of Fall River's large Azorean families. But the Confortis left my mother and titia cold. They never could identify with what they saw as the Portagee-like Wops of Beattie Street. In the Christmas Eve movies my mother and titia look ill at ease amidst the drinking and smoking and merriment. By ten o'clock, if not earlier, my mother announced that we had to leave. "It was getting too late for the kids" was the usual excuse. We gathered our jackets, kissed our grandparents good-bye, and were led by my mother and titia from the festivities and subterranean warmth of the Conforti homestead into the frosty night and back to dark, chilly Bowler Street. Always his own man when it came to the Confortis, my father stayed behind until after midnight.

One Christmas Eve, after we had bid farewell to the collective Confortis until the next Fourth of July, there was a knock on our door. It was Manny Santos Jr., the third-floor tenant, a fidgety oddball who gave me the creeps even before his parents committed suicide. He came to wish us a Merry Christmas. My mother stood in the doorway talking to him about the revelry on Beattie Street in a way that made a frightful impression on me. "They are sitting around smoking and drinking," she unloaded on Manny. "That's like sticking a pitchfork into your veins," she said excitedly as she drove two fingers into her arm. Manny simply nodded. I can only imagine how my mother's life, and ours, would have been different had she been prescribed drugs that fine-tuned her nervous constitution, dialing down her distress.

Yet, I can't simply issue my father a pardon. I have another revealing home movie that he shot. He loaded a three-minute film into his Kodak camera when my sister along with her cousin, my father's niece, made their First Communion. When I look at the film now, I simply shake my head instead of my fist. The girls walk back and forth, side by side, in the yard of the house that we would move to from Bowler Street. They wear white dresses and stockings. My father's camera slips like a divining rod, fixing on my cousin and excluding all but my sister's right shoulder, arm, and leg. He holds the camera steadily, only to catch himself and put my sister back in the frame. Then the dowser effect returns. My kind sister, the proverbial good egg, would grow up to be a nurse, a devoted parent, and loving wife. Her favored cousin would turn to drugs as a teenager, then resort to crime to support her addiction, and find herself in and out of jail. She would die suddenly and alone in her midfifties from years of abusing her body, including selling it to men who would have her.

Though he was reticent about the operation of the barbershop, occasionally my father carried home stories. "A niggah came in for a haircut today," he related one evening. "I sent him to Eighth Street," he said, where there was a small black community with its own barbershop. "I couldn't risk losing customers by cutting a niggah's hair." I fully accepted his justification. "Two sailors came in today from Newport," he told us another time. "They wanted Mohawk haircuts because they were goin' on a long cruise."

Sailors strolled through my early life as if Fall River was a set for *Navy Log*, a popular 1950s television show. Fall River was the largest city near Newport; buses ran regularly between the cities. World War II had led to the buildup of the navy in Newport, and it remained an important base through the 1950s and beyond. Fall River became something of a liberty city, accommodating the sailors who sought booze and women. Whenever I walked downtown, I had to pass the establishments that catered to sailors, as well as some locals, and constituted Fall River's modest tenderloin. On or near lower Bedford Street stood the notorious Pier 14, followed by the Army and Navy Café, the Narragansett Room, the Wilbur Café, and, just across Main Street, the Latin Quarter. Military police patrolled the streets and sailors' haunts. They wore white helmets and armbands with the letters "MP." They also carried intimidating billy clubs at their sides.

Newport sailors were notorious for getting into fights and for propositioning local females, who could ruin their reputations by being seen in the company of "anchor crankers," as some locals dubbed the servicemen. The father of friends on Bowler Street worked as a bartender at the Wilbur Café. A fight broke out one night. A sailor half his age pummeled the bartender, badly breaking his nose and leaving him with a huge shiner. When I saw him the next day, he looked like he had gone a few rounds with the fabled Rocky Marciano.

The presence of sailors on the streets and in my father's barbershop represented only one way our Fall River remained tied to Rhode Island. In the 1950s, my father found time to bring us to the Rhode Island beaches he loved. After the war, Fall River's barbers cut their workweek to five and a half days, closing their shops on Wednesday afternoons. My father had resisted this change; he wanted to keep working six full days a week. The Master Barbers' Association prevailed on the barber supplier for the city to cut off rogue shop owners like my father. He yielded. By the midfifties, the barbers had reduced their workweek to five days. This time my father fell in line. He closed his shop on Wednesday.

Without a car, there was little he could do with his newfound leisure time. Three or four times each summer, we took the bus to Island Park in Portsmouth, Rhode Island, where we spent the afternoon. As a young man, my father had frequented this spit of sand on the rock-strewn shore of the Sakonnet River. Island Park's proximity to Fall River had made it a working-class getaway. It was devastated by the sneak-attack hurricane of 1938, among the worst in New England history. The storm claimed nineteen lives in Island Park and destroyed nearly two hundred homes. Ruins along the river were still visible twenty years later.

My father was a terrific swimmer in his vintage maroon woolen suit. It was scanty and tightfitting and looked like my bag of marbles. I never learned to swim; my father never tried to teach us, except by saying, "Relax, and just do what I do." We watched the Old Stone Bridge, which linked Portsmouth and Tiverton, open for the smallest crafts cruising on the Sakonnet River. By late afternoon traffic began to back up as civilian employees of the navy in Newport headed toward Tiverton, Fall River, and places beyond. Sometimes my mother, aunt, and sister joined us and we stayed late, cooking hot dogs and hamburgers on the beach. More typically, we caught the five o'clock Island Park bus to downtown Fall River, picked up the Bedford Street bus, and were home by six o'clock.

Our annual day trip to beautiful South Shore Beach in Little Compton, Rhode Island, bred more excitement and required more planning. My father hired a customer of his to transport us back and forth. His name was Leo Jean. He owned a driving school and had tried unsuccessfully to teach my father how to operate an automobile. Several times we saw Leo Jean's car turn the corner from Quarry onto Bowler Street with my father behind the wheel as stiff as the Flint's statue of Prince Henry the Navigator. We jokingly yelled, "Dad's driving! Run for cover!" The car lurched to a stop before our house. "I just couldn't get the hang of the clutch, brake, and gas pedal," he would later admit in defeat.

For our yearly excursion to South Shore with Leo Jean as our chauffeur my mother packed lunch and supper for the whole family. We were usually at the beach before nine o'clock; it was only a half-hour drive from Fall River. We loved the waves, smooth sand, and tidal pool. Leo Jean returned around six thirty and brought us back, we city kids badly burned from being out in the sun all day without sunscreen.

There were two other annual trips that broke up our summers while we lived on Bowler Street and for a few years thereafter. We took in a Red Sox game at Fenway Park, sometimes during the week of the Fourth of July, my father's only vacation time. He worked fifty-one weeks a year. Once we went by train to Boston and carried our lunch, which we ate in the Public Garden. More typically, my father invited a friend or a brother-in-law with a car to join us. My father paid all the expenses, including the tickets, lunch, and parking. One time the driver said, "Let me get the peanuts." We arrived early to watch batting and fielding practice. I must have been seven years old when I first walked up from under the stands and saw the sea of green, dominated by what would much later be celebrated as the "Green Monster," part of the enshrined New England quirkiness and defiance of fashion that Fenway Park came to betoken. I never tired of being delivered from the dingy bowels of Fenway Park to the emerald world of graceful athletes in white uniforms with red trim, numerals, letters, and stockings. On the way home we stopped at a Mattapan landmark stand that sold foot-long hot dogs. My father continued to play deep pockets for a day. "This is on me," he insisted to no protests from our driver.

My father didn't teach me how to swim, but he tutored me in the fine points of baseball and loyalty to a team whose motto through almost the entire decade of the fifties could have been, "We aim for mediocrity, and lily-white rosters, always hitting our mark." It didn't discourage him. He displayed eight-by-eleven pictures of his beloved Red Sox players in the window of his barbershop. We watched games from Fenway starting with our Admiral television. He fell asleep each night listening to the Sox on a radio that I still have, a wedding present from his best man. Our annual trip to Fenway Park was the high point of my fervor for the Red Sox, a devotion begun in childhood on Bowler Street that has long outlasted my formal Catholic faith.

There was one other annual summer trip that injected a brief thrill into our routine lives of unsupervised play in the street and sitting before the television in our tenement. In North Dartmouth, approximately halfway between Fall River and New Bedford, Lincoln Amusement Park continued to draw largely working-class people out for a day of fun and fried, greasy food. Streetcar lines had developed the park to generate passenger revenue as well as profits from amusement rides and games of skill or chance. National acts played in its ballroom. Jimmy and Tommy Dorsey performed on July 4, 1955. There was an outside pavilion that presented free acts such as Eddie and Richie Zack, Armenian country and western singers from Rhode Island, of all places, the most urban state in the Union! The short, swarthy Zacks drew a crowd at Lincoln Park. They were local celebrities; their Country Jamboree aired weekly on Providence's Channel 10. Besides such free entertainment Lincoln Park offered customary rides, a "Tunnel of Love," and a fun house with a large window on its second floor where compressed air blew up the skirts and dresses of females for park-goers below to ogle.

We often made our outing to Lincoln Park on Labor Day afternoon. We mounted the bus at Stafford Square, the large intersection at Pleasant and Quarry Streets that served as the portal to the heart of Flint Village. We were at Lincoln Park in less than twenty minutes. It was a creaky, begrimed place like many faded southern New England amusements parks. But it clung to life as the playground of an increasingly downscale clientele. For me the colorfulness of the park-goers proved more alluring than the paint-chipped, rusting rides. The park attracted people like us and people who were object lessons for us. It had its share of young and old "Stellas" who wore tight shorts and suggestive or revealing tops and dangled cigarettes from their lips. Young and older men donned white undershirts and some rolled-up packs of Camels or Chesterfields in their sleeves. At Lincoln Park we rubbed shoulders with lower-middle- and working-class people in all shades of civility and coarseness. We ate clam cakes, French fries, and doughy pizza smothered in a sweet tomato sauce.

I looked forward to visiting Lincoln Park, joining its human spectacle, and leering freely at the Stellas who surrounded me. I experienced temporary reprieve from a life of social conformity and respectability monitored by my mother and titia. I think they tolerated rather than enjoyed a few hours among inexpensive amusements and overly expressive fun seekers at Lincoln Park.

I always wondered how much my father's ego was bruised by his inability to learn how to drive a car—a simple manly skill. The parade of bumper stickers during the 1950s as Fall Riverites like most Americans took to the road must have added to his sense of humiliation. I know it made me feel deprived when I saw cars proclaiming they had driven the Mohawk Trail, climbed Mount Washington, stopped at the Edaville Railroad, visited Canobie Lake Park, and paid their respects at LaSalette Shrine. Then, too, my father had to listen patiently as barbershop talk inevitably turned to travel near and far.

I don't think he ever visited one of the popular drive-in theaters that operated in and around Fall River beginning in the 1950s. Some of my Conforti aunts and uncles saw to it that we kids would not be denied this new movie-viewing experience. My brothers and I occasionally took turns going to a drive-in theater with them. I went twice. My father never came. What would he have done—sat in the backseat with us kids?

In 1955, approaching the age of fifty-two, my father would finally become a homeowner, perhaps a compensation for failing to conquer the automobile. We would move a few dirt lanes away. He would no longer have to raise his vegetables on Beattie Street, and we would no longer have to live under the Sanfts' oppressive gaze.

Four

"UP THE FLINT"

After we packed up our things on my tenth birthday, we moved less than a quarter of a mile, but we crept closer to the heart of the Flint—Fall River's Fall River. The largest and densest of the city's mill villages, the Flint's streets ran parallel to or at right angles from the Quequechan River. Many of these streets were choked with shoddy wooden tenements tossed together after the nearby banks and marshlands of the Quequechan gave way to rapid industrialization beginning in the late nineteenth century. Fall Riverites referred to going "up the Flint." Following the course of the Quequechan, the Flint's terrain rises gradually for two miles, from flat Stafford Square through the Pleasant Street business district, past the statue of Prince Henry the Navigator, and arrives at its modest apex on Bogle Hill. Far more than Bedford Street, Pleasant Street formed the Flint's commercial hub. In a half-mile stretch, it made available all the goods and services befitting an inward-looking mill village, the size of a small city, at the far East End of Fall River: a five and ten, a movie theater (the Strand), clothing shops, markets, ethnic restaurants and bakeries, the ever-popular New York System and Coney Island hot dog joints, jewelers, dentists, doctors, barbers, furniture dealers, shoe stores, and a cobbler. For many residents of the Flint, Fall River's central business district lay far downstream.

The Flint was the only Fall River mill village that acquired the name of an individual. Growing up in the Flint I had only a vague notion that there was some historical figure behind the curtain. His name was John D. Flint. He spearheaded the development of the village that bore his name. He began his career as a furniture merchant, real estate speculator in a booming city, and investor in mill stock. In 1872, he built the Flint Cotton Mill, threw up wooden triple-deckers, and recruited families of workers from Canada. Relying on steam power, Flint and other investors continued to construct mills well east of the Quequechan's falls. More triple-deckers and workers from Canada followed. In 1888, when he was sixty-two years old, a local paper singled him out as one of the richest men in Spindle City. By then Flint had earned his seal of success and worth in Fall River—a mansion in the Highlands.

One of his legacies was that the Francos outnumbered the Irish and Portuguese in Flint Village. We referred to the Francos as "clannish." Many lived in well-defined ethnic neighborhoods, spoke French as their primary language into the second and third generations, married within their group, and chose French Catholic education over the public schools. In the upper Flint the Francos erected an impressive fortress to their tribal faith. Adjacent to the statute of the Marquis de Lafayette and the park that carried his name, the Francos built the most beautiful Catholic house of worship in Spindle City. Notre Dame de Lourdes Church was completed in 1906, the year John Flint died. Constructed of granite and crowned with two soaring copper-clad spires, it served as a landmark not only for the Flint but also for Fall River as a whole. The Francos of the upper Flint went on to establish Notre Dame Grade School, Monsignor Prevost High School for boys, Jesus Marie Academy for girls, and St. Joseph's Orphanage. All of these buildings clustered around the church.

The lower Flint was not known for its religious piety. The Quequechan and Massasoit cafés catered to the Flint's more hard-boiled working class and its shady hangers-on. A little further down Pleasant, beyond the Bluebird Café, stood the Crown Café and "Hotel," a bar with several shabby rooms on the second floor where customers could repair for the night, or for shorter stays. The Davis School was located in the middle of the lower Flint. A three-story redbrick building with grades 6 through 8, the school had been built in 1873, when the Flint began to take shape as an important industrial village. The Davis School had a reputation for a student body with some of the toughest kids in the city, who would just as soon trade punches as curses. The three grades were filled with graduates of the Flint's elementary schools.

We could see the roof of the Davis School from our new home; the building was only a five-minute saunter away. Yet no one from my family ever darkened its threshold. Instead, we walked a mile away from the Flint to attend an Irish Catholic school. I was the only one of my brothers drawn to the Flint. During my teens Lafayette Park became a second home. In retrospect I see my behavior as a modest and fleeting act of teenage rebellion—an identification with Fall River's working-class kids, a refusal to follow in my older brothers' footsteps, and a resistance to march in lockstep with my parents' aspirations for their children.

✣

Filled with anticipation, I barely slept the night before we moved in 1955. My birthday present, an eight-week-old mutt from the local pet shop, occupied the bed with Doc and me, pissing on us a few times. (The puppy would grow into old age at our new address while I grew into young manhood.) We made a big stride forward with homeownership that included central heat and hot running water for the first time in our lives. Yet we also took a step back toward a kind of first-generation immigrant way of life, not unlike what my father and his siblings experienced on Beattie Street. Our new home was on a "street" appropriately named Way. It was no more than a rutted 25-feet-wide dirt lane, perhaps 1,500 feet long. Only six houses occupied this bypath, two on our side and four on the opposite side at the other end of Way Street. Italian families owned them all.

We purchased the largest property on Way Street, a corner lot. Diagonally across Doyle Street, the friendly Souza family occupied two small houses—one pinkish, the other shit brown. The houses defied architectural classification. They were shoehorned onto a postage stamp–sized lot. The Stafford Mills sprawled behind us, and its burned-out concrete parking lot, our new field and court of dreams, stood across Doyle Street from our yard. We now had plenty of room to play without spying landlords and intrusive squad cars.

I only recently learned from my brothers the full financial details that led to our becoming homeowners. I had known that my mother and titia came up with most of the down payment for the property. By 1954 they had finally settled my grandmother's estate in the Azores, selling her house and land. When Titia contributed her half of the $2,000 in proceeds to purchase 83 Way Street, she punched the ticket that gave her permanent admission to our household, joined at the hip with my mother. This arrangement continued the awkward family triangle from Bowler Street. I don't recall my father ever having a conversation with Titia. He never said much more to her than "Merry Christmas" and "Happy New Year."

My mother, of course, confided in Titia constantly, especially when my parents' marital relationship went into cold storage. On a luminous Memorial Day in 1957, I marched in the annual parade with my Little

League teammates decked out in my white "Comets" uniform with red trim and letters. I returned home only to step into the middle of a heated marital spat. My father wanted to borrow money against the value of the house, perhaps to invest in the stock market. He had a broker, and at one point bought stock in the Studebaker Car Company shortly before it turned into a financial demolition derby. He needed my mother's signature on the bank document, but she was balking, wanting to know the purpose of the loan. "What is the money for?" she demanded, her petite figure bobbing back and forth like a gamecock. "You don't have to know," my father angrily repeated as if his patriarchal prerogatives were under assault. This only poured accelerant on the dispute. After all, I now know, he contributed only $1,000 toward the purchase of the house, though he did become responsible for the $24 monthly payment on the ten-year mortgage. Tempers surged and a high-voltage argument echoed through the house. At one point my mother turned to Titia, whose name was not on the deed to the property and who passively occupied a ringside seat to the quarrel. "My poor sister," she exploded, "gave us her money so that we could buy this house." In the end my mother scribbled her name on the document, but she and my father remained testy and barely spoke for what must have been close to a year. I hated these long periods when iciness took up residence in our house. My father was old school, the patriarchal Primo role so inbred that even a hardwired, spunky, high-strung wife could not housebreak him. Yet my mother usually held out until he offered a peace token.

When serious marital squabbles erupted like what ruined my Memorial Day when I was twelve years old, my mother grabbed her pillow, leaving my father to sleep alone. She moved into a small room shared by my sister and titia. My mother took my sister's bed, forcing her to sleep in a twin bed with Titia for months on end. Once again Titia, long accustomed to life's slights, uncomplainingly accepted the new fallout from Conforti domestic tempests.

In return for a $6,400 selling price, we moved to a place riddled with flaws and unsightliness. We bought the small, boxy house, on a large lot with scattered outbuildings, from an Italian family named Cerce (pronounced chur-chee). The immigrant father had built this poor man's estate and raised a family of sons and daughters, who had grown up and left home—except for Dominic. We called him "Turkey" because it almost rhymed with Cerce.

Turkey was the Cerces' man-child—their retarded, horribly deformed youngest son, and another maimed soul who roamed Bowler Street. He could hear but he couldn't speak, except to make indecipherable guttural sounds. His lantern jaw seemed to be locked open and he constantly drooled. When we cruelly called him "Turkey, Turkey," he tried to chase us, but he could only shuffle, not run. We dreaded falling into his clutches and having him slobber over us like a St. Bernard. During the summer he would make the rounds of Bowler Street trying to sell quarts of blueberries that he had picked in the East End woods. But people were reluctant to buy them because they feared he had dribbled over his pickings.

Turkey's father was an industrious immigrant. Unfortunately, George Cerce built from necessity not skill and he relied on a lot of scrap wood. The house resembled a bungalow constructed on the fly. Mr. Cerce piled shoddy construction on top of flimsy foundation. So much so that our family adopted a motto when we set out to do some work like trimming with hand shears the 350 feet of four-foot-high hedge on three sides of the property: "Don't do a Cerce job," my father or brothers would say. If we didn't complete some task satisfactorily, we faced censure: "That's a Cerce job."

In moving to Way Street we exchanged living space for land, not unlike what Nonnuzzo had done thirty years earlier. The three bedrooms were much smaller than those in our Bowler Street tenement. We four brothers crowded into one of the rooms aided by a bunk bed. The living room and main bathroom were half the size of what we had been used to. There was no kitchen or dining room on the first and only floor. Mr. Cerce had attached an unheated sun porch to the front of the house. He also added a picture window to the living room's south side that framed a patch of grass and a sweeping view of the burned-out Stafford mill yard. Far from lending the house some curb appeal, Mr. Cerce's architectural afterthoughts gave the dwelling a quirky appearance.

To make the house habitable for his large family, Mr. Cerce converted the basement to living quarters. Only a single support, a steel lally column (one of two that underpinned the house), broke up the space occupied by the kitchen, dining, and sitting areas. My parents had a semipartition built that enclosed the column and created a cozy family room. The Cerces, like us, must have spent most of their time in the basement. As his family grew, Mr. Cerce built a cinder-block addition to the back of the house. This proved to be another Cerce job. The addition included an unheated wash-room followed by a claustrophobic half bathroom with a shower slightly larger than a phone booth and an undersized radiator that meant we froze in the winter. Beyond the expansive cultivable land, for my father there was another feature to the Cerces' slapdash house that proved a selling point. Under the unheated sun porch, Mr. Cerce had built a concrete wine cellar.

The structures scattered around the yard were the handiwork of a poor Italian immigrant—seemingly a peasant at heart. A crude outhouse was conveniently located in the middle of the garden, saving a trip to the bathroom when Mr. Cerce toiled outside. It was equipped with a thick 1948 Sears Roebuck Catalogue whose pages were put to good use. A large, windowless, tar-paper shed lay at the back of the yard and served as a chicken coop. It was connected to a long chicken yard. Mr. Cerce used scrap boards of different sizes attached to chicken wire as fencing for the yard, with the back fence marking our property line. An ugly screened-in summer kitchen and smokehouse occupied space near one of the yard's four grape arbors. Finally, a poorly constructed garage filled another corner of the yard. Oddly, one of the house's three cesspools lay partially under the garage, its murky contents visible after the building settled with a tilt.

Never did ham-handed Mr. Cerce make more of a hash of things than when it came to plumbing. For this he earned a lifetime "Cerce job" award. He added cesspools behind the house as his family grew. During heavy rains the cesspools regularly clogged and backed up. Plumbing problems controlled our lives, especially during the first years on Way Street. To reduce water flowing into the unreliable trio of cesspools, my father issued a house rule: "Don't flush the toilet every time you piss." When it rained, flushing became more fitful. We were conservationists before our time.

My father and I engaged in hand-to-hand combat with the main cesspool during our first spring on Way Street. I was home on Wednesday afternoons, his day off, because of overcrowding and double sessions at the Brown School. We loaded an old wine barrel on our rusted wagon. My father attached a pail to a chain and lowered it into the deep. He then pulled as if he was hauling lobsters instead of turds. He dumped the pail's contents into the barrel. When it was half full, we headed to the sewer two hundred feet away on Doyle Street. He pulled and I made sure the barrel didn't tip. "Don't let 'er slip. Keep ya grip," he urged me. He pried open the manhole cover, we dumped the barrel's contents, and then we returned for a refill.

After three and a half years, my father laid down his weapons when it came to skirmishing with balky cesspools: the wine barrel, chain, and bucket; a ladder and baseball bat that my brother Bill used to unclog the main line flowing into the largest cesspool; and the restrictions on flushing the toilet. My father decided to hook up to the sewer on Doyle Street. We boys dug the long, three-and-a-half-feet-deep trench to the edge of our property, and a backhoe made quick work of the rest.

Still, plumbing problems dogged us. We took off the grate in the shower drain, the low point in the plumbing, and jammed the fat end of a baseball bat into the hole to prevent water from backing up. Sometimes we used a sandbag. Our house was built on fill with a high water table. During downpours, water seeped through the foundation. I can remember having breakfast with my bare feet dangling in two inches of water. The television was nearby. I could only think, How come Ozzie and Harriet never had plumbing problems to contend with, let alone jerry-rigged cesspools? When dry, the basement was a warm refuge in winter (except in the washroom and shower) and cool during the summer. But in becoming homeowners we made no headway toward suburban living.

Way Street surpassed Bowler in eyesores—and not only because it was a narrow, rutted dirt lane with no tar surface at all. The Covel Laundry stood across the street from us, a mere thirty-five feet away. A long, wooden structure with peeling, white paint and a sagging roof, the laundry must have been at least fifty years old. On warm summer nights the women operating the pressing machines would throw open the doors on the side of the laundry facing us. We would fall asleep to the hiss of the pressing machines and the chatter of the women as they wrapped up the evening shift of their humdrum jobs.

Little did we know that the business, like the run-down building, was tottering toward collapse, victim of the fifties' "white" appliance revolution that even brought an electric washer and dryer into our home. A few years after our move into the Cerce house, the laundry fell silent. Then vandals preyed on the abandoned building. They broke windows, smashed open doors, ransacked the interior, and salvaged anything of value that they could carry. It is amazing that no one torched the derelict building; it probably would have taken our house with it, and that may have deterred potential arsonists. Year after year the laundry rotted; its peeling paint littered the ground, and its roof shed shingles and threatened to collapse under the weight of heavy snow. No one seemed to care, least of all us. We grew accustomed to the eyesore as we did to a stripped, rusted, 1940ish, black Chevrolet coupe that met its end on a spot of grass behind our property. Perhaps we were distracted from the front and back rot by the goings-on next door.

The property of Angelo and Antoinette DiMarino adjoined ours. Angelo was a short, burly Italian immigrant in his mid- to late fifties who worked as a laborer. When he cleaned up and took off his work hat on Sundays, he revealed his "farmer's tan." Angelo built a stone house like he had known in southern Italy. Working as a laborer, he collected rocks of different sizes, colors, and composition and mortared them into place over a period of years. He was no craftsman, but then he was forced, like Mr. Cerce, to work with a grab bag of material. His stray rocks occupied the place of George Cerce's scrap boards. Angelo's house had its own misshapen character. The assemblage of myriad rocks—some of which protruded, others of which he set evenly in cement—gave the house a crooked appearance, the sure sign of an amateur builder. In other words, a Cerce job stood next door to our Cerce job. Antoinette was Angelo's American-born Italian wife. She too was beefy, and she had a husky voice, as if she had been a career carnival barker. Like us, the DiMarinos lived in their basement—with one difference. They had a dirt floor. The DiMarinos were friendly, if a tad too earthy, neighbors.

One day, about a year after we moved, a tow truck dragging a decommissioned Eastern Massachusetts Street Railway bus suddenly appeared on Crane Street, behind our yard. The truck backed the orange and black bus into the DiMarino yard, parking it right on our property line with the door facing away from us. Once again, no one seemed to mind, especially after Angelo, in a burst of artistic inspiration, painted the bus green. His creativity did not stop there; he had a well-thought-out plan. He turned the bus into a chicken coop, with the door opened during the day and closed at night. He collected the chicken manure from the bus and fertilized his plants.

Angelo grew the best vegetables in the neighborhood—not just because he was the only one with an ample supply of chicken shit. He too had a cesspool, but his intimacy with it was different from ours. As if heaps of chicken manure were not enough to fertilize his garden, he fed his plants human waste. In the summer we could always tell when Angelo was practicing his master gardening. No one called the board of health, just as no one apparently complained about the derelict Covel Laundry or the abandoned black coupe. It would be too much to say that fatalism banked the course of life in Fall River. Yet people, including us, did seem to accept things the way they stood.

Since the DiMarinos had no children, they grew more vegetables than they could eat or preserve. They shared their good fortune with us and other neighbors. We tossed their gifts into the backyard underground swill can whose cover was opened by stepping on a lever. Like two generations earlier, a Portuguese immigrant garbage man arrived on a set day each week almost as punctually as the train in *High Noon*. He lifted our pail, maggots and all, out of the ground and emptied it into a large bucket that he carried on his shoulder. When the bucket was full, he dumped its contents into the back of a waiting truck and continued his rounds.

Antoinette was a gregarious woman who sometimes dropped in at breakfast time for coffee. My father didn't seem to mind. She was rough around the edges, but she was Italian, unpretentious, and friendly. My mother was cool to Antoinette and Angelo. They confirmed what we had repeatedly heard when my father was not around: Fall River's cellar-dwelling Italians failed to measure up when it came to personal hygiene.

Somehow word got back to Antoinette that my mother did not want her visiting because she wasn't sufficiently scrubbed. To Antoinette's credit she confronted the issue head-on. One summer morning after my father had left for work, Antoinette knocked, walked into our basement, and declared in her deep bass voice, "I heard you think I'm too dirty and you don't want me in your house." Antoinette sounded more hurt than angry. My mother was cornered by this frontal assault. "No, no, no," she stammered, "that's not true." "Well, you know, I'm just trying to be friendly when I visit," Antoinette responded, though our hefty neighbor also had a roomy appetite for gossip to fill her idle days. "I know," my mother said. "You're welcome in my house." "I just wanted to get this thing out in the open," Antoinette offered. "You know, things like this can cause hard feelings." My mother again assured Antoinette she was welcome. She seemed to be mollified, but her visits dwindled. I don't think my mother visited Antoinette's house more than a few times.

Though there were stretches of harmony between my father and mother,

on the whole she seemed disheartened by her marriage. She sought solace in her sister and overinvested in the lives of her kids. The move to
83 Way Street must have added to her disappointment with how her life
had unspooled. She found herself living next to earthy, even peasant-like
Italians, in a shoddily built handyman special with perennial plumbing
problems and a yard that required years of labor to tidy up.

And this small domestic world was bounded by blight: Angelo's chicken
coop, the junked black coupe, the rubble-scarred Stafford mill yard, the
crumbling Covel Laundry, and Way Street itself. In this dirt crossroads of
the Flint I found security and hours of happiness with my brothers and
friends on new makeshift playgrounds. But I was not home free. Life in
and around 83 Way Street only deepened my feelings of being an outsider to "normal" American living, which aggravated the ungainliness of
adolescence. Home ownership had not brought us a Cape Cod, Garrison
colonial, or California-style ranch or even a well-built bungalow. It had
not even entitled us to good plumbing. We might as well have kept Mr.
Cerce's outhouse, perhaps upgrading it with the soft pages of an old phone
book in place of his Sears Roebuck Catalogue.

In my father's moral universe too much boyhood idleness came close to
a hanging offense. He now had a small peasant estate and a captive labor
force in my brothers and me. "Start turning over the garden," he would
command annually during Fall River's cool, breezy early spring. We each
took a turn with the pitchfork, and so did he. Using hand shears we were
responsible for trimming the thick hedge that swept around three sides
of our property. Then there was the hundred feet of small hedge that
separated the expansive garden from the scrawny lawn.

My father never ran out of jobs to keep us busy. With the lure of television, he feared we would go soft, that we would not be steeled for success in Fall River as he had by the struggles of his immigrant family, the
Depression, and the relentless labor that he poured into launching his
barbershop. "Go to Bevilacqua's stables and get manure for the garden,"
he would order before he left for work. My brother John, the most studious
and who was headed for the seminary, was immunized from such labors.
My brother Bill and I mounted two bushel baskets on our all-purpose
wagon and set off for the stables, located a block off Bedford Street, where

there were piles of horseshit free for the taking. We filled the bushels and headed for home, Bill pulling the wagon and me balancing the bushels as we negotiated Bedford, Quarry, Bowler, and Way streets, spilling pieces of our valuable cargo here and there.

We made regular trips to the Varley Waste Company, which was just past the suffocating dump on North Quarry Street. We used our wagon to deliver accumulated newspapers and magazines to the company, earning 50 cents to a dollar for our efforts. But there was an added payoff for me at the waste company. Workers had pulled pictures from "girlie" magazines and pasted them on the wall above where they weighed the waste that arrived. The Varley Waste Company introduced me to what passed for pornography in the 1950s, mostly women naked from the waist up. The provocative pictures made the trip worthwhile, but I had to make sure that I didn't gaze too long. Then I would have to confess my mortal sin to the parish priest. The same was true of the magazines I occasionally stumbled on in the Stafford mill yard that had been discarded by workers.

Every six months or so my father marshaled the whole family to clean the barbershop, usually after it closed at 6 p.m. but sometimes on Sunday when painting was involved. We mopped the floors, polished the chairs and display case, washed the walls, and shined the mirrors. Our reward was a "feed" at the Eagle Chinese Restaurant next door.

For all the nationalities and ethnic cuisines in Fall River, Chinese restaurants dominated dining out in the city. Fall River may have claimed more Chinese restaurants per capita than any other place in Massachusetts. From downtown to every Fall River mill village, Chinese restaurants of varying quality and reputation thrived during my youth. With a steady clientele of mill families, Mark You was the standard bearer of Chinese food up the Flint. Like many Chinese restaurants in Fall River, Mark You made dining out a working-class bargain by including bread and butter, French fries, and coleslaw with all meals.

My father wanted work that would keep us busy year-round and teach us how to handle money, which, of course, he controlled. He conscripted us to take charge of a paper route with eighty-five *Herald News* customers. There was just one kink in the hose: the paper route was more than a mile from Way Street and several blocks from the Sacred Heart School, where we boys went after leaving the Brown School. My father's logic entailed a certain perversity, or careful calculation, which we didn't question. "You can deliver the papers after school," he told us. We didn't attend school on Saturdays, during vacation weeks, and all summer; however, we still had to trek over a mile, deliver our newspapers, and retrace our steps home. And when a snowstorm blew in, we couldn't rush home from school. We had to report for duty; after all, our customers needed to know who had dropped dead the previous day and how the local sports teams had fared.

My father set up a succession system for delivering the papers. My older brothers John and Bill first took charge. When I arrived at Sacred Heart School, John had graduated, so I replaced him. Then Doc succeeded Bill. We trudged Fall River's streets in all kinds of weather, a dirt- and print-begrimed, white canvas newspaper bag draped over a shoulder. No doubt my father saw our responsibility and the miles of walking we compiled each week as a kind of grindstone that would sharpen our work ethic and thereby give us a footing in the laboring life of the real Fall River. We found a means to partially subvert his calculations. He knew how many customers we had and the price of the paper, 42 cents per week. But we never told him how much we received in tips. With a mingling of guilt and delight, we dipped into the weekly tips to buy things we seldom or never had at home: potato chips, ice cream, and Mounds and Snickers candy bars. On cold days we stopped at the Stafford Square Diner for hot French fries sold in a brown paper bag that was saturated with grease by the time we finished eating. At Christmastime the tips grew tenfold. We splurged on malted milk shakes and a few games on a pinball machine.

My parents made financial sacrifices to send their sons to the coed Sacred Heart School and their daughter to the all-girls Sacred Heart Academy. My mother took in sewing and began a part-time job at the Portuguese Moonlight Bakery on Bedford Street. She worked a few days a week from 3 to 6 p.m. and all day on Saturday. She remained in character behind the bakery counter: punctilious, nervously energetic, and effortlessly switching back and forth between Portuguese and English. While she was on the job, hapless Titia was in charge of the home front. We toyed with poor Titia. Her love for us tilted toward indulgence, not maternal prerogative; she was clueless about flexing surrogate parental authority. We ran circles around her and laughed off her toothless threats. Frequently Titia consulted central command at the Moonlight Bakery.

"Agnes," she would say, "the boys are acting up, and they won't do anything I tell them." One of us would take the telephone. We were beyond the discipline of the strap, so my mother would plead with us to behave until she came home. Sometimes she tried to bribe us with the promise of pastries from the bakery. "I'll bring home some malasadas," she would hold out, referring to an inexpensive Portuguese dessert consisting of fried dough covered with sugar.

We all appreciated the price my parents paid to send us to the Sacred Heart School. The paper route was our penance for their sacrifice — a penance far more onerous then the three Hail Marys and Our Fathers typically assigned by the priest regardless of how many impure thoughts stirred my imagination and stoked lust in my heart. Yet the Sacred Heart School and its nearby paper route were also intended to orient us, geographically and socially, away from the Flint's hub, away from the Davis School and its bare-knuckle roughnecks. There was a Catholic school in the Flint, Espirito Santo, where I would begin my teaching career. It proved too Portagee for my parents' taste. In choosing the distant Sacred Heart School and the neighboring paper route, my parents wanted us to have sustained contact with the "respectable," assimilated, middle-class Irish.

My father loved the Irish. Father Sullivan had been my father's patron at Holy Rosary Church, and many of my father's customers were Irish professionals: lawyers, teachers, dentists, and businessmen. In fact, the Irish had succeeded the Yankees as Fall River's power brokers. They had even taken over much of the Highlands, along with some upwardly mobile Jews. The Irish bishop himself lived triumphantly in a former Yankee mansion on Highland Avenue.

Sacred Heart parish edged into the Highlands but was not really part of it. The parish stretched from a working-class quarter bordering lower Bedford and Pleasant streets to a solidly middle-class neighborhood with a small mix of doctors and lawyers. There was only one Catholic church in the Highlands. Holy Name, the city's newest parish, was established in the early 1920s as the Irish professional class began to migrate toward the Highlands. The church was a white clapboard, colonial revival building with pseudo-Greek columns and a cupola with a small cross on the top. It resembled St. Francis Xavier, the Kennedy family church in Hyannis. I only set foot in Holy Name once, as a teenager to attend the Requiem Mass for the mother of a coach. Compared to my stucco St. Anthony of Padua with its colorful interior, Holy Name had the look and feel of a Protestant church. Each year the diocesan newspaper, *The Anchor*, published individual parish contributions to the Catholic Charities Appeal. Holy Name always topped the list. Someone has coined the term "CWASP," Catholic white Anglo-Saxon Protestants, to describe well-off, highly educated, and assimilated members of the faithful, the Kennedys and the late William F. Buckley being only the most prominent and wealthy. Less affluent Irish CWASPs, not WASPs, formed my Fall River's entrenched establishment.

Holy Name had no school. Kids from the parish attended Sacred Heart, the nearest Irish school. A few non-Irish good students like us were also admitted. Then there were a handful of students who belonged to Sacred Heart parish and who were of mixed marriages, sometimes Irish and Portuguese. I always felt marginalized at Sacred Heart. My classmates took to calling me "Toni," the name of a popular women's hair permanent and a reference to my naturally dark, curly hair. But it also labeled me as "Tony," the Wop, the Manny of the Italians. Then one day in the seventh grade during social studies, the subject of Portugal came up. The Irish nun matter-of-factly informed us, "Most of the Portuguese in Fall River have Negro blood." In 1958, the black Portagee had not yet been administered the last rites. The alien figure remained alive and kicking up dust in Fall River's sacred and secular precincts. After school, I told my short-fused Portuguese friend, Ronnie Gomes, what Sister had said. "You tell that bitch that I know plenty of black Irish," he railed.

I hated Sacred Heart School, the prejudiced purgatory of my early adolescence. In Sacred Heart's spiritual economy, good Palmer Method penmanship seemed to rank second only to devoutness. I failed miserably on both counts, my left-handed scrawl refusing to yield to stylized Palmer cursiveness. I got along with my Irish classmates, though I made no lasting friends at Sacred Heart. From a few swells I heard talk of dancing school and piano and tennis lessons. I have forgotten, or repressed, the names of my Holy Union nuns, except for "Millie."

Sister Ann Mildred was the scourge of the eighth grade. Square-jawed Millie zealously embraced her assignment: to put the finishing touches on Sacred Heart students by lacquering on guilt day after day. Some layers stuck. Millie, the school's nun in jackboots, gained notoriety throughout the upper grades. When I was in the seventh grade, I heard that she lifted a student by the front of his shirt, slammed him against the blackboard, and held the bug-eyed victim there while she delivered a tongue-lashing. If thumbscrews had been available, I am sure Millie would have put them to good use bringing to heel anyone who displayed a trace of insubordination.

I was one of those students, and Millie was the last chance the Holy Union nuns had to bully me into shape. My schoolwork had begun to flag in the seventh grade. I wore a red tie on St. Patrick's Day. I remained a tractable student in class, but the ever-vigilant nuns detected a change in my attitude. Perhaps, as the darkest and only brown-eyed Conforti sibling, my Negroid blood was finally manifesting itself. "Why can't you be like your brothers?" I was admonished several times. Millie sanctimoniously luxuriated in her scolding and her scorched earth approach to education. "I do what I do for your welfare," she dinned into us. "No one will care for you the way I do after you leave this school."

I survived Millie's reign of terror but not Catholic education. Unlike my two older brothers, after Sacred Heart I would never set foot in a Catholic school again as a student. A decade later, I would accidentally find myself teaching the fourth grade at the Flint's Espirito Santo School. I tried to make some amends for what Millie and Sacred Heart School had visited upon me.

Before then, however, I found minor satisfaction for real and imagined slights at Sacred Heart and for feeling like a Portagee while delivering newspapers in a middle-class Irish neighborhood skirting the Highlands. My dad's beloved Father Sullivan had a sister who was a physician in Fall River. Dr. Doherty lived in the Highlands and belonged to the city's CWASP class. She had a son named Ricky, a Holy Namer who graduated from Sacred Heart School two years ahead of me. One day, Dr. Doherty mentioned to my father that Ricky was set to attend Portsmouth Priory in the fall. This Rhode Island institution was an exclusive Catholic prep school. It resembled St. Paul's, Groton, Phillips Andover, among other private WASP institutions founded in the late nineteenth century by New England Brahmins and Brahmin wannabes who shunned public schools, which were becoming more ethnic and immigrant. The priory's academic rigor posed no serious problem to Ricky. Rather, his mother was concerned with team sports, which, following the character-building model of the Brahmin prep schools, the priory valued. Unfortunately, Ricky played no sports. "Send him down to Columbus Park," my father offered. "My boys will play baseball with him and he can pick up the game."

Arrangements were made for us to meet Ricky a few times a week at 10 a.m. Dr. Doherty would arrive from the Highlands in her big blue Lincoln Continental and drop off Ricky. He carried a new, pricey Rawlings glove, the Cadillac of baseball gloves in the 1950s and '60s. We had ancient mitts, small, fat gloves with no rawhide between the fingers, from the 1930s when my father coached baseball for Holy Rosary Church. Ricky wore a new baseball cap to protect his pale, freckled face. The hat was a tip-off that Ricky would soon remind us of the Little League's minor league. The visor stuck straight out like a duckbill. Seasoned baseball players rounded their visors the way major leaguers did.

We all liked Ricky. He was an earnest, quiet, unpretentious kid. He wanted so badly to learn, but he was hopelessly lacking in any athletic ability for baseball, and probably for sports in general. He was stiff in his movements, fielding ground balls by stooping from the waist rather than bending from the knees. At bat he had an awkward sweeping swing that led him often to flail at the air. His mother would return at noon to pick him up. After a couple of weeks she stuck her head out of the car window and asked, "How's he doing?" "He's doing okay," we would say. "He's learning."

The sessions lasted about a month. Ricky and his mother must have realized the futility of trying to learn in a few weeks a game of skill that we had played for years. It was the first time I felt that I had some experience, knowledge, and ability that outshone a privileged Irish kid, a Sacred Hearter via Holy Name. I resisted gloating over my minor triumph because Ricky was such a likeable guy. Yet, I did feel satisfaction, winning one over a kid who came from what I would later more clearly understand as the CWASP world of the Highlands. ✓

The disastrous Ricky affair took place at Columbus Park, but after we moved to Way Street the Stafford mill yard became our main "pickup" game playground. We played baseball on its concrete surface, marking out bases and a homerun line with bricks from the original building. Closer to our house, on a perfectly flat stretch of mill-yard concrete, we erected a ten-foot-high basketball hoop with a square backboard. We kept the court clean of snow all winter and used a push broom to remove rainwater.

Of course we made new friends: the Saravo brothers, Henry and Joey, members of a rough-edged Italian family who also lived in their basement; Billy Souza, who attended Fall River's Portuguese Baptist Church and whose other distinction was that he had two thumbs on one hand; and Irv Gitlin, a Jewish boy who regularly joined our basketball games. Above all, I became a close friend of John Kershura, who was three years older and half a foot taller than me. Whether it was baseball, basketball, or stickball, he relished vanquishing boys who were much younger and smaller than him. We called him "Kosher" because his Polish last name took too long to pronounce. He retaliated with cruel names for his mill-yard teammates and opponents: uncouth Henry Saravo was "Garbage"; Billy Souza was "Thumbsie," a play on Pumpsie Green, the Red Sox first black player, who joined the team in 1959; and Irv Gitlin was "Jew Boy," one of Kosher's nicknames that neither my brothers nor I used, though it didn't seem to bother Irv.

We played football on a strip of grass behind our house where the old Chevrolet coupe had expired. When games broke out on Sunday afternoons, Al Ciullo, a thirtyish married neighbor with no kids, joined us and played quarterback for one team. He passed and ran the ball, but we tagged rather than tackled him. It may seem strange that a grown man would play football with ten- to thirteen-year-old kids. Today, that would be so suspect that no sensible male would attempt it. But Al was a decent man who played exuberantly with us as if we were the children he never had.

Al would die fifty years after our football games, and my brother Doc would send me his obituary. I would be shocked to learn that Al had been a youthful hero in World War II. He was born in 1926, so he could not have been more than nineteen when World War II ended. He was not yet a man when he served as a machine gunner with the frontline infantry in Europe. He earned the Bronze Star for valor in combat. Perhaps his war experience explains why he settled into a machinist job in East Providence and into the simple life at the dirt corner of Bowler and Crane streets in the house where he had grown up. He was content to plant the garden his father had cultivated, to make wine in his cellar, to play bocce in the dirt street with old Italian men on Sunday afternoons in summer, and to switch to football with us in the fall. I can still smell the Sunday dinner garlic and wine on Al's breath when we huddled to make up plays. Little did I understand how what Al had done and seen and heard about while still a teenager shaped his life, including the boyish pleasure of playing football with neighborhood kids.

Early one summer evening my grandfather stormed into our house unannounced and angry. There had been a blowup with my grandmother and Aunt Edith. I had seen Nonnuzzo fuming with them before. He would grab his chin and pull down quickly, the signal that he had reached his frothing point and a gesture that seemed to restrain him from lashing out physically at them. This time he vowed not to return to Beattie Street. "I belonga here," he said, "in the homea my oldest son." My father smiled and called Beattie Street to find out what happened. Nonnuzzo insisted he would not return. He sat watching television with us smelling of Parodi Cigars, the cheap, stinky Italian stogies that he smoked and chewed on when they hung from his mouth unlit. My father let Nonnuzzo sit and stew for a couple of hours. While Nonnuzzo let off steam, I could see my mother worrying quietly about how this Beattie Street squabble would end. My slightly built father, the smallest of the Conforti men, remained the Primo who carried decisive weight in the domestic affairs of Beattie Street. He finally persuaded Nonnuzzo to return. His oldest son escorted him home.

Two years later, in 1959, Nonnuzzo lay on his deathbed. He had suffered a heart attack or stroke on Quarry Street. We saw the pool of blood in front of Giaconni's Grocery Store, where he had fallen and cracked open his head. He was waked at Silvia's Funeral Home on Bedford Street. A Portuguese family ran Silvia's, but it served both the Azorean and Italian communities. In Fall River each ethnic group had its own funeral parlors, but the Italians of Bedford Street were not numerous enough to support one of their own.

My mother made something of a peevish scene at the wake. The euphemistically called "Home" was laid out with an inner room, where the casket was placed and the family sat to greet mourners. There were also seats for the nonfamily mourners in the inner room. Through a wide doorway, there was an outer room for large wakes like my grandfather's—his eight surviving children having in-laws and many friends.

I was fourteen years old when, along with my siblings, I followed my mother up to Nonnuzzo's casket; we knelt two at a time and said prayers in silence. Instead of joining the Confortis, my mother chose to sit with friends and to do so in the outer room. We simply followed her. This insult to the Confortis may have been in retaliation against my father during another polar frost that gripped my parents' marriage. Or perhaps my mother saw her behavior as a way of separating herself from her Dago in-laws by sticking a thumb in their eyes. My aunts and uncles were livid. My aunts Natalie and Rose came over and said firmly, "Agnes, you belong with the family not out here." "No," she replied, "I'm not budging. I'm staying right here." My aunts tried again but to no avail. I remember sympathizing with my mother, sitting by her side like a loyal son. In retrospect, my only explanation is that I grew up constantly exposed to a bill of particulars enumerating my father's and the Confortis' Portagee-like flaws. I was still too young to express anything but solidarity with her, even though I had great affection for the Confortis.

A few years before this incident, my mother faced a problem with her side of the family that challenged her identity as a dignified, assimilated Portuguese woman. In 1954, one of my mother's Azorean cousins immigrated to Fall River with her husband, two daughters, and a son. They were proud to have Americanized relatives in the city. Manuel Jr., the oldest child, was around seventeen. He had dark skin and a wide cheery smile. He worked on a farm and wore a broad-brimmed straw hat. Influenced by television, I saw him as a sombrero-clad Mexican-looking exotic. We would occasionally meet him as we hiked to and from our paper route. He would smile and yell in Portuguese from across the street, "Hi cousins," eliciting chortles from us. He continued to greet us heartily even after we stiff-armed his family.

The immigrant cousins settled on the first floor of a triple-decker around the corner from Orange Street, where my mother and father had grown up. My mother first welcomed Mabel and her family to our tenement on Bowler Street. She even gave her immigrant kin clothes. But then the relationship soured.

It began, I think, a couple of summers after we moved to Way Street. Mabel invited us for supper at her tenement. My father didn't join us because he worked late. Mabel was a nervous host, excited to serve her American-born relatives and eager to put her best foot forward. My mother was also on edge. In many respects, she faced a generational dilemma.

Extending charity to an immigrant cousin's family represented one thing. Engaging "greenhorn" relatives on level ground disrupted her identity as an assimilated Portuguese-American woman. We were invited to sit down at the table in Mabel's kitchen with its worn linoleum floor. Just before we did so, Manny and his two sisters took the gum they were chewing and placed it on the top of the refrigerator for later retrieval. Supper went downhill from there. The table was set with reused bottles as drinking glasses. There was conversation in Portuguese; the family had understandably not yet acquired facility with English.

We made it through the meal and left, commenting endlessly on their greenhorn ways. My mother failed to return the invitation. Mabel and her family never visited our house on Way Street, I am sure. My mother remained loyal to her parents' friends from St. Michael as their numbers dwindled throughout the 1950s. Yet, sadly, we had nothing to do with Mabel and her family after that one meal. We sometimes saw them from a distance at St. Anthony's.

The immigrants of the 1950s and early '60s presaged the new wave of Azoreans who would arrive in Fall River after the abolition in 1965 of the exclusionary quotas of the 1920s. In the main, these new Azoreans were, like my grandfather Jose Bento and Mabel's family, hardworking immigrants who injected vitality into an exhausted mill city. Of course, many new Azorean women flocked into sweatshops while their husbands found low-skill, low-wage jobs. But talented, enterprising Azoreans also settled in Fall River. One, Manny Moniz, lived around the corner at the far end of Way Street. He remodeled a spacious house into the neighborhood's most attractive home by far. He formed a carpentry crew and did some work for my parents. I remember him saying in his halting English, "I will send one of my mans over." We found this amusing, like the gum and bottle episode at Mabel's house.

Even their fellow Portuguese referred to the new Azoreans as "greenhorns." I had mixed, confused feelings about Manny Moniz. He was a greenhorn who was economically better off than us, living in an attractive house that we had to pass whenever we visited Beattie Street. As our reaction to Mabel and her family suggests, the new immigrants exposed fault lines in Fall River's Portuguese community. Portuguese identity and social relations acquired a new complexity in parishes like St. Anthony's.

The church seemed to have only a handful of Cape Verdeans and families from mainland Portugal, groups that would have enriched but also confounded Portuguese racial and social identity. Nevertheless, in my mind, a sometimes muddled immigrant-ethnic ranking took hold at St. Anthony's. There were second- and third-generation Azoreans like us who were assimilated in varying degrees. Next, came the Portagees—the less successful, minimally educated Portuguese, many of whom continued to live in cheap triple-deckers. Then there were the greenhorns, whom perhaps most Portuguese, including us, slighted or disdained even as some skilled, industrious immigrants such as Manny Moniz prospered impressively. And all Fall River Portuguese, regardless of their social position, remained vulnerable to disparagement as black or dirty Portagees. Little did we all know that the day would come when continued Azorean and Cape Verdean immigration combined with later Brazilian arrivals would make Portuguese the major second language spoken in what had been Puritan-Yankee Massachusetts.

My father despised idleness, whether among his boys or within himself. Beyond tending his garden and battling persistent plumbing problems, he looked for other ways to keep busy on his midweek day off. He launched a sales venture around the time we moved to Way Street. To this day it saddens me, like the fact that he flunked out of driving school.

Sometime in the early 1950s my father got his hands on a package of the obscure Hoffritz Razor Blades. We would repeatedly hear what became part of his sales pitch. "The blade gave me the cleanest, smoothest shave I ever had." He found out that no one marketed the blades in southern New England, not that the German company had any plans to make a splash in the United States. He apparently secured the rights to be Hoffritz's point man in southeastern New England. Then, a large storage cabinet arrived that he placed in the basement next to our rumbling but dependable old furnace. He stocked the cabinet with perhaps more than fifty boxes of blades, twelve packages to a box. For his new enterprise, my father purchased a satchel to carry his goods to barbershops. He then set out to persuade the barbering fraternity to accept his merchandise. If he could convince barbers to try the blades and offer them for sale, he was sure the Hoffritz product would sell itself. Never mind that he would be competing with Gillette, which advertised extensively on major sporting events such as the popular Friday night fights. Soon Schick would offer more competition.

My father seems to have had a business plan in his head. Since so many barbers in southern New England were Italian, he believed he had an edge convincing his compatriots to carry the blades. He started in Fall River. He talked barbers he knew personally into carrying the blades at no cost and to display them with other grooming items. The barbers would receive a percentage of the sales, a no-expense incentive to push Hoffritz on their customers. We sometimes delivered boxes of blades to local barbershops when they ran out.

My father had set his sights on Boston and Providence and cities in between like Pawtucket and Brockton. He was an ambitious salesman with no personal transportation. He often hitched rides with customers who were going to one of his target cities. Sometimes he used the bus. Once in Providence or Boston, he traipsed from shop to shop. Sometimes he took one of us with him. I am sure he wanted to teach us about work, about the importance of persistence and determination. He may have also reckoned that having a kid as a sidekick might win him sympathy.

I went with him once to Brockton. It was in the spring of 1955; we traveled with a customer of his who had business in the city. I vividly recall walking into a one-man barbershop decorated with photographs of hometown hero Rocky Marciano. After my father introduced himself by name and as a barber from Fall River, he delivered his sales pitch. "Have you ever heard of Hoffritz Blades," he asked, to which the Italian barber's answer was no. Then came a description of how the blade gave my father the best shave he had ever had. "I can leave a box with you at no cost. Just try them and encourage your customers to try them." He pulled out his card so the barber could contact him when he needed a new supply, which would be mailed promptly. Otherwise, my father promised to check back the next time he was in Brockton. I don't recall what this barber's profit would be or whether he accepted my father's offer. Most of the time I was engrossed with the autographed pictures of Rocky Marciano in the cozy shop.

My father viewed Providence as his potential gold mine, or at least as a silver lode. It was large, close to Fall River, and held a high concentration of Italian barbers. He came to know and like the city, pounding its pavements Wednesday after Wednesday, while we were doing the same on our paper route. Surprisingly, he met substantial resistance among Providence's Italian barbers. Then one day a chance opportunity fell his way. He let it melt in the palm of his hand.

Between calls on Providence barbers, he stopped in a bar for a drink. He happened to sit next to someone he had coached at Holy Rosary twenty years earlier. Delighted to see my father, the man asked him what he was doing in Providence. "I'm tryin' to get barbers to carry a line of excellent blades called Hoffritz," he explained. "But I'm findin' the most resistance among my own people." The man pulled out a scrap of paper, scribbled something on it, folded it and handed it to my father. "Take this to Raymond Patriarca's business on Atwells Avenue." My father knew the street well; it was the main artery through Federal Hill, Providence's largest Italian neighborhood. Patriarca, the head of the New England Mafia, operated out of a vending machine business called Coinomatic. It was apparently a means of laundering money. "I walked in," my father related, "and there was these goons hangin' around. One asked me what I wanted. I told him and handed him the note. He said, 'wait here' and went into a backroom. I was so scared I left before he returned."

Of course, word from Raymond, as he was referred to, would have thrown open many doors for my father in Providence. The Mob boss was at the height of his power. My father sought the support of his fellow Italians, but not if it meant getting mixed up with the Mob.

My father did not give up his Hoffritz dream easily. He continued to peddle the blades for at least a decade, that is, into his midsixties, while he ran his barbershop the other five days. Besides the opportunity to turn a profit with the potential to grow over time, the Wednesday excursions got him out of the house on his day off and away from my mother and aunt. I doubt he made much money, especially a return equal to his steadfast itinerant salesmanship. He did have regular customers, however, to whom he mailed or delivered boxes of blades.

Like the barbershop, I came to take the Hoffritz escapade for granted, preoccupied as I was with sports and bad teenage skin. Yet Hoffritz Blades were a part of our lives — through my father's absences, through the stacks of boxed blades, and through the local deliveries we made. I sensed something futile, even farcical in my father's reprising the role of the Jewish peddler of the era and the Fuller Brush man. From the vantage point of hindsight I see no humor, just a determined man without a car but with an outsized work ethic who sadly chose the wrong product at the wrong time.

Unlike my brothers, whatever industry and tenacity passed through my bloodlines and permeated my family culture I diverted to organized sports beginning at the age of twelve, my last year of eligibility for Little League. Athletics were all important in Fall River. Winning teams brought distinction to a downtrodden city. This was especially true of Durfee High School athletics. We all knew that the Durfee basketball team won the New England championship in 1948 and repeated the feat in 1956. Miss Connors, principal at the Brown School, had posted photographs of the latter team on the fifth-grade bulletin board. The starting five—composed of two Portuguese and single Lebanese, Polish, and Irish players—were giants in my eleven-year-old eyes. In 1957, the Durfee baseball team claimed the state championship. Two players signed professional contracts, including Russ Gibson, the catcher for the Red Sox when they won the American League pennant in 1967. Durfee football games, like its basketball contests, were community affairs. Games with Thanksgiving rival New Bedford and Catholic opponent Monsignor Coyle of Taunton overflowed with spectators. For athletic-minded males growing up in Fall River, Durfee High sports loomed as a path to personal and city laurels—and sometimes to elective office.

With the exception of football, Fall River had a rich infrastructure of organized baseball and basketball that preceded or competed with high school sports: numerous Little Leagues; several Babe Ruth Leagues; junior, senior, and adult Catholic leagues; Park League; and American Legion Baseball. Except for American Legion, I would play in all of these baseball leagues, including as a teenager in the adult Catholic league with grown men! I also played in several basketball leagues. After getting a late start in Little League because I was a timid middle child fearful of playing against older boys, my athletic confidence surged as my school grades went into free fall. Through organized sports, I was increasingly drawn to the heart of the Flint, Lafayette Park, and identification with working-class ethnic kids.

One episode and one coach stand out in my memory of pre-high school organized athletics. I was a mediocre shooting guard and decent defender on St. Anthony's Junior Catholic Youth Organization basketball team. We had a tall center named Manny Papoula, who would later star for Durfee and earn a basketball scholarship to Boston College. We swept to the Fall River championship and advanced to the diocesan finals against St. Mary's of Taunton, where the game was played. The referees were blatantly against us, favoring St. Mary's on every close play. Our coach mildly questioned a call, and he was slapped with a technical foul. We lost the game. "Shit. Shit, shit! We got screwed," I grumbled to Johnny and Gerry Lima, brothers and teammates who were my close friends. Their father Manny coached our team and treated me like one of his sons. "You bet your ass we did," Gerry replied. Someone who was leaving the game overheard our angry exchange. He mentioned that St. Mary's had a "Fighting Irish" pastor whose philosophy was "We never lose." It would be too much to say that the referees were in on a fix. In part, the crowd influenced the local men in stripes. But most of us felt that there was no way that Irish St. Mary's was going to lose on its home court to a bunch of Portagees from Fall River.

George "Sneaker" McDonald, my coach in the Flint Babe Ruth League, would have been a humble, patient priest had he found himself drawn to that vocation. Instead, he devoted his life to the youth of the Flint. If ever a saintly man walked the streets of Fall River, his name was Sneaker McDonald. He was a member in good standing of the Flint's respectable working class. He later became a cop, and a benevolent one at that, who gave many a teenager a second chance. He was the other face of Fall River's Irish Catholicism from the blood-chilling Millie. Sneaker was to me something of what Father John Sullivan had been to my father—a man who had faith in me and believed I would amount to more than a decent athlete.

We called him Sneaker, but no one knew how he acquired that moniker. He never raised his voice, but he could be firm with his players. He wanted to win, but not at the cost of teaching values like teamwork and hustle. He often took troublesome individuals and with a fine touch nurtured them as persons and players. He treated us with respect and we responded in kind—and won a lot of games in the process.

Sneaker did more to distinguish himself as a mentor and coach than any of the numerous dedicated men I played for in three sports at many levels of competition in Fall River. At the end of each season, he hand wrote letters to his players' parents. Based on my letters for the two years I played for him, Sneaker penned positive evaluations focusing on character development, not athletic achievement. These letters cheered my parents because my grades continued to tank while my older brothers' soared. My mother and father were no longer placing bets on me to win, place, or show as a student. Thus they were pleased to read what Sneaker wrote, which they let me see. The letter for my last year of Babe Ruth baseball when I was fifteen began, "Once again this is a letter that I look forward to writing." It was filled with words like "gentleman," "team player," "co-operative," "respectful," and "leading by example."

I only partially recognized my likeness in Sneaker's portrait, for I had long learned to salt my speech liberally with four-letter words like my Flint friends. I occasionally played pranks with them, under the cover of night, turning over a few trash barrels set out for the next day's collection, for example. Then, too, my body was a riot of hormones.

Sneaker was the coach who fought for me to receive the Most Valuable Player Award only to see ethnic politics triumph. I did earn a trophy, however. More importantly, his letters to my mother and father were a kind of merit badge, a substitute for what I never had a chance of achieving because my parents couldn't afford a Boy Scout uniform.

Beginning with the Flint Babe Ruth League, Lafayette Park joined the Stafford mill yard as the terra firma of my sports-centered life. With Portuguese, Lebanese, Irish, and French working-class teenagers, I joined pickup games of baseball, touch football, and wiffle ball in the park and watched endless rounds of poker played for small change. At fourteen, I learned that a Franco girl, who virtually lived at the park in summer, had a crush on me. She became my first girlfriend; part of our bond was mutual bad skin. Our dates consisted of occasional Sunday afternoons at the Strand Theater and huddling in Lafayette Park during the winter with trips to a nearby corner store to buy candy and get warm. The courtship lasted over a year. My next female relationship would have to wait until the start of my senior year at Durfee, after my skin suddenly cleared up as if I had bathed it in Lourdes water.

⊰ *Five* ⊱

FAITH

Catholics dwarfed other religious groups in my Fall River the way granite mills dominated the industrial landscape. The three-volume definitive history of the city, completed in 1946, reported that Fall River was 80 percent Catholic. Ten or fifteen years later, that number must have crept upward toward 85 percent. Twenty-seven churches ministered to the faithful during my youth: nine Irish, seven Portuguese, six French, two Polish, one Italian, one Lebanese, and one Ukrainian. Fall River's Catholicism was as tightly entwined with ethnicity, class, neighborhood, and extended family as the inner threads of the old, coverless baseballs that we wrapped with black friction tape.

My study of Puritanism would later offer an escape from this entanglement. I would come to see New England's formative religious faith as solely residing in Protestantism. I would miss the forest through the leaves. New England has been a majority Catholic region for more than a century. Mill cities from Lewiston to Lawrence and well beyond abounded with Catholics. There was no single moment when the scales fell from my eyes and I realized that there is more than one New England conscience; that my religious heritage mattered; and that like tens of thousands of New Englanders, my habits of heart, with their own geyser of guilt, represented an authentic regional tradition.

My father, mother, and titia were all devout ghetto Catholics. That is, they had boarded up their minds and nailed them shut to any religious ideas and influences that did not stem from Catholicism. Evangelist Billy Graham would be the only exception. Their religious life was a closed book stamped with the Church's imprimatur.

My father had not always been such a pious Catholic. My grandparents seem to have had a typical southern Italian attitude toward the Church. It was there for life's turning points—birth, marriage, and death. I never saw Nonna or Nonnuzzo in church on occasions when I attended Holy Rosary with my father.

Like my mother and titia, my father never missed Mass on Sunday or Holy Days of obligation. And like them he dutifully adhered to days of abstinence. When it came to Lent, however, my father did not win bragging rights in our family. I gave up candy and held on for seven weeks despite ever-present temptation. My father sacrificed his daily pack of Philip Morris. Then he retrieved his tobacco pipe from a bureau drawer where it had gathered dust for a year. The pipe supplied his daily nicotine fix until Easter Sunday. I found this amusing, another blemish on his fatherly figure—like his inability to synchronize a car's clutch, brake, gas pedal, and steering wheel.

Father John Sullivan did more than help my father open his barbershop. The humble Irish pastor who spoke Italian rescued my father from his tepid Catholicism. He imbued my father's faith with the puritanical Catholicism so characteristic of the Irish-dominated American church.

Father Sullivan became pastor of Holy Rosary in 1929 and energized a small, flagging church. He reached out to the youth of the parish and beyond by transforming the church basement into a boys' club. He tapped my father to coach a highly successful basketball team for twelve- to fourteen-year-olds that was called the Piccolinis (nice small boys). My father also coached a baseball team that played in Columbus Park. He kept a scrapbook of the Piccolinis' impressive string of victories in the early 1930s, before he opened his barbershop. I paged through his Depression-era album as a teenager, and it spurred me to start one of my own.

My childhood and teen years were sprinkled with references to and stories about Father Sullivan, a narrative of a holy man who walked on stilts, if not on water. "He was the finest man I ever met," my father pronounced whenever an opportunity landed his way. I remember one story he told about Father Sullivan when someone, whom I can't recall, was visiting our house on Way Street. A woman parishioner came to Father Sullivan seeking permission to marry a non-Catholic who had no intention of converting. Father Sullivan discouraged the idea and told the woman she should reconsider, my father related. "The woman went away disappointed and determined to try again. She revisited Father Sullivan, who tried again to persuade the woman to change her mind, telling her he would not sanction the marriage. The woman persisted and Father

Sullivan lost patience. "You want a man so bad, you'll marry a niggah," he told her. She reported Father Sullivan to the bishop. But my father leaped to the pastor's defense. "He was only expressing his love for the Church."

Father Sullivan's powerful influence on my father reinforced his deep affection for the Irish and instilled in him one dimension of the Catholicism that he imparted to my siblings and me. When an Italian priest from Fall River became pastor of Holy Rosary, he could never measure up to Father Sullivan's humility and holiness in my father's eyes. He left Holy Rosary for an Irish Catholic Church near the heart of the Flint. When I came to know Father Sullivan, this lion of ghetto Catholicism, he was a feeble old man living out his days in Fall River's Catholic Memorial Home in the Highlands. My father sustained a devotion to his benefactor. He visited Father Sullivan regularly to cut his hair and shave his blotchy, jowly cheeks. One of us often tagged along. I can still see my father plying his trade with a straight-edge razor and hearing the scratch, scratch, scratch as he carefully worked down to Father Sullivan's throat, never drawing blood. Father Sullivan spoke slowly, the only man I ever heard refer to my father as "Orlando." It was a sign of the formal distance that the priest maintained with his acolyte, upholding the Church's hierarchy even as his days wound down.

My mother and titia did not need the intervention of a priest to change the course of their religious lives. They were always devout, unquestioning ethnic Catholics; their Portuguese identity was milled into the grain of their faith. I don't recall them ever attending Sunday Mass at any church but St. Anthony's. To do so was almost their equivalent of dropping in on a Protestant service.

My mother had the kind of rich devotional life that was common among Catholic women in the 1950s. For years she continued her novena, nine days of worship, to St. Anne for her ostensible intercession in my sister's birth. St. Anne Church stood second only to the Flint's Notre Dame de Lourdes in stateliness. It was the mother church of French Canadians in Fall River.

My mother turned to St. Anne Church because it had been declared a shrine—a place where a miracle occurred and where supernatural power was presumably still housed and accessible to the laity. When a cornerstone for the church was laid during the blessing ritual, a platform collapsed. The priest who guided the church's founding was grievously injured. He prayed to St. Anne, promising that if he were healed he would name the church for her. He made a complete recovery.

Not finished until 1906, St. Anne's upper level was made of striking blue Vermont marble. Its twin steeples soared 155 feet, another sacred Fall River landmark like Notre Dame that broke up a skyline owned by smokestacks. In 1928, a perpetual novena devoted to St. Anne was established at the church. Evidence of St. Anne's cures, especially of the lame, adorned the church's walls. I remember crutches and leg braces like those worn by polio victims in the 1950s. Such magical Catholicism captivated my imagination and sustained my faith, not the calcified religiosity of Sacred Heart School. I would race to St. Anne's as a teenager, hoping that its holy water and the saint would cure my acne when a dermatologist could have turned the trick.

Stretching from the fall into early winter, my mother made her annual novena once a week for nine consecutive visits to St. Anne's. The churchly shrine was in Fall River's South End, at least two and a half miles from our house. She often walked back and forth, dragging one of us on her pilgrimage, sometimes in the bitter cold and probably figuring that this was an added sacrifice that St. Anne would appreciate. After all, my mother might need the saint's services again.

On occasion when the weather turned especially frigid, my mother managed to secure a ride. I went with her one time with Manny Diaz. He owned a fish market on Bedford Street across from "Your Meating Place" and around the corner from St. Anthony's. Manny was my mother's age, a handsome ladies man, the Lothario of Bedford Street, I would later learn. I have no doubt that he had designs on my mother. She was slim and still attractive even after bearing five children.

When Manny arrived in his truck, my mother pushed me in first, a buffer between them. He dropped us off at St. Anne's. We entered the church, dipped our fingers in the cold holy water, and made the sign of the cross. Perhaps, I imagined, this liquid was more spiritually potent than ordinary holy water, something akin to Lourdes water. The dimmed lights, the banks of flickering candles, the hint of incense in the air, and the miraculous evidence on the walls all stirred my youthful faith in our religion's enchanting power.

We joined a handful of others who had braved the bone-chilling night and forgone the popular Milton Berle show to pray for their own intentions or to give thanks for blessings bestowed. My mother prayed for about an hour, lit a candle, and repeated the sign of the cross with holy water; then we stepped out into the cold. Manny was waiting. It was Christmas time, and he asked, "Do you wanna go see a house that has beautiful lights and decorations?" My mother hesitated and then yielded. We drove about a mile and stopped in front of a house that had more Christmas lights than I had ever seen. As we were leaving my mother turned to me and said, "Don't tell anybody that we did this." It was as if she had done something illicit, deviated from her religious mission, gone on a date with Manny. Like the men who pursued her before marriage, Manny had no success denting my mother's moral armor. Later it became the talk of Bedford Street when he left his wife, abandoned his business, and ran off with another woman.

My mother's novena to St. Anne represented but one thread in the tapestry of her devotional life. She and Titia said the Rosary every day, my mother nervously working her fingers through the well-worn black beads that had belonged to my grandmother. Usually after supper my mother announced, "I'm going to say my Rosary." This meant she was not to be disturbed for the fifteen or twenty minutes of rote praying, when the Rosary beads doubled as worry beads. She retreated to the bedroom that Titia and my sister Betty Anne shared. The bureau held a little shrine to my Azorean grandparents. There were photographs and a votive candle that was lit every night and burned until bedtime. A crucifix hung over the bed as it did in the other two bedrooms. My parents' room also had a painting of the Last Supper. Palms were saved in drawers or they were fashioned into crosses by Nonnuzzo and stuck in the bedroom crucifixes.

My mother made sure we wore other amulets, convinced as she was of their power to protect us. We progressed from scapulars, to medals pinned on our undershirts, and finally to chains with images of St. Joseph, St. Christopher, St. Anthony, or the Blessed Mother dangling from our necks. The sacred artifacts of our faith also included pictures of a soft Anglo-looking Christ and images of Mary and the saints that were given out during catechism at St. Anthony's. Once we enrolled at Sacred Heart School, we were exempted from parish catechism; the school became a source of sacred images.

St. Christopher, the patron saint of travelers, was the beneficiary of a devotional revival during the 1950s and '60s, as America became a nation on wheels. For a contribution to Father Keller's *The Christophers* show, which aired on Sunday morning, you received a small, white plastic statue of the saint that attached to a car dashboard. It announced your faith and created something of a religious congregation on wheels regardless of the kind of car you drove. Our 1950 Ford sported a St. Christopher icon. John and Bill drove the heap sixteen miles back and forth to Taunton, where they attended Monsignor Coyle High School. They never had a serious accident that I recall.

The saints brought the divine closer to my life. They made the supernatural accessible, not remote. They bypassed the priest and churchly sacramentalism and enabled me to appeal directly for spiritual and mundane intercession to the divines who were once mortals. The saints were saints because they had performed miracles that were investigated and documented by the Church. From St. Anthony to St. Anne, a canonized crisis intervention team or first responders stood on call ready to entertain offers like my mother's: "If you do this, then I'll do that."

The feast of St. Anthony (the "festa" in Portuguese) was a major event in our lives and another facet of lay devotion, this time enmeshed with ethnic and neighborhood identity. Our church held the celebration on the third weekend of June, more or less near St. Anthony's feast day on the thirteenth. The festa usually coincided with the end of school, which swelled my boyish excitement for this seasonal religious rite. Born, raised, and ordained in Portugal, St. Anthony (1195–1231) joined the Franciscan order and spent the end of his short adult life in northern Italy; Padua claimed him as one of its own. St. Anthony was credited with impressive miracles. In one of the most celebrated, he was said to have reattached the foot of a young man who had kicked his mother and cut off his appendage in repentance. Thirty years after St. Anthony's death, the people of Padua opened his crypt to place his relics in a new temple. A miracle had apparently occurred. The corpse had been reduced to dry bones, but befitting a holy man who had been a renowned preacher, St. Anthony's tongue was perfectly preserved, as pinkish as the day he was born. Naturally, Paduans put the tongue on display, drawing pilgrims to the miraculous relic. When it lured me, long after my Catholic childhood, the tongue would evoke warm youthful memories of a magical Catholicism: my mother's devotion to the saint; the constant invocation of his name in our home; and the annual festa.

For the celebration, strings of lights encircled the church grounds.

Nightly outdoor band concerts enlivened the Portuguese stretch of Bedford Street. St. Anthony's Band entertained the crowds while the curious circulated through the church hall where donated items were sold or auctioned off. Despite its name, St. Anthony's Band was not officially affiliated with the church. The musicians had their own clubhouse in the parish, and during the summer they performed in the festas of other Portuguese churches in southeastern New England. Many parishes hosted brass bands like St. Anthony's, adult and teenage musicians who were hired for concerts and processions during parish celebrations. My brother Bill, a clarinetist, joined St. Anthony's Band when he was fifteen; he spent his summer weekends playing at Portuguese feasts in nearby Massachusetts and Rhode Island.

Peopled filled the sidewalks for the procession through the streets of our parish, the highlight of St. Anthony's festa. The procession took place on Saturday evening, one of the rare times when my mother spared money so that we could buy popcorn, cotton candy, or ice cream from the vendors who lined Seventeenth Street, which bordered the church grounds. Several brawny men of the parish—construction workers already showing the tanned skin that would darken as the summer deepened—broke out their shiny polyester Sunday suits and mounted St. Anthony's statue on their broad shoulders. The priests and altar boys, dressed in their Sunday regalia, marched directly behind the statue, which was positioned in the middle of the procession. Members of Church sodalities, as they were called, fell in line ahead of and behind the statue. They were mostly women, some of them dressed in black and carrying Rosary beads and candles with cardboard protectors against the evening breeze. St. Anthony's and usually one or two other bands split their musical duties from the front to the back of the procession. People genuflected as the statue of St. Anthony made its milelong journey from Seventeenth Street across Bedford, up Plain, left on Pine and left on Davis, and then back up Bedford, reaffirming boundaries of the parish—an urban, ethnic village.

With the exception of my father, who would have nothing to do with the Portagee feast of St. Anthony, none of us missed the annual procession. As an altar boy, my brother John marched regularly. My mother was a faithful observer of the festa rather than a participant, even though she had been one of the founding members of a women's sodality. I think she saw the procession as a little too public and Portagee for her refined social tastes, what with its promiscuous mingling of immigrants and second-generation Azoreans.

I marched only one time, when I was eighteen and playing for St. Anthony's Senior Catholic Youth Organization (CYO) baseball team that would come within one game of winning the city championship. St. Anthony's pastor complained to our coach: "The church pays for uniforms, bats and balls, equipment, and new hats every year, but the team doesn't show its appreciation by marching in the annual procession." Our well-liked coach, Ray Nobrega, relayed Father Lauriano dos Reis's displeasure with us. We agreed to march. We took our place somewhere after the statue but ahead of the women dressed in black. As we were heading up Plain Street, Claude Rego, who was marching behind me, said, "You have some admirers." I turned my head to see a couple of teenage Irish girls whom I recognized from my three years of confinement at Sacred Heart School. It was a fantasy to think they were admirers. The Irish, French, and Polish Catholics in Fall River did not have festas with street processions. There weren't enough Italians in the city to support a festa. Columbus Day substituted. Festas in Fall River were the exclusive practice of the Portuguese. I am sure my "admirers" saw me as a Portagee foot soldier. At eighteen, I felt that way.

Beyond and above St. Anthony and his fellow saints loomed the Blessed Mother. Many Portuguese in Fall River proclaimed their faith with a statue of Mary, usually located in the front of their houses. Some people created little shrines by purchasing or building an enclosure that sheltered the mother of mercy on three sides. The most practical minded recycled discarded claw-foot bathtubs. They were partially buried and nestled Mary's statue, a porcelain and iron fortress against blizzards and hurricane force winds. These displays of "Mary on a half shell" or "Mary in the bathtub" were ridiculed, mostly by Fall River's non-Portuguese. Homeowners planted flowers (sometimes artificial) around their statues or shined a light on the Blessed Mother at night. This public devotion in Fall River served as a marker of ethnicity, not just Catholicism. The religious shrines that sprouted in front yards across St. Anthony's parish were too Portagee or greenhornish for my mother. The Rosary and private petitions to the Holy Mother and the saints moored her devotional life.

St. Bernard of Clairvaux has summed up the maternal role of Mary in the Catholic devotionalism that I knew: "If you fear the father, go to the son. If you fear the son, go to the mother."

Apparitions of the Blessed Mother brought the divine down to earth. Even more than the saints, Mary's apparently miraculous forays into secular time helped span the chasm between God and his earthly subjects that even the sacramental Church could not adequately bridge. Growing up I was familiar with only three of the Blessed Mother's scores of Church-recognized apparitions and alleged apparitions. In nearby Attleboro, there was a shrine to Our Lady of LaSalette, the French village where she appeared in 1846. Each Christmas, the Attleboro shrine drew visitors with a spectacular arrangement of lights. I made my first trip to the shrine when I was in high school. I went with friends to see the lights, not to pray for the Blessed Mother's intercession in an illness or other life crisis as believers did year-round. It was common for those seeking help to walk on their knees up the steps that led to the shrine.

I was more familiar with Our Lady of Lourdes (1858). The story of the apparition was made into a movie in the early 1940s, and it remained popular into the 1950s. I saw *The Song of Bernadette* either at the Flint's Strand Theater or at the Sacred Heart School. It was an account of Bernadette Souibrous, to whom the Blessed Mother appeared eighteen times. Water from the shrine, people testified, possessed miraculous healing power. I would later learn that what became the University of Notre Dame was founded in 1842 by a French, not an Irish, priest. He imported Lourdes water, which he sent to petitioners who contributed money to build the school, "Notre Dame du Lac," and a church. The school became the "Fighting Irish" only after the Sons of Erin overwhelmingly dominated the student body and faculty.

The Marian apparition that transfixed me as a teenager was Our Lady of Fatima, a village in Portugal. The Blessed Mother did not mind globetrotting. Her encounters with early subjects ranged across the Catholic world: France, Portugal, Italy, and Mexico (Our Lady of Guadalupe), for example. As a consequence ethnicity infused Mariology, worship of the Mother of God—the near Goddess of Catholicism. For Fall River's Portuguese, Our Lady of Fatima prevailed as a luminous figure of devotion.

Warner Brothers made the story of Our Lady of Fatima into a feature film in 1952. I remember seeing it in the Strand Theater some years later as a young teenager. I came to know the story as thoroughly as the Baltimore Catechism and to accept its details unquestioningly. I filed Fatima alongside the intercessional work of the saints—another way my enchanted faith brought the divine near at hand, into the everyday world. The "secret" distinguished Fatima from other apparitions. Mary bestowed a revelation, part of which was to remain sealed until 1960.

The Blessed Mother's apparition first appeared to three children, shepherds aged eight to ten, on May 13, 1917, while war raged in Europe. She told the children to return to the same place on the thirteenth of the following months. On July 13, the Blessed Mother delivered her message to the children, telling them not to reveal it. Word began to spread throughout Portugal, and crowds descended on Fatima. Then on October 13 the "Miracle of the Sun" occurred before thousands of people, a sign of the apparitions' authenticity, which only the children could see. I remember the Miracle of the Sun as one of the inspiring highlights of the film. The sun danced in the sky and seemed to fall toward earth. The panicked multitude began to scatter in all directions like ants whose hill was suddenly disturbed. The lame fell to their knees, and as the sun stopped its gyrations and returned to normal, these pilgrims rose and tossed their crutches aside. They were cured.

The movie *The Miracle of Fatima* popularized the details of the apparitions. Lucia, the oldest of the children, became a nun and conveyed the mysterious final secret to Rome in a sealed envelope, directing that it not be opened until 1960. But the papacy refused to reveal its contents. My Flint friends speculated on the secret message. As more than one said to me, "Whenever the Sister was asked about the envelope, all she'd do is cry." Some predicted that 1960 would mark the end of the world.

Rome's secrecy only fueled apocalyptic rumors. They centered, as I recall, on July 13, the date of the original revelation. On that refulgent summer day in 1960, I was stationed at my usual post—Lafayette Park—dressed in newly fashionable Bermuda shorts, a jumpy fifteen-year-old, especially attentive to the sky and landscape. Nothing happened. The heavens failed to open; the earth didn't quake; and the sun stood impassively against a placid blue sky. Yet the uneventfulness of that day did not shake my faith in miraculous Catholicism or in the wondrous drama of Our Lady of Fatima. (When the secret was finally revealed in 2000, the Church claimed it predicted the attempted assassination of Pope John

Paul II, which occurred on May 13, 1981, the month and the day of the Blessed Mother's first apparition in Fatima.)

Whenever we began a writing assignment or submitted homework at Sacred Heart School, we were required to inscribe "JMJ" at the top of the page. "Jesus, Mary, and Joseph," the real merciful, accessible Catholic Holy Trinity: the son, the mother, and the saints. The Holy Union nuns encouraged devotion to Mary and belief in the intercession of the saints. Yet they embalmed personal piety in the Baltimore Catechism and parochial swipes at Protestantism. I learned the doctrine of transubstantiation, namely, that through the Sacrifice of the Mass, the priest converted the host and wine into the actual body and blood of Christ. Protestants viewed Communion as merely a symbolic reenactment of Christ's sacrifice. Because Catholics believed the Eucharist was the bona fide body of Christ, we were to swallow the wafer whole rather than chewing it like cannibals devouring human flesh. In preparation we made our own sacrifice, fasting after midnight and cleansing our body once confession had sterilized our souls.

My sixth-grade teacher brought home the doctrine of transubstantiation with a story that also illustrated the sacrilegious, atheistic animosity of Communists toward the Church. "Some Communists received Communion under false pretenses," she related. "They kept the hosts in their mouths, walked out of church, and removed the body of Christ. They took the hosts home, attached them to a wall, and repeatedly stabbed Christ's consecrated body." Of course, the illogic of this story is that atheists didn't believe in God, let alone transubstantiation. But Sister had an answer for this: "They wanted to show their hatred and contempt for the Church."

Transubstantiation and Holy Communion left an opening to shorten one's Sunday or Holy Day of obligation, especially in summer. Since Christ's sacrifice and communion composed the heart of the Mass, one might head for the exit when they were completed. All that remained of the Mass was the priest's post-Communion mopping-up operation and his blessing. If one sat or, even better, stood in the back of the church, one might steal away barely noticed, quickly bypassing the holy water. I didn't occasionally resort to this maneuver at St. Anthony's until well into high school, assured by my friends, "You've gone to Mass and met your obligation." Staying long enough to put money in one of the two rounds of collections helped ease my conscience.

"Offer it up," Millie and her handmaidens exhorted us when it came to the catechism of life's physical and emotional afflictions, like my parents' brittle marriage. The Holy Union nuns strove to cultivate a Catholic sensibility of silent suffering, whose benefits would accumulate on one's moral slate, if not on one's cemetery slab. Militant Millie especially enjoyed wielding the sword and shield of ghetto Catholicism against a Protestant religion that didn't stick to the ribs. Indulgences, the body of Christ in Communion, the Marian apparitions, and the intercession of the saints all had no place in Protestantism. (Though unbeknownst to me, some Episcopalians would have disagreed.) "Why, the Protestants even had to close many of their churches in the summer for want of attendance. The Catholic Church," Millie drummed into us, "had a firmer grasp of human nature. Attendance at Mass under the pain of mortal sin showed the wisdom of the Church fathers."

The catechism of sin, a cavalcade of human frailty, represented another unsettling subject. I knew we were to avoid occasions of sin and that "idleness was the devil's workshop." But how was I to stay clear of the Varley Waste Company and its lurid photos when my father ordered my brother and me to carry newspapers and magazines there? Then I could not always recognize the moral daylight between venial and mortal sin. Even Millie never devised delicate euphemisms for masturbation. I somehow felt that "pulling your pud," as some referred to it, resided at least in the foothills of mortal sin, within the shadow of the big ones: missing Mass on Sunday or a holy day of obligation; eating meat on a day of abstinence; failing to make one's Easter duty; and not wearing green on St. Patrick's Day. What about a fleeting "dirty" thought or sudden arousal?

It was my misfortune to become trapped in the riptide of puritanical Irish Catholicism just as I was wading into puberty. When in doubt, I assumed the worst. Sacred Heart School launched a thousand ships of guilt in my soul. Father Andrew Greeley has accurately observed, "There were Catholic puritans long before there were Puritans."

On the first Friday of every month the Sacred Heart student body attended Mass and received Communion. In preparation, we went to confession on the preceding day. Sometime late in the sixth grade, I began to tote up sins by the thousands: every time I had lusted for a woman in a bathing suit on television, for example. I piled on dirty thought after dirty thought no matter how quickly it took flight. I left nothing on the cutting-room floor.

I entered the confessional, pulled the purple curtain closed, and waited for the priest to abruptly slide open his screened window. "Bless me father for I have sinned. It has been one month since my last confession and these are my sins." I gave a kind of life history of my sins, all those I had forgotten to confess now churned up by the catechism of Sacred Heart School. "I have had ten thousand impure thoughts. I have looked at five thousand dirty pictures." Before I could go much further the priest stopped me, probed the state of my soul, and then indicated that what I confessed was not anywhere as serious as I was making it. The priest was an Irish curate and sounded authoritative because he did not speak with an accent. He helped lift the lion's paw of guilt off my conscience; my anxiety receded. Though I never made a confession like that again, my moral ease did not last. I was a frightened kid on the cusp of adolescence who failed to measure up to my older brothers intellectually and morally. John was headed for the seminary, and I never talked with him or Bill about the emotional tumult of my Sacred Heart initiation.

First-of-the-month confession was an assembly line. Classmates made judgments about the gravity of your sins according to the amount of time you spent in the confessional. Some breezed in and out, though I knew they cursed like the sailors who roamed Fall River's streets and told dirty jokes. My weighty confession drew snickers from classmates about my secret sinful life that required hard duty from the priest.

The Holy Union nuns shamed us into contributing money for the missions. The church designated mission month each year. We had been well tutored in the belief that there was no salvation outside the Catholic Church. We had a moral obligation to contribute to the missions. In foreign countries people were starving for food and spiritual nourishment.

The nuns ginned up mission contributions by dividing classes into two teams. They competed in the course of mission month to see who made the largest "offering." The reward was a week with no homework. The nuns kept a daily tally on the blackboard. They badgered, even coerced, us for four weeks to cough up money. After all, indulgences were at stake, not just a break from homework. Only the self-sacrificing nuns, parish priests, and Church hierarchy seemed to have advanced reservations on the express flight to heaven. The bulk of the laity would be fortunate if they landed for an extended layover in purgatory. The nuns taught us that even if we received absolution in confession for our mortal sins, we still had to do time in purgatory, still owed penance for our grave misdeeds and our never-ending venial lapses. Depending on how much money we forked over for the missions, we might slice years off our confinement in purgatory.

During mission month, everybody wanted to be on Peggy Connors's team. Her father was a doctor. She lived in a big, old Victorian house on the edge of the Highlands, and she benefited from a liberal weekly allowance, with more cash available as needed. She far outdistanced competitors in the monthlong mission footrace, but she wasn't sanctimonious or snooty about her contributions. She was well liked, including by me.

One year her team was losing on the last day in spite of her healthy donations. She came to the rescue of her teammates just as the clock was ticking down. She reached into her wallet, walked to the front of the class, and slapped a five-dollar bill on the nun's desk. She hit a grand slam in the bottom of the ninth inning with two outs and her team behind. No wonder I remember so clearly this dramatic conclusion to mission month. I was also on the losing team.

Far more than during mission month, Sacred Heart School's religious pulse quickened during Lent. Especially under Millie, "sacrifice" and "guilt" resounded off classroom walls more frequently and forcefully. We abstained from meat on Wednesday and Friday. (Of course, if St. Patrick's Day fell on a Lenten Wednesday or Friday, the bishop issued a terse dispensation from the Highlands, a verbal snap of the fingers that didn't seem quite right to me. The Irish could now eat corned beef, and we could now eat whatever meat we wanted.) During Lent we sacrificed a half hour of sleep to attend compulsory 7:30 a.m. daily Mass at Sacred Heart Church. On Fridays, classes prayed at the fourteen Stations of the Cross. School was canceled on Good Friday, but we knew our duty—a prayer visit to church between noon and 3 p.m., the hours set aside for venerating Christ's crucifixion.

Easter's rituals, traditions, and mysteries now reside in my lost religious world. Yet yearly memories of Easter still warm the blood: Lenten sacrifices and self-discipline that once appealed to the temperament of a budding athlete; colors — saints' statues in St. Anthony's shrouded in maroon on Good Friday, priestly vestments that changed from purple to all white during Holy Week, a florist shop of lilies decorating Sunday's altar; and the sweet smell of my mother's massa with an unshelled egg lodged in the center of the round loaf as if it was giving birth.

Monsignor Joseph Sullivan was the pastor and patriarch of Sacred Heart parish. We referred to him as "Papa Joe." Over six feet tall, with an erect posture, a ruddy red complexion, and a full head of carefully combed white hair, without a speck of dandruff on the shoulders of his black clerical coat, Papa Joe embodied churchly authority and commanded respect. He took the time to distribute quarterly report cards, at least in the upper grades, and to say a few words to every student in a low sonorous voice that seemed to well up from the caverns of his chest.

He would open the classroom door without knocking. Our nun would immediately bow her head, as if the bishop had suddenly appeared. Papa Joe even pressed Millie's sheepish button. The nuns were spared the ritual of kissing Papa Joe's ring, a ritual reserved for higher-ups. We were trained to leap to our feet as soon as the patriarch appeared and greet him with "Good morning, Monsignor," for he usually made his rounds before noon. We sat quietly with our hands folded on our desks until our names were called. We hustled to the front of the room, where Papa Joe sat at the nun's desk. She retreated to the corner and stood meekly like some miscreant morally quarantined from the rest of the class. Papa Joe offered words of encouragement, asking us to do our best and improve less than "A" grades or correct conduct problems. We scurried back to our seats. When he was finished we shot up, he blessed us, and we thanked him.

My relationship with Papa Joe and the three curates at Sacred Heart Church was formal, involving report cards, confession, and Communion. But my brothers and I had a more intimate association with Father Manuel Andrade, the curate at St. Anthony's. He belonged to the same priestly brotherhood as Papa Joe, but their physical appearance and bearing could not have been more different. Short, squarish, and portly, Father Andrade had a heavy beard whose five o'clock shadow arrived promptly after noon. His head and large face were round and plump. He had yellowish Chiclets-sized teeth and spoke with a slight accent.

Father Andrade's family and my mother's had been neighbors on St.

Michael. Once a month or so, he visited her and Titia for a couple of hours on his day off. Whether on Bowler or Way streets, whenever we saw his big, black Mercury we had to stop our play, even on the sunniest of summer days, and go home. There we sat quietly while the grown-ups exchanged news and talked about the Azores, interspersing their English with Portuguese. In summer he wore a Panama hat. Sometimes when he broke up our games, Johnny Kosher would snort, "Why do you have to go home every time that Mexican arrives." And it was true: Father Andrade resembled chubby Sergeant Garcia on *The Mark of Zorro* television show. Father Andrade drew especially close to my brother John during the several years he served as an altar boy. Occasionally on his day off he took us boys on trips — to Plymouth and several times to the beach.

Father Andrade would be transferred around the diocese. He left Fall River for New Bedford, and then, still a curate, he returned to the city. He was assigned to Espirito Santo, the Flint's poor Portuguese parish. Only late in his clerical career did he become a pastor of another modest Portuguese church in Fall River's South End. The Irish diocesan hierarchy seemed not to think highly of Father Andrade, though in the era of priestly sexual abuse he was not even a bit offender.

Still, I suspect he wrestled with dark impulses that may have gained at least a toehold on his psyche. I say this because, though he never came close to molesting us, he did develop a repulsive ritual of physical contact that my mother tolerated whenever he paid a call. At the end of his visits to Bowler and Way streets, Father Andrade would get giddy. "Now it is time for a 'contribution,'" he announced. This meant that we each took turns kissing him on his bristly cheek and inhaling Aqua Velva, the cheap aftershave that he splashed on his face. I found this disgusting, but it delighted Father Andrade.

Yet whatever demons dueled for his soul and whatever humiliations he inflicted with his kissing ritual, Father Andrade would turn out to be a pious, generous, workaday Azorean parish priest who was never implicated in any church scandal. One summer when my Uncle Tippy was having some trouble finding me a good job, Father Andrade tried to get me construction work with his brother. Father Andrade would become responsible for my first teaching position. After a stroke and retirement, he would nevertheless show up for my father's funeral to concelebrate the Mass. The stroke had scrambled his brain, and he had to be led through the Mass by his fellow priest. When he died a few years later, time had already proved a solvent for the disgust of my youthful physical contact with him.

Beyond crucifixes and other sacred accessories in our home, there were three more religious fixtures: *The Anchor*, the diocesan newspaper; Bishop Fulton Sheen's weekly television show; and Billy Graham's crusades, which were broadcast a couple of times a year.

At some point in the late fifties Fall River's Bishop James Connolly issued a directive from the Highlands: pastors were to lean on their parishioners to subscribe to *The Anchor*, which was published weekly. My father complied. I found the tabloid-sized paper interesting on several scores. It published parish contributions to the annual Catholic Charities Appeal, offering an economic profile of diocesan churches. I paid special attention to Fall River's rankings. Then, too, I scanned the paper's small sports section that focused on the athletic activities of Catholic high schools and of Stonehill College, the only institution of Catholic higher education in the diocese. But another part of the paper jumped off the page: the weekly Legion of Decency film ratings. They ran from "A: Morally Unobjectionable" to "B: Morally Objectionable" and "C: Condemned." Category C was Catholicism's scarlet letter, the Church's puritanism on horseback. We courted mortal sin and eternal damnation if we sat through a movie labeled with a C. The Church had an "Index" of forbidden books long before "Banned in Boston" became shorthand for a New England still saddled with the toxic by-product of the region's Puritan past. Nonetheless, the guilt culture that I, and tens of thousands of other New Englanders, inherited had little, if anything, to do with Nathaniel Hawthorne's ancestors.

Of course, the term Banned in Boston originated with Yankee descendants of the Puritans in the late nineteenth century. These self-appointed moral police saw to it that municipal authorities banned certain books, plays, and magazines in the "Athens of America." Irish Catholics increasingly seized the reins of local government. Banned in Boston may have been initiated by descendants of the Puritans, but Irish Catholic hands soon gained control of the throttle. In Boston and Fall River, and Massachusetts as a whole, the presence of religion in the public square became principally

Catholic. After all, in the Bay State the Church was chiefly responsible for the defeat of legislation to create a lottery (1935) and of a referendum to liberalize birth control laws (1948).

The Puritans' notorious Blue Laws still ruled in my Massachusetts of the 1950s and '60s. Most major commercial activity in the state remained prohibited on Sunday. The retail sale of alcohol was illegal, and bars were only allowed to open after noon. Blue Laws were clearly a Puritan legacy. Nevertheless, the majority Catholic Church, whose laymen dominated the General Court, extended the longevity of Blue Laws. Like Banned in Boston, Blue Laws had a double religious life.

My Fall River's version of Banned in Boston seems now to have involved self-censorship. Theaters in Fall River were fearful of antagonizing the Church and provoking a boycott in such an overwhelmingly Catholic city. Most apparently chose not to show condemned movies. There were six theaters in downtown Fall River in the 1950s before most were picked off one at a time by television, despite free dinnerware, Panavision, and 3-D. Only the Empire showed condemned films from time to time. Occasionally we went to the Empire when it ran "decent" movies. But the theater still had a moral stench about it.

One movie I recall from the condemned list in *The Anchor* was titled *The Roman Spring of Mrs. Stone*. I would view it years later on television. Adapted from a Tennessee Williams novel, the movie is about a late mid-dle-aged widow played by Vivian Leigh who goes to Rome and has an affair with a gigolo played by Warren Beatty. There is no nudity or profanity in the film. I'm sure there were more lascivious movies on the condemned list, but Hollywood itself practiced self-censorship in the 1950s. I never questioned the authority of the Legion of Decency, though the need to know the condemned movies meant that careful perusal of suggestive titles awakened less than pure thoughts.

I can't remember Bishop Sheen discussing the Legion of Decency. We watched his long-running show *Life Is Worth Living* and then the *Fulton Sheen Program* as faithfully as we tuned into Lawrence Welk and Ed Sullivan. Bishop Sheen's program was not about the "don'ts" of Catholicism. The most frightening words I remember him uttering had to do with the threat of Communism. Bishop Sheen's show was an inspirational, theatrical performance. He transformed his ecclesiastical wardrobe—cassock, purple cape, skullcap, and gold cross—into a stage costume that he skillfully exploited. When he skated across the stage sweeping his cape behind him with one hand, he took on the character of a Catholic Superman. He possessed piercing eyes, and he paused dramatically, staring into the camera after he made a compelling point.

Bishop Sheen was a facile thinker and speaker who personified the authority of the Church but not its ghetto Catholicism. He preached more of hope than guilt. He relied on parables, dappled his preaching with humor, and embodied passion and intelligence. He always ended his show before a live audience with a soft inspirational landing. Far more than St. Anthony's immigrant priests, Bishop Sheen made me proud to be a Catholic and bolstered my youthful trust in the Church. When I started watching Bishop Sheen, I retrieved my rosary and clutched its beads for the half hour he was on the air.

Bishop Sheen's sermonizing, his well-honed oratory, contrasted sharply with the thin gruel I along with countless Catholics endured each Sunday. The Sacrifice of the Mass, not the priestly sermon, defined Catholic worship. Typically the priest made some announcements from the pulpit and then slogged through what was all too often an arid, ad-libbed, ten-minute commentary on the biblical passage for that Sunday. Sometimes parish business, usually pleas for more money, filled the pulpit slot. I remember reading in a sports magazine about Billy Martin, the fiery, Portuguese Italian second baseman of the New York Yankees, and the two times he took the great Mickey Mantle, an Oklahoma Baptist, to a Catholic church. Martin complained that on both occasions the "sermon" had to do with finances. That ended Mantle's exposure to Catholicism, at least from Martin's hands.

From time to time a mission priest outshined St. Anthony's men of the cloth. Mission Week was part of the devotional life of Catholic parishes. Priests who usually belonged to a religious order made the rounds of churches holding nightly meetings with parishioners, mostly women like my mother. Mission Week was designed to shore up the laity's faith. The mission priests I heard were usually skilled preachers because they had to win an audience and make sure its members returned the following night. The visiting priest often took to the pulpit on the Sunday before the start of Mission Week, enabling him to do a little preacherly grandstanding while St. Anthony's outclassed Azorean priests looked on.

Parish priests even came up short at Requiem Masses. I was fourteen and nineteen, respectively, when Nonnuzzo and Nonna died. I remember Father Joseph Pannoni, the pastor of Holy Rosary, delivering stock sermons in his lumbering manner. He said nothing about my grandparents' lives—nothing of their immigrant pilgrimage or of the tests of fortitude that lay in wait for them. Requiem Masses were occasions for priests to remind mourners of the Church as the means to salvation. Eternal life offered by the Church, not the liturgy of my grandparents' lives, took center stage in their Requiem Masses.

Billy Graham inhabited a radically different house of God from Bishop Sheen. Yet the evangelical wunderkind and the seasoned bishop shared one thing on short rations at Sunday Mass—inspired preaching. No wonder he was the only Protestant my parents and I listened to.

Billy Graham riveted me because he was such an exotic religious figure. His verbal pyrotechnics disturbed me. He muscled in on the Catholic guilt already lodged in my emotional life. He wore no clerical garb. He grasped the Bible as his spiritual guide, not a specific church or a human religious hierarchy of authority. His silver tongue repeated a mantra: "The Bible says . . . . The Bible says . . . . The Bible says . . . ." He offered a blend of judgment and mercy, the proverbial stick and carrot. His message was Christ centered, with no mention of the Blessed Mother or of the intercessionary power of the saints. He was Protestant to the core. His religion of the word, of the sermon, of the Book of God, in effect reduced ceremony, ritual, and sacramentalism to old shavings.

I didn't know what to make of his call for a personal commitment to Christ as the road to salvation. I thought salvation flowed from the Church and the grace it dispensed via the sacraments. I was also puzzled by Graham's summons to the audience to make a decision for Christ immediately. As a sign of this commitment he asked members of the audience to leave their seats and come to the front of his stage for counseling. People streamed forth as if there had been one huge Mass and it was now time for Communion.

I am sure watching Billy Graham and listening to his Sunday evening radio show as I tried to fall asleep deepened my homegrown Catholic adolescent feelings of sinfulness. Graham may have had a hand in my becoming an academic specialist on Protestantism. He represented a pared-down American religion that made my dense ethnic, sacramental, saint-flushed, familiar Catholicism seem Old World.

Given its twenty-seven Catholic churches distributed throughout a city that remained a patchwork of mill villages, Fall River's sacred geography took some time to comprehend. I first became familiar with the neighborhoods. Then I began to understand the mix and proportion of ethnic groups in each quarter. Next I gained a sense of how class differences intersected with place, ethnicity, and religion. Each year I took notice in *The Anchor* of parish-by-parish contributions to the Bishop's Fund. My Sacred Heart social experience accelerated my learning curve, and so did my CYO exposure to basketball and baseball teams from churches throughout the city.

In descending order, Fall River's socioreligious hierarchy consisted of the Irish, the French, and the Portuguese/Polish. But within each group there were gradations, subtle and not so subtle social differences often telegraphed by humble or stately church architecture. The Highlands' Holy Name stood at the head of Irish churches. Sacred Heart, St. Mary's Cathedral located in the center of the city, and St. Patrick's in the South End seemed to cluster in the next tier. More architecturally modest churches, such as the Flint's Immaculate Conception and the South End's St. Louis, fell toward the lower end of Irish parishes.

Among the French, Notre Dame and St. Anne's Shrine towered above other parishes. St. Roch was Fall River's most modest French church. It adjoined St. Anthony's parish and did not field any CYO athletic teams.

I had some difficulty sorting out the seven Portuguese churches. Fall River's Portuguese community remained heavily working class. Its parishes mostly differed by population and the size of their church buildings. Santo Christo, the oldest and largest Portuguese parish, had a modest but attractive church. It was located in a working-class tenement district at the bottom of Columbia Street near the waterfront. Santo Christo boasted of consistently excellent basketball and baseball teams. St. Anthony's and St. Michael's in the North End may have been the next most populous parishes. The Flint's Espirito Santo and small churches toward the South End fell below these three. Of course, some Fall Riverites saw no reason to make distinctions among our churches. We were all Portagees in their eyes. "What are the only geese that can't fly?" a trite local joke went. "The Portagees."

My grasp of Fall River's religious topography developed slowly. Yet I learned early on, thanks in large measure to Sacred Heart School, how my faith was enmeshed in ethnicity, class, family history, and place. St. Anthony's was my home parish, but as a Conforti, ethnic and family ties also attached me to Holy Rosary.

My unwavering faith in the institutional Church would survive the first two years of college, only to erode rapidly thereafter. It would require much more time to grope my way out of Catholicism's interlocking communal cubicles. From non-Catholic institutions of higher education I would learn that I possessed a sovereign self, an individual mind, and a critical intelligence capable of subjecting everything to scrutiny, especially the ethnic-religious constituents of an identity that was a product of descent, not consent. Without that education I could never have written this memoir, never viewed myself as distinct from, and more than, the sum of the socioreligious attributes that composed my narrative of origins and identity. In a sense, higher education Protestantized my mind. Intellectually and morally I would become a free agent. "Trust thyself: every heart vibrates to that iron string," Ralph Waldo Emerson would preach to me.

And yet I would only experience a halfway conversion, my self-determination never whole. I have remained uneasy about publishing this memoir, for example, because of what Catholicism impressed upon me: the place to talk about one's self is in the confessional, not in public. (This lesson was reinforced by my status as an anxious middle child in a patriarchal ethnic family.) When I came to a key passage in James Joyce's *Portrait of the Artist as a Young Man*, I would know why the protagonist, Stephen Dedalus, stops short of completely breaking religious rank. Stephen concedes to a close classmate that he has lost his Catholic faith. His schoolfriend asks Stephen if he intends to become a Protestant. Stephen replies, "I said I had lost my faith, but not that I had lost self-respect." I would put it differently. Losing my faith would represent the collateral damage of gaining a secular American higher education. Converting to Protestantism would constitute too much of a betrayal of where I came from and of who my beloved, if flawed, people are and have been.

So a kind of cultural Catholicism persists, along with a moral sensibility not quite equal parts guilt and social responsibility. I have been locked in dialogue with my Catholic faith—and guilt—all my life, especially, I came to realize, when I was devoting decades of study to the lives and writings of American Protestants. Fall River's Catholicism, an entanglement of the sacred and secular as dense as a tropical forest, gave me a tradition to push back against—which is better than having no tradition at all. Thank you, St. Anthony.

Fall River, Mass. Bird's-eye View looking East.

Early twentieth-century photo of Fall River, with Notre Dame church in the background.
Collection of the Fall River Historical Society

STAFFORD SQUARE, SHOWING STAFFORD MILLS, FALL RIVER, MASS.

9383

Early twentieth-century postcard. We lived behind these mills.
Collection of the Fall River Historical Society

Early twentieth-century photo of Flint Village. Collection of the Fall River Historical Society

The Bentos in 1912, shortly after the family was reunited
and my mother was born.

The Confortis in the backyard of their house, c. 1925.

My father and mother pose with John, Bill, and me on
the front porch of our triple-decker in 1946.

My mother and Titia standing on the side
of our house in 1963.

St. Anthony's Junior CYO champions in 1958. The author is in the back
row with Coach Manny Lima's hand on the shoulder.

First Team All Bristol County Linemen, 1962.
Tackle Ray Landry is on the left; author is on the right.

Durfee baseball, 1963. The author swinging
toward a 400 batting average.

⊰ *Six* ⊱

ASPIRATIONS

The moment when I knew I wanted to attend B. M. C. Durfee High School and first dreamed of playing for its athletic teams remains a red-letter day of my childhood. It was Thanksgiving 1954, and I was two months shy of my tenth birthday. We were still living on Bowler Street, with our move to Way scheduled after the holidays. My father took my brothers and me to the traditional Durfee–New Bedford football game. The late fall day dawned sunny and crisp, and the stark November landscape was arrayed in its understated beauty. We set out to walk the mile and a half to Alumni Field. People were burning leaves, and the once common fragrance of fall accompanied us much of the way. Fans packed the stands. They grew boisterous when the teams took the field—Durfee outfitted in black helmets and jerseys with red numerals and three red stripes on the sleeves. New Bedford was trimmed in crimson and gold. Our "Hilltoppers" prevailed, and my brothers and I imitated Durfee halfbacks on our way home. We stopped for a short visit with Nonna, Nonnuzzo, and Aunt Edith. My mother and titia had a traditional Thanksgiving dinner ready for us when we arrived home.

I closely followed Durfee's athletic glories for the next four years. And then Sacred Heart clinched my decision. I was determined to attend Durfee with the sole purpose of wearing the red and black. Thankfully, my parents didn't interfere, perhaps grateful that they would not have to piece together another Coyle High tuition for such an unpromising student. My father did let out, "You don't have to be a bad student to be a good athlete." Then he laid into the Durfee stars and students who spent hours in the poolroom under his barbershop, taking breaks at the Eagle Restaurant for a chow mein sandwich and a Coke for a quarter. "I see these guys come and go everyday," he fumed. "They have nothin' bettah to do than waste their time in a poolroom." As long as I was playing sports for Durfee and St. Anthony's CYO teams, I was sufficiently busy in my father's eyes. I didn't have to work after three years on the paper route.

Following New Bedford, Taunton's Coyle was Durfee's chief athletic rival, in part because the Catholic school attracted more than a bus full of Fall River residents, my older brothers included. It may seem surprising that a large city so overwhelmingly Catholic as Fall River did not have a diocesan secondary school. (Bishop Stang High School in North Dartmouth, between Fall River and New Bedford, did not even open until 1959.) Perhaps the strong Catholic influence at Durfee diminished the need for a separate school.

My 1963 *Durfee Record Book* documents the heavy Catholic presence on the faculty. During my senior year, approximately 40 percent of Durfee's 110 teachers were Irish. If one adds the French, Portuguese, Polish, and Italian members of the faculty, the number of Catholic teachers at Durfee probably nudges the 80–85 percent of the faithful in the city. The three principals of Durfee during my four years were all Irish: one died in my freshman year; another was promoted to superintendent after my junior year. Two of the three Durfee vice principals were Irish. The dean of boys, the assistant director of guidance, and even the six-member office staff were all Irish.

In subtle and not-so-fine-grained ways, I now realize, Catholicism infiltrated Durfee High. A priest always delivered invocations over the intercom, such as for Thanksgiving. The football team had a tradition of attending Mass at St. Mary's Cathedral before our annual Thanksgiving game with New Bedford. One Durfee principal placed an image of the Sacred Heart of Jesus on his office wall. When he was made superintendent, he carried the icon a few blocks away to his new headquarters in the Highlands. I would confront it when I visited him in 1970 to discuss a teaching position. It was approximately two feet by three feet and hung directly behind his desk. Jesus's eyes were always fixed on you when the superintendent spoke in the ex cathedra voice of public education in Fall River. His words seemed to issue directly from the exposed Sacred Heart. With his icon the "pope" of education in Fall River made a pompous proclamation of his piety in a way that violated the separation of church and state. Yet no one protested as far as I could tell.

The ethnic Catholic takeover of Durfee would have probably unhinged the benefactor who brought my high school into existence and who attempted to control its early operation. During my freshman year I learned a few facts from an official outline of the school's history and traditions that were given a high sheen to promote student-body pride.

Here was another Fall River story that we were never told. Had I known more details it would not have diminished my loyalty to and affection for Durfee. After all, the school now belonged to us ethnic Catholics, not to the Yankee Highlanders who established Durfee at the pinnacle of their power—largely for themselves. I would only learn the full story of the school's founding decades after I left Durfee. A quick sketch reveals the moral and political machinations of Spindle City's blue blood elite.

Major Bradford Durfee married Mary Brayton in 1842, a year after his wife Phoebe Borden Durfee died. Little did the newlyweds know that the Fates had their designs on him. As we have already seen, the robust, versatile Durfee died after battling the devastating Fall River fire of 1843. He left behind his wife Mary and a son Bradford Matthew Chaloner Durfee, who was a month old. Mary turned over her financial affairs to her lawyer brother John, whose savvy, diverse investments swelled the Durfee fortune.

Here the tale makes a hairpin turn. Bradford Matthew Chaloner (B. M. C.) Durfee grew into manhood as a shadow of the father he never knew. The major had been a handsome man with a muscular physique formed during his early years as a ship carpenter and blacksmith. The son was a sickly, homely looking soul. But his unattractiveness did not prove an obstacle to the life of a playboy once he inherited his fortune at the age of twenty-one. He toured Europe, wintered in the Caribbean, and flaunted his wealth in Newport during the summer. His life of indulgence, however, did not last long. He died of a stroke in 1872 at the age of twenty-nine. His bereaved mother went into seclusion.

At one point during his short existence in the lap of luxury, B. M. C. Durfee uttered several words about doing something for the education of the city's youth. He never managed to find the time to divert a pittance of his bountiful wealth for such educational improvement. It took his mother eleven years after her son's death, during which her fortune mounted even more than her grief, to make Fall River a grand gesture. Mary Brayton Durfee Young (she had married a former Congregational minister) offered the city a block of prime land on Rock Street, the major thoroughfare connecting the Highlands to downtown. The land consisted of a knoll, a kind of stepping-stone into the Highlands. Mrs. Young would pay to build and equip the finest high school in Massachusetts and provide it with a $50,000 endowment. The school would be named for her deceased son. Young, a former teacher, stipulated that she would have a say over the curriculum and appoint a self-perpetuating group of trustees to approve the hiring and firing of teachers and expenditures from the endowment. Though the conditions infringed on city authority, especially the responsibilities of the school committee, public officials accepted Young's offer.

Begun in 1883, B. M. C. Durfee High School was completed four years later at an estimated cost of $750,000, an astounding sum for the time. A red tile roof formed a beautiful contrast with the Renaissance-style gray granite edifice. At the south end, the clock tower rose nearly two hundred feet above the base of the building. It chimed twenty-nine times each morning, B.M.C.'s age when he died. An observatory with a powerful telescope was located at the opposite end of the structure. With John Brayton and two of his siblings among the first five-member group of trustees, Mary Young's family retained control of the high school.

The building faced Rock Street, home of the Yankee establishment's most imposing houses of worship: First and Central Congregational churches and the Episcopalian Church of the Ascension. In other words, Durfee's grandeur complemented the neighboring Protestant churchly pronouncements of wealth and power. Durfee High, then, was part of an impressive architectural gateway to the Highlands. The school was never intended for the children and grandchildren of the immigrants who labored in the mills. Tellingly, "Hilltoppers" became the school's nickname; it was a kind of proxy for "Highlanders" when most Fall Riverites were "hillsiders" or "flatlanders."

A generation after Durfee's completion, education in the city began to change. A technical high school, offering business and vocational courses, opened across the street from Durfee in 1913. With the school committee and not private trustees now in control, the two high schools merged in 1918. The increase in the age of compulsory school attendance to sixteen and the loss of mill jobs beginning in the mid-1920s launched the growth of Durfee's student body. When I entered Durfee in the fall of 1959, I joined approximately 2,300 other Hilltoppers.

Unlike the teeming activity around Durfee's two buildings, the once mighty Protestant churches on Rock Street were in survival mode, monuments to a Fall River that was drawing its last breaths. The churches probably leaned on their endowments to cling to life while Catholics strengthened their grip on Mary Brayton Durfee Young's school and their dominance of Fall River's civic and religious landscape. Beyond the name of the school all that remained of Mrs. Young's memorial to her star-crossed son was the chiming of the bell in the tower each morning. For me, it became nothing more than white noise at the start of the school day.

Durfee was more than four times larger than Sacred Heart School and far less rigid. But the Catholic leaders of Durfee knew how to institutionalize order and discipline. The main job of the vice principals seemed to be standing outside and monitoring students as they changed classes between the Durfee and "Tech" buildings. The latter was a four-story redbrick structure that dated from 1930. Teachers patrolled the corridors between classes. They also circulated through the cafeteria ready to apply a hammerlock on any students who threatened to duke it out.

Remarkably there were no fights outside or in our cafeteria during my four years at Durfee. Occasionally, someone rang the fire alarm. The most brazen student prank occurred during my junior year. An enormous hall occupied the third floor of the old Durfee building and covered almost its entire length. The space served as a study hall, with the capacity to hold perhaps three hundred students at a time. A cadre of teachers watched over students, who worked on assignments or penned love letters to sweethearts. One day the enforced silence was broken when a thinly disguised Jack Sullivan, a gregarious alumnus of Sacred Heart, burst into the room armed with a plastic machine gun. "Rat-tat-tat," he repeated, moving his gun back and forth across the students. An accomplice yelled out, "You get 'em, bugsy."

Sullivan then bolted from the room with teachers racing after the prankster. They didn't catch up with him. He ultimately had to pay with a suspension for what I, and others I am sure, would remember as a brash joke. Sullivan became something of a daring folk hero for disrupting the orderly march of time at Durfee.

The school was an unusually well-run place for a large, diverse institution. The Irish principals and vice principals and the overwhelmingly Catholic faculty had learned their lessons when it came to student discipline. Some assuredly did so from their education in Catholic schools such as Sacred Heart.

The freshman class was the smallest of the four grades at Durfee. Students in Fall River's North and South ends attended ninth grade in junior high schools. The Flint had no junior high school. Most of its students spent the first of their four years at Durfee, along with Portuguese kids from below the hill in the center of the city. They lived too far from either junior high school. I became friendly with working-class Portuguese and Lebanese kids from the Flint.

During the fall of our freshman year we received something of an orientation to the school from Alice Harrington. She was a guidance counselor who would become a vice principal before I graduated—the two goldbrick jobs at Durfee. Once a month during the fall semester she took over our general science class. Miss Harrington was in her midforties, I guessed. She had a reddish complexion and accompanying flaming hair. She spoke to us kids from the Flint and below the hill in a patronizing manner. She exaggerated her pronunciations as if she was tutoring us in the proper diction of a foreign language. I realized that part of her mission was to teach us verbal etiquette, to put us on the path toward success by making us self-conscious of our Fall Riverese, a hard local dialect of New Englandese. After all, we were downscale ethnics—heavily Portagee—from the frayed-collar Flint and from below all of Fall River's hills.

New Englanders, I would later come to realize, often insert the letter *r* where it doesn't belong and drop it where it does belong. Law becomes "lore," for example. Conversely, *r* disappears, as in "mock the date for the pahty." Some Fall Riverites spoke in a rough-edged, class-inflected, local New England dialect. Perhaps Miss Harrington heard Durfee students who said things like "For Rivah is a bettah place to live than New Beffid." She was trying to teach us good diction, to wean us away from the Fall Riverese that she assumed formed our verbal gravitational field. I resented Miss Harrington. I was no Flint Portagee or Wop. I inherited my mother tongue from a proud American-born daughter of Portuguese immigrants.

Miss Harrington distributed a little red handbook with black print on its cover. It offered a synopsis of Durfee's origins and the reason for the daily chime ringing as well as the school's rules. "When you are asked where you go to school," she advised us, "don't say Durfee. Say Bradford Matthew Chaloner Durfee High School." This implied, I gathered, that Durfee was the equal of, and probably superior to, other schools. Its official name even had the lilt of a prep school Harrington seemed to suggest. We ignored her; we went with Durfee.

I loved Durfee right from the start, though I spent most of my four years off the school's academic grid. After Sacred Heart, Durfee proved wonderfully liberating, even though the school was run with a firm hand. Freed from the Holy Union nuns, I continued my downward academic spiral, reserving self-discipline for the athletic field, not the classroom. Unlike Sacred Heart, Durfee enrolled a motley cross-section of Fall River where one could find a comfortable niche. I joined the working-class jocks, some of whom were academically challenged, rather than the preppy athletes, who were mostly good to excellent students.

The Durfee faculty was a "Whitman Sampler" of local humanity: the inspired, the competent, and the misfits; jocks, recovering jocks, and screwballs; and teachers doing their time and playing their political cards until a better-paying administrative position opened at Durfee, or at junior high or elementary school. Graduates of nearby Bridgewater State Teachers College, Providence College, and Durfee College of Technology probably outnumbered other members of the faculty. Bradford Durfee College of Technology, a forerunner of the University of Massachusetts at Dartmouth, had evolved from an arm of the textile industry into a significant source of teachers for the Fall River School System. Durfee Tech was a one-building college that opened in 1904 on land donated by Sarah Brayton. Like the Durfee Mills, the school was a memorial to her ill-fated brother-in-law, Major Durfee. Its mission was to teach the "theory and practical art of textile and kindred branches of industry."

As college enrollments grew in the 1950s and '60s, Durfee Tech became an inexpensive commuter school for Fall River students of meager means. My brother Bill graduated from Durfee with a major in textile technology. He compiled an outstanding academic record that earned him a fellowship to the Institute of Textile Technology in Charlottesville, Virginia. Engineering was another of the modest school's stronger programs.

Many graduates of Durfee Tech managed to join Fall River's teaching ranks, though the college had no education programs and therefore no student teaching or path to the required state certification. If you majored in math you could teach that subject at Durfee. A mechanical engineering degree might lead to a high school mechanical drawing position. A major in textile technology could secure one a job teaching chemistry. Then there was the ever-popular gut major at Durfee Tech—business administration. This opened a path to teaching business courses at Durfee or social studies classes at the junior high level. If that was a stretch, one of my older baseball teammates at St. Anthony of Padua majored in business at Durfee Tech and somehow became a Latin teacher in junior high! It was common knowledge that in many cases you needed to know someone to receive an appointment or especially a promotion at Durfee or any Fall River school. Insular power brokers who followed their own playbook had replaced Mary Brayton Durfee Young's educational overlords.

Despite a deeply politicized appointment process, Durfee boasted many inspired teachers. My best instructors taught English. Even though I had all but decommissioned my mind and placed it in mothballs, I was continually assigned to good, though not the best, English classes. One sign of this was the presence of Jewish kids, typically from the Highlands and usually serious students. Four of the top ten academic graduates in my senior year were Jewish.

The Jewish students who were sprinkled in my English classes were headed for places like Boston, New York, and Syracuse universities, not the Ivy League. We had enthusiastic college prep English teachers, like "Big Jim" Donnelly. I was assigned to his class during my junior year.

A graduate of Providence College, Big Jim stood six feet five or so, was passionate about literature, and possessed a good sense of humor. When he caught a student who was distracted and looking down, he would say, "Whaddayah doing, staring at my big feet?" At one point, he decided that everyone should read a book by Hemingway. He gave no other guidance, except the date the paper was due. I went to the local bookstore. It only had *For Whom the Bell Tolls*, a bit bulky for someone of my literary bent whose preferred reading consisted of sports magazines and newspaper sports sections. I never thought of using the high school library, which I had not visited since a brief freshman orientation. The exterior of the public library, a museum-like granite structure, proved more daunting, even though my father served on the board of trustees. He had resisted his appointment, telling John Arruda, Fall River's first Portuguese mayor, "I know nothing about libraries." "That's okay," the mayor responded. "I want you on the board." Well I knew nothing about libraries either. I simply turned in a biographical report on Hemingway, one of the few times I just took a pass in Big Jim's class.

The head of the English Department, Miss Carroll was a dedicated sixtyish Irish spinster. "I'm a teetotaler," she revealed during one class my senior year, as if we needed to be told. She loved teaching and tackled with enthusiasm English classics like Thomas Hardy's *Return of the Native*.

I had serious trouble with Algebra II. I just could not see its usefulness. I also intensely disliked history. In our sophomore year we studied Western civilization with Jack McCann, another graduate of Providence College, where he had pitched for the baseball team. He served as coach of Durfee's freshman baseball team. I liked him because he was young and a former athlete. But he deployed his tongue as a blunt instrument, like most of Durfee's coaches. I was a good hitter, but not fleet of foot, especially for my slender build. One time he gave me the steal sign, and I made it successfully to second base. A teammate told me that he said, just short of my hearing, "That's it Conforti; steal second base and take your ass with you."

When I took his yearlong Western civilization class as a sophomore, he found another occasion to humiliate me verbally, this time well deserved. We were studying about the Roman Empire and the head of the History Department, the constitutionally choleric Dorothy Sullivan, was observing the class, apparently as part of McCann's pretenure evaluation. His pedagogy involved assigning us a chapter in the bulky textbook and then grilling us the next day. He called on us by our last names, with no Mr. attached. That would be too formal for our class backgrounds, even though our school had a preppy-sounding name. In the midst of the discussion, he turned to me. As usual I had no answer because I had not read the chapter. "Conforti," he sliced into me, "we can't even interest you in your own people."

I found this mystifying: my "own people." It was true that I was descended from Italian immigrants and that my father spoke the language. Yet not one member of my family ever returned to Italy or expressed a desire to do so within my earshot. What had Italy done for my grandparents but push them on an epic trek from home? My "own" Italian and Portuguese people could be found in a country bounded mostly by Bedford and Pleasant Streets.

Hazel Donnelly taught American history in my junior year. She was the wife of Big Jim and also a very good teacher. She tried to discuss current events like President Kennedy's news conferences. She was animated in class and labored mightily to make history meaningful to her students. Yet I could not get past my distaste for the subject. History, as someone has observed, seemed like just one thing (and king) after another. My mind was never more off-line, as one might say today, than in history class. In frustration and thinking the flaw lay in her, Mrs. Donnelly said calmly to me, "Why is it that you do good work for my husband and not for me?" I had no answer.

The best thing I can say about my history classes, and many other courses, at Durfee is this: I didn't drool on my desk. I did, however, spit on a desk, my only act of misbehavior during the four years when I barely registered an academic pulse at Durfee. It happened in my sophomore geometry class when we had a substitute teacher. Durfee had an ever-changing stable of substitutes. Some were waiting for the political dice to roll their way, enabling them to join the fraternity of permanent appointees. For others, young and middle-aged, substitute teaching served as a holding pattern while they figured out what they wanted to do, though a goodly number didn't show promise of gaining much yardage in life. The substitute who appeared in geometry class looked to be in his thirties. He was a tall, lumpish, phlegmatic redhead with horn-rimmed glasses that slid down his snout of a nose. He was physically imposing but awkward to the bone, and mild mannered—a patsy for students who enjoyed toying with substitutes because there were no repercussions. He lost control of the class, and the smell of the kill was too strong for me not to join in making sport of the poor man. As the class ended and I got up to leave, he yelled at me. In defiance, I spit on a desk.

The substitute told a teacher-coach who knew me. I was stopped a few days later. "Joe, what's this business of spitting on a desk," he shouted at me. I just lowered my head in embarrassment. "How would you like it if I told your father," he threatened. "I wouldn't like that," I responded meekly. "Well shape up then," he upbraided me as he walked away. I wasn't afraid of physical punishment at my father's hands. I worried that I had let him down, shamed him. Sleepwalking through my classes was one thing, especially since my parents had understandably developed such low academic expectations of me. Disobedience in class and disrespect for teachers represented weightier wrongdoing that reflected on parenting. After I was warned, I reverted to the respectful, if now academically anemic, student I had always been. I never again presented a disciplinary problem for a regular or substitute teacher at Durfee.

And heaven knows there were plenty of opportunities given some of the teachers who were, to varying degrees, off kilter or who courted classroom dereliction. My Spanish teacher ranked near the top of Durfee's incompetent oddballs. I gave up on Latin after one year, switching to Spanish and figuring my familiarity with Portuguese might help me. The instructor wore the same rumpled suits day after day. A recluse Italian who never belonged to the Bedford Street community, he was in his fifties, paunchy, and pale with an owl-shaped face and slicked-back threadlike strands of thinned-out dark hair. He was a person about whom one could say confidently that he seemed old, and odd, from an early age.

His idea of teaching was to assign grammar exercises in our textbook or to have us listen to tapes through individual headphones. Either way, students conducted running conversations, which he proved unable to silence. He hovered over us with a clipboard close to his chest, repeatedly making marks on it. In an unguarded moment when the class resembled a "koffee klatch," I snuck a peek at his clipboard. It was filled with religious crosses, apparently keeping track of his constant praying. He was a religious fanatic, obsessed with saving his soul and in the process losing his students year after year. At graduation, we should have awarded him the palm for classroom ineptitude.

"Pop" Conlon was another easy target, but I resisted amusing myself at his expense. The senior member of the faculty, Mr. Conlon must have been in his midseventies. He was a good man and a knowledgeable teacher of economics. But he was nearly as hard of hearing as the poor souls laid out at Silvia's Funeral Home. He wore a primitive aid with a wire that snaked down from his ear under his shirt to a volume control device attached to his belt. He would ask a question from the textbook. "How do you define laissez faire?" A student would raise his hand and answer loudly: "That is an economic system in which government intervention is weak." Pop would try unobtrusively to turn down the volume on his hearing aid. The next question might be about trust busting or the Federal Reserve. A student who was in on the game would answer in a low voice. Pop would turn up the volume on his hearing aid. And so the class proceeded.

I liked Pop, whose first name was James. He was interested in Durfee sports and even collected tickets at football games. When I won the outstanding lineman award in my senior year, he saw fit to congratulate me and to tell me that Donald Trevisano, after whom the trophy was named, had been a student of his.

My athletic career, the reason I went to Durfee, did not begin promisingly. In fact, it barely left the gate. I was the sole, nervy freshman to try out for the Durfee basketball team, a perennial powerhouse. I hoped to make the junior varsity team. On Tuesday and Friday nights Durfee played before an always-overflowing crowd at the armory in downtown Fall River, where the national guard drilled. The junior varsity warmed up the crowd before the main event. Junior varsity would have provided enough athletic glory for me to start my Durfee career. I failed to make the team, however. I accepted the reality: basketball was not my best sport. I joined Durfee's freshman squad, where I was a starting guard and did well. Then I switched to St. Anthony's Senior CYO team and reunited with the fatherly Manny Lima.

My monthlong tryout for the Durfee basketball team, though it ended in failure, offered a close-up view of a Fall River legend during his last year of coaching. Luke Urban (anglicized from Urbanski) graduated from Boston College, played both professional football (in the old NFL) and professional baseball for the Boston Braves. Appreciative Fall Riverites affectionately called him "Lukey." His players often felt otherwise. Lukey coached football, baseball, and basketball for two decades. He had a blowtorch for a mouth. He berated his players and sometimes assaulted them. But in the 1940s and '50s he guided Durfee to its greatest athletic achievements up to that point. More important, Lukey made Durfee athletics a source of community pride for a city that had little to lift its spirits. Durfee athletic teams commanded respect; they couldn't simply be discounted like our diminished city.

I participated in his basketball drills and observed him closely in the late fall of 1959. Lukey sustained a high-decibel harangue of his players for two hours. I heard the same booming soundtrack every day. With perfection his goal, nothing was ever done right. Sometimes he would get so agitated that he choked and coughed up phlegm, which he spit into a handkerchief. An upper classman, a star baseball player who hated Lukey, turned to me and said, "How'd you like to be the person who has to wash those handkerchiefs?"

At the end of my freshman year, Lukey gave up coaching—and abusing players as well as handkerchiefs—for a sinecure as athletic director. His legacy of coaching like a schoolyard thug endured, however. It was almost as if a capacity to demean mostly working-class athletes became part of the job description to coach at Durfee. Lukey's successor as basketball coach would retire the local trophy for ridicule. Tom "Skip" or "Skippy" Karam became a legend in his own right. Over four decades he would win league and state championships, sometimes with undersized, overachieving players.

Karam served as an assistant football coach, where I had the most contact with him. I feared and loathed him, along with many of my teammates. He was a son of the Flint. His father, an industrious Lebanese immigrant, had labored in the Berkshire Hathaway Mills for forty years and risen to assistant night foreman. His mother worked as a seamstress in a Flint sweatshop, the well-known Fall River Knitting Mills.

Lukey didn't swear at his players as far as I could tell, but Karam had a mouth as foul as the Quequechan River. He became a central figure in a very good book about Durfee's basketball success, entitled *Fall River Dreams*. The author, Bill Reynolds, is a sports writer for the *Providence Journal*. He tells many stories about Karam that resonate with me from my years at Durfee. One day at practice, as Reynolds describes it, Karam was belittling the two centers on the basketball team. "'It takes balls to play inside,' Skippy had said to both Callahan and Jones, pointing to his crotch. 'Jonesy, you've got one, and Callahan, you got none.'" Parents in Newton, Lexington, and Cohasset would never have tolerated the verbal manhandling of their sons that Durfee athletes endured.

Karam was driven not only by the fact that he followed legendary Lukey but also because he was a working-class native of the Flint and a marginal student who made it into Providence College through the intervention of his parish priest. I always felt that he should have been called "Chip" Karam. He clothed himself in class consciousness and a seeming fear of failure. Given his mill-family Flint background, there was one thing I never understood. Why did he have to treat his players as if he were an autocratic foreman and they were lowly unskilled greenhorns on the graveyard shift at the Durfee Mills by the Quequechan?

(Six years after I graduated from Durfee, I would briefly join the ranks of substitute teachers at the high school while studying for a master's degree at Brown University. The first time I saw Skippy he let loose his acid tongue as if I had repudiated my roots in the Flint. "From Columbus Park to Brown University, Joe, that's pretty good," he said, his words coated with sarcasm and resentment.)

Don Montle was different. He succeeded Lukey as football and baseball coach. But he shelved the Durfee hand-me-down of the coach as petty tyrant. Montle could prod his players, raise his voice, and ignite the competitive fire in his belly. However, he never relied on curses or the regular practice of raining insults on his players. He had played for Lukey and gone to Springfield College, then the MIT of physical education. After graduation he had become a successful coach in another state. He returned to his hometown in the spirit of local boy makes good. Coach Montle became my mentor. During my senior year the guidance counselors were missing in action, and not just for students with a low pilot light like me. I requested application materials from Durfee Tech. I thought of majoring in business and then taking the familiar exit ramp into the Fall River School System and perhaps an assistant coach position. Coach Montle would steer me toward his alma mater.

My relationship with him had not started smoothly, however. Actually, it fizzled like a cheap Roman candle. He had a rule that he spelled out before the first football practice my sophomore year. "Listen up! Listen up!" he would bark in the locker room before he had something to say. Silence fell over the players equipped to do battle in the August heat and humidity of Coach Montle's first year at Durfee. "If you decide to quit the team, just be man enough to tell me to my face. Otherwise you will not be able to play football or baseball for me in the future."

Fifty or so players and I then took the field. I walked away after three days of grueling double sessions. I had played for many teams, usually two at a time, in multiple Fall River leagues and had never quit. I persuaded myself that it was not the physical grind of practice that led to my quitting. Rather, I was simply a helmet among the crush of players, a short skinny nobody as I had been a year before during my futile tryout for the basketball team. Yet that failed to explain why I had gone all wobbly when it came to looking Coach Montle in the eye. I guess it was like having to face my father for spitting on a school desk.

I later saw Coach Montle spurn the pleas of players who had quit on him as I had and who wanted another chance. Fortunately for me, I was such a small fry that he had forgotten my name by the following spring. I was helped by the fact that, from Ferreira and Furtado to Pineau and Pieroni, vowel-heavy ethnic names romped through the Durfee student body. Coach Montle must have lost hold of my name in this explosion of vowels, especially as final flourishes. I joined the baseball team for the first of my three seasons. I redeemed myself in football, playing part time for the varsity my junior year and serving as captain of the junior varsity team. I started every game in my senior year and served as de facto cocaptain.

Like basketball, Durfee baseball was usually competitive with any team in Massachusetts. I rode the bench my sophomore year, but hit four hundred in limited playing time my junior year. Baseball was my best sport. My natural position was as a catcher, where I had played in Babe Ruth League and CYO. We already had a very good catcher, however, one of two players who became professional minor leaguers. I could hit, but Coach Montle had a hard time finding a position for me. Finally, in my senior year he stuck me in left field and I hit four hundred, batting behind our leadoff man and spraying line drives all over the field. If we were ahead, he often put in a defensive replacement for me after the seventh inning. Despite my glittering batting average—second only to the best, highly scouted player on our squad—I just didn't have quite enough at bats to make All Bristol County first team. I had to settle for second team, which at least earned me an all-important photograph in the *Herald News*.

The previous fall and winter my photograph had also appeared in the newspaper. In football I made first team All Bristol County. My picture showed up again when I received the outstanding lineman award. Such small-pond triumphs preserved a Durfee athlete's memory for a generation or more. Decades after I graduated from Durfee, my brothers would often tell me when they met someone who remembered me as a Hilltopper jock. That's what Durfee sports once meant to a Fall River hungry for some respect.

My sports accomplishments compensated for my deep feelings of inadequacy as a student. I not only played the role of a dumb jock but also came to believe that, academically speaking, I was an empty sack. From playing on athletic fields, I aspired, by my senior year, to compete eventually from the sidelines, perhaps alongside Coach Montle.

I remember a preseason scrimmage in my senior year with a team from Rhode Island. Across the line from me I saw a tall, pudgy galoot. He had about as much athleticism as the dummy bags we blocked in practice. I was able to get a good angle on his doughy body and push him off to one side or the other depending on the play. About halfway through the scrimmage, after the whistle was blown ending a play, the Rhode Island coach came charging forward. "Look at him. Look at him," he screamed pointing at me. "Look how small he is, and he is pushing you all over the field," he derided his lineman. Coach Montle, who was smallish himself, beamed. In the afterglow of this incident I could do no wrong in his eyes. The Rhode Island coach's outburst served as a defining moment for me. It clarified my preferred self-image as an undersized overachiever for whom doggedness on the athletic field was essential. In a sense, I resembled Skip Karam, a product of the Flint with modest natural ability who always had to prove himself. This self-concept would stalk and drive me once I was roused from my academic stupor.

When our baseball team entered the state playoffs, we sometimes traveled to affluent Boston suburbs where athletic facilities inscribed class differences. Natick, I remember, had a campus with a low-slung sweeping building surrounded by manicured playing fields and other modern athletic appointments. Such new suburban schools left the old Durfee High building as an antiquated memorial whose architectural significance was mostly lost on us. Heading toward Boston, our teams knew that we would travel a considerable social distance in a fifty-minute bus ride from Fall River. At home we did not play on preppy fields of dreams. Our small redbrick clubhouse was a Depression-era Works Progress Administration project. Alumni Field, which performed double duty as a gridiron and baseball diamond, was a mile and a half from the high school. We often held our football practices in Alumni Field's parking lot, which was as much dirt as grass. During a practice in my junior year, I fell on a large cinder, which pushed through the space between my facemask. It ripped a gash on the side of my nose that required seven stitches. I was a Hilltopper. I proudly wore around school my black sweater with red stripes on the sleeve and my first varsity letter sewn on by my mother. I was more than willing to bleed for Durfee, but not from a cinder in a parking lot!

In high school I reunited with Alan Robillard, my childhood friend from

Bowler Street. He had grown into a six-foot, two-hundred-pound sack of potatoes. He was a backup tackle on the football team and the good-natured recipient of much hazing. Alan had developed an especially fleshy upper body. Players began referring to him as "Jugs." When he undressed and headed for the showers, the locker room frequently broke out in the chant of "Jugs-Jugs-Jugs-Jugs." Someone stole into his locker and drew breasts and nipples on his shirt with a felt-tipped pen.

Like many of us, Jugs must have carried away something from his athletic experience. He would graduate from Durfee Tech and become an officer in the marines. He went on to pilot helicopters in Vietnam and to win the Distinguished Flying Cross for his bravery. None of his high school chums would dare call him Jugs again.

During my junior year, less than a decade before that valor, Jugs, two other football players, and I went through what was considered a rite of passage for young men in eastern Massachusetts. We visited the Old Howard Burlesque Theater, for us Boston's main fleshpot. Its garish lights cast spooky shadows on the flophouse world of Scollay Square. I was chosen to approach the ticket booth because, my friends argued, I looked older than seventeen. The woman in the booth barely made eye contact as I asked for four tickets. We were waved through, just like thousands of pimply faced teenagers who had handed over their allowance or money earned cutting lawns, taken their seats, and tried to hide the bulge in their pants. In between raunchy comics, tarted-up representatives of full womanhood danced for twenty minutes, concluding their acts in a G-string with pasties on their nipples. The star stripper boasted of "twin 45s." The show more than lived up to our erotic expectations. In June of 1961, a couple of months after our visit, the Old Howard caught fire and was quickly demolished. A Boston era and the site of a momentary teenage thrill had gone up in smoke.

The winter before our erotic outing in Boston, I engaged in the only fistfight with one of my brothers that I remember. I now regret but more fully understand how I felt and behaved. John and I had an argument, perhaps over TV. I don't recall. It progressed to a shoving match. This time I was determined not to back down. John was two and a half years older than me. He was always bigger and stronger when we were growing up. Now we were about the same height, but I was heavier and more muscular.

Between football seasons I had been working out with weights at the Durfee gym.

The fight moved toward the door, and we found ourselves outside in the winter's cold trading punches. I avoided hitting him in the face because he wore glasses. I pummeled his body. He grabbed me and we continued to land blows. He pulled away with tears in his eyes. "Come on, come on! You want more?" I muttered under my breath. He turned and went into the house. We didn't speak for months. Eventually, we patched things up and never had a serious disagreement again. My pent-up fury toward Primo, toward the first in the family and first in class, had ruptured. I finally topped John in something. That is why I remember it in high definition. Nine months later I felt similar rage on the football field when we drubbed Coyle—those shits who were too good to attend a public high school like ours.

In 1958, I traveled to Springfield College with a twelve- to thirteen-year-old Fall River YMCA all-star basketball team. We played for the New England championship in our age group and we won. Four years later, as a junior at Durfee, I accompanied Coach Montle and a handful of Durfee football teammates for Springfield College's winter homecoming, when there were athletic events all day. In my senior year, Coach Montle took a few other footballers and me back to Springfield. He brought film of football games and tried to impress Springfield's head coach with my blocking ability. "See how he is moving that much bigger player around," Coach Montle pointed out. Springfield's coach hardly responded. Given my size he was understandably not enthusiastic about my prospects as a college lineman. That Saturday there were much bigger potential recruits on his schedule. I saw them roaming around campus in jackets, ties, and close-cropped hair. They resembled muscular marines who had just finished boot camp. My trips to Springfield, ninety miles from Fall River, were the farthest I had been from home.

Coach Montle was trying everything he could to get me accepted at his alma mater. He knew I had B and C grades, with a few Ds sprinkled in, and modest SAT scores. I had taken the SAT cold, never practicing by sitting for the PSAT or studying the sample questions that came with the registration materials. It was the fall of 1962; my mind was on the football season and my girlfriend. Even the gravity of the Cuban missile crisis was partially lost on me. As a backup to Springfield, Coach Montle suggested Dean Junior College in Franklin, Massachusetts, rather than Durfee Tech. Again he took several players and me to visit Dean. It was a thriving school, like many of the private junior colleges of the era. This was before public two-year schools became common and were rebranded with the more uplifting, inclusive name "community" colleges — like the overnight marketing switch from "used" to "preowned" cars. I was accepted to both schools. I would be heading to western Massachusetts again, thanks to another coach, who, like Sneaker McDonald, believed in me.

I skipped my senior prom, after a serious female relationship dissolved over the course of my final year. Gail, who was a year behind me, initiated it. She was everything I was not: a good student; preppy; fair skinned and freckled with blue eyes and light brown hair; a resident of a nice part of the city made up of single-family homes; and a Protestant. Destiny called; she became a cheerleader. I fell for her and she returned the affection. But after several weeks I found myself treating her shabbily, frequently losing my temper, as when she would not let me drive her parents' car on one of our dates. By late winter I had pushed her away, even though I continued to feel more deeply for her than for anyone else I had dated. In retrospect, it seems, I did not trust that anyone like her could have strong feelings for someone like me: a jock from the Flint with a honeycombed brain who often felt like a Portagee-Wop and who, at that point in my senior year, still worried about getting into college. Better to push her away than to suffer the ultimate arrow of rejection.

I graduated from Durfee, worked at the Brayton Point Power plant all summer, played baseball for St. Anthony's at night, and left in September for a week of freshman orientation. My father was thrilled that I was going to Springfield, perhaps knowing that I was set on a course to secure a job as a teacher and coach, the latter of which had brought him so much success and satisfaction at Holy Rosary Church in the 1930s. Coach Montle had assured him, "Joe will have ten jobs to pick from when he graduates from Springfield." None of us knew that, even after four years at sports-absorbed Springfield, I would never earn a living in a gym or coach an inning of baseball or a minute of football.

Two mottoes bracketed Springfield's identity. The unofficial one was self-mocking and perhaps what we would now call sexist: "Springfield College, where the men are men, and so are the women." "Spirit, Mind, and Body," Springfield's official motto, derived from the New Testament Book of Ephesians. It was emblazoned in triangles across campus. The college traced its roots back to the School for Christian Workers founded in 1885. Five years later it became the International YMCA Training School, not to be rechristened Springfield College until 1953. Like the "Y," the school had been part of the Social Gospel—the late-nineteenth-century reorientation of mainline Protestantism toward an emphasis on Christian service in this world, especially in America's rapidly expanding cities. The school had educated outreach workers, coaches, and administrators for YMCAs that were being organized across the country and around the world.

Basketball had been invented at what became Springfield in the winter of 1891–1892 to occupy men between football and baseball seasons. At the time, collegiate sports represented a form of "muscular Christianity." The gridiron, basketball court, and baseball field became high-minded arenas—manly sites of self-discipline, sacrifice, teamwork, and fairness.

In the fall of 1963, "Spirit, Mind, and Body" remained more than a distant echo of muscular Christianity at Springfield. It persisted as a living creed, even if "Body" had edged out "Spirit" and "Mind" for primacy. Still, there were many Springfield students, a decent number headed for Protestant seminaries, who did not drink, smoke, or swear and who went to church every Sunday. We unfairly referred to them as "Triangles," translated squares—refined translation, assholes. Nevertheless, an admirable ethos of service pervaded the student body. Yet so did an anti-intellectual fungus—a kind of mental mildew. Physical education and various community leadership programs probably made up half the majors on campus. The other half was dispersed among students in education, the liberal arts, and even premed. Springfield attracted mostly individuals who, in varying degrees, integrated service not money making into their professional goals. There was no business major.

Though I didn't let on to my parents, I was miserable during my first semester and I would only reconcile myself to Springfield after two years or so. I couldn't walk out of my dorm room without tripping over peers who were "All Conference" this and "All State" that. The athletes were bigger, faster, and better than me, as I discovered when I tried out for the freshman football team. I had lost some weight over the summer working forty hours a week in a very hot electric power plant and playing baseball for St. Anthony's at night. When I went to pick up my equipment, the freshman coach sized me up and asked, "What position do you play?" "Guard," I responded. "Stay low. Stay low," he grinned.

Except for a few fast halfbacks, I was the smallest member of the more than fifty players who showed up for the opening practice. The coach put me at linebacker, a position I had never played. Much bigger linemen all but made a meal of me. The first game was at another school. I did not make the traveling team.

Swimming loomed as a formidable hurdle. I must have been the only physical education major in the class of '67 who could not swim. I worried about this deficiency when I was first accepted to Springfield. But in the enthusiasm over my admission, I consigned this handicap to some darkroom of my mind. Soon, I would have to confront it. Given Springfield's background and character I am still amazed that I was allowed to graduate without learning how to swim.

There were many very good students at Springfield, as there were during the 1960s at schools of varying academic reputations. (Two of my classmates, twins who were baseball players, became nationally known neurosurgeons, for example.) Springfield had selective admissions. Even among physical education majors, there were many bright students, individuals like Don Montle who wanted to be counselors as well as coaches, who wanted to form character, something that had not yet passed its appointed time in 1963. Springfield also had more than its share of students, particularly among physical education majors, who strutted around campus and carried themselves in class as if they were still in high school. "Jock," with all the trimmings, was their primary identity; it was all but tattooed on their bulging biceps. In them I saw reflected an image of who I had been at Durfee. It was not an appealing picture—more so because the self-image remained fresh and clear in my mind's eye, not faded like the photos in my father's Holy Rosary album.

Springfield was on a ten-week trimester system. That meant I had two and a half months to learn the academic ropes and dust off my cobwebby brain. My gray matter needed to be assigned to the educational equivalent of extended spring training. I didn't have time to limber up. Instead, midterm exams stared at me in five weeks, finals and term papers in ten. At the end of a dreary trimester, during which I was homesick and depressed, I landed on academic probation.

I immediately transferred out of physical education into teacher education, with, of all things, a history major and English minor. I had quickly modified my plans. I would become a high school history teacher with some coaching on the side. I never revealed to my parents that I tried to transfer from Springfield to a state school after the first trimester. My letter of inquiry failed to elicit a response. Coping with the surge of baby boomers, colleges confronted more students than they could handle. I remained at Springfield from sheer inertia.

Liberated from physical education, recoiling from a student body intoxicated with sports, I began to swim against the anti-intellectual tide instead of learning the breaststroke. I gradually turned bookish. I went home for the summer with a copy of Julius Huxley's *Religion without Revelation*. My father saw it. "Why are you reading that Fosdick?" he asked dismissively. I had no idea at the time that he referred to Harry Emerson Fosdick, who had been the liberal minister of the progressive Riverside Church in New York City. The message was clear. For my father college was not an opportunity for growth and reassessment but an avenue to a decent, secure job. Above all, I was to preserve the faith descended through him from Father Sullivan.

After my initial disastrous trimester, my grades began to climb steadily. I gained my academic footing during freshman year and began to hit my stride as a sophomore. In the first trimester of my second year, I almost made the dean's list, which I would later achieve. Grades were sent home to parents and placed in students' college mailboxes after the holidays, when the second trimester started. On my birthday a few weeks later, I used the hall phone on my dormitory floor, the only one available, to call home. At the time a widely reported cheating scandal rocked the Air Force Academy. "How'd you get those grades?" my father asked. "You didn't cheat, did you?" That was my happy twentieth birthday from my father. The telephone exchange stung, reminding me of the limited academic achievement my parents expected from me. Far from boiling over, however, the call only stiffened my spine to prove myself in college and graduate school. During the next ten years, I would continually resolve to earn my academic chops in classroom after classroom and then beyond.

In the end, Springfield turned into a good place for me. It enabled me to purge the toxins associated with a life too long fixated on sports. At the same time, I realized that Springfield was far from the academic major leagues, or even triple A. Proving one's self at "Muscle Tech," as some locals referred to Springfield, remained small beer.

By sophomore year, my seeds were ready, to paraphrase Thoreau. I read extensively outside of assigned books. I started with classics such as *The Brothers Karamazov*. I then shifted my focus to American authors: Twain, Fitzgerald, Hemingway, and especially Thomas Wolfe. The college bookstore had a general reading section that I scoured regularly. I saw a title that intrigued me, *You Can't Go Home Again*. *Look Homeward, Angel* was also on the shelf. I read both hefty books my sophomore year and followed them with Wolfe's more than nine-hundred-page *Of Time and the River*. Then I devoured the biographies and critical literature on Wolfe that our library held. For the first time I reveled in knowing a topic in depth, something more than the Red Sox team statistics, and then forming my own critical judgment.

Wolfe was out of fashion in part because his voluminous writing sprawled like a Texas cattle ranch. Nonetheless, his lyrical prose moved me and cultivated my appreciation for the power of language. Wolfe did more. He quickened the rewiring of my neural circuitry, alerting my senses to the mundane yet miraculously momentous ebb and flow of American daily life: "A woman's laughter in the dark; the clean hard rattle of raked gravel; the cricketing stitch of midday in the hot meadows; the delicate web of children's voices in the bright air." Wolfe's aspiration to write the great American novel, to imaginatively summon the sprawling continental nation in all its diversity, was Whitmanesque, I would later come to realize. Wolfe did not produce the great American novel. But in the ungainliness of his work—in its energy, its formlessness, its verbal excess, its hunger for experience, and its abandonment of home—Wolfe's writing seemed to mimic the dynamic world-turned-upside-down America that was aborning in the 1960s. Wolfe prodded me toward American studies.

I went home at the end of my sophomore year with my mind undergoing a kind of long overdue retrofitting. My Uncle Tippy Carreiro again found me a good summer job—this time as a laborer for the Fall River Gas Company. I almost relished the thought of people, especially former classmates, driving by Conforti the ditch digger, the dead-ender, the jock who had fouled out of life. I continued to read Wolfe that summer and to be transported by his prose poems. I also pushed on to such writers as Nathaniel Hawthorne, Theodore Dreiser, Henry James, Sinclair Lewis, Sherwood Anderson, John Steinbeck, and especially Henry Miller. I began my parole from ignorance's imprisonment.

⽗

For a relatively small faculty, Springfield had its share of eccentrics, though not among the legion of crew-cut physical educators. In my junior year, Woodrow Wilson Sayre, a philosopher, joined the faculty. He closely resembled his grandfather, the twenty-eighth president of the United States. He possessed his grandfather's facial features and reddish Scots-Irish complexion. Sayre had a gold-plated academic pedigree. He had taught at Tufts University, where he was denied tenure for his refusal to publish scholarship. He then joined the Springfield faculty and encountered a student body that, in the main, represented a significant falloff from Tufts.

One day he arrived in class with his hand covered in a hastily wrapped bandage. "Got into a little car accident on my way here," he reported. "Then we had a disagreement and it lead to this." He held up his hand almost proudly for the class to see. He was a professor to remember: a philosopher, the grandson of a president, who punched rather than reasoned his way out of a dispute and who displayed his wound as a badge of honor.

The same year Sayre arrived, another eccentric, a historian, joined the faculty and turned out to be an important mentor to me and to other serious history majors. Frank Carpenter, like Sayre, rebelled against the conventions of the scholarly guild. He studied for a doctorate in Chinese history at Stanford but burned out from the grind before completing his dissertation. He then went to work in Washington as an East Asian specialist for the State Department. After a decade, he left Washington for Springfield.

Carpenter taught modern European history and Chinese history. He would arrive at class in a jacket and tie and begin lecturing, wandering around the front of the room without consulting notes. He removed his jacket and then loosened his tie. Next he pulled his tie off and then rolled up his sleeves. By that time the class ended or else he might have continued disrobing.

Carpenter took five or six students under his wing. He encouraged us, invited us to his house, and worked with us individually. Once again a mentor who believed in me stepped into my life at a critical juncture.

One of Carpenter's coterie of students was my best friend, Bill Stueck, who experienced his own intellectual awakening at Springfield. Bill's middle name was Whitney. A descendant of the inventor of the cotton gin, Bill came from a well-established Connecticut family. His father graduated from the other MIT and owned a small manufacturing company. Bill was a blunt disciple of the radically libertarian Ayn Rand. I had never met anyone like him. Self-confidence, intellectual rigidity, and an indifference to what others thought of him formed Bill's personality—an inflexible trinity of his own making that supplanted Springfield's more supple "Spirit, Mind, and Body." He strutted around the dorm, telling classmates that they were full of shit or that they were assholes. He visited me in Fall River between our junior and senior years. We were watching television with my parents and a Billy Graham crusade was under way. Bill professed his indifference and casually announced, "I'm an atheist anyway."

Bill had enrolled at Springfield primarily to play baseball. Like many of Springfield's nonphysical education majors, Bill had a very good academic record in high school and could have chosen to attend a better school. He was a six-foot-two, fire-balling, right-handed pitcher who could have signed a professional contract out of high school. He chose Springfield because it had excellent baseball teams, players who regularly became professionals, and a legendary coach. Bill quit the team after two years, turning his back, as I had, on the life of a jock. He came to see that Ayn Rand fundamentalism had curdled his thinking. Under Frank Carpenter's tutelage Bill began to set his sights on graduate study in history, and so did I.

When it came time for me to plan a semester of student teaching, I lost heart. I just didn't possess the confidence to stand before a class and to be observed by a teacher and a Springfield supervisor. I transferred from a secondary education major to a liberal arts degree program in history.

Under Frank Carpenter's influence I had begun to balance my extra-curricular reading of literature with works of history. He encouraged me to buy a series of inexpensive paperbacks. Each volume was devoted to a major topic such as *The Age of the Reformation, The Age of Reason*, or *Liberalism: Its Meaning and History*. The books contained approximately one-hundred-page essays by leading scholars and a series of primary sources. I bought and read several of the volumes, including one on the medieval era. During my senior year, I enrolled in a medieval history course. On the first essay examination, I briefly discussed something about serfdom that had not been included in any of our lectures or readings. I was not trying to impress the instructor, though history exams amounted to serial regurgitation contests. He seemed as much startled as impressed. "I have never had a Springfield student who displayed such independent knowledge," he complimented me after class. I felt like the day on Durfee's football practice field when I was singled out for pushing a much bigger lug all over the place.

Three of Frank Carpenter's students—including Bill Stueck and me— applied for master's degree programs in history with the goal of strengthening our academic credentials and gaining intellectual purchase after graduating from sports-defined Springfield. Carpenter took one student to Tufts and told the history graduate advisor, "If Paul does not succeed never accept another recommendation from me." He was admitted. Bill Stueck enrolled in the master's program at Queens College in New York City. I was accepted at Temple University in Philadelphia. I had no money to attend Temple. I was heavily in debt to the National Defense Student Loan Program, which, along with my summer earnings, parental contributions, and college work-study, paid for my Springfield education. Stueck and classmate Paul Pickowicz got a head start on me.

At best there were only twenty to twenty-five secondary education and liberal arts history majors in my class. Stueck, Pickowicz, and I, representing more than 10 percent of these graduates, would each go on to write multiple books that would be published by leading university presses, the gold standard in academic scholarship. We each would achieve the status of distinguished professor at our universities. None of us could have predicted this while we were at a college that we arrogantly derided as "Dinkfield."

Those accomplishments would take decades to attain. In the meantime, I graduated cum laude, wishing that I could have erased my first trimester if not my entire freshman year. I decided not to attend graduation, selfishly depriving my parents of celebrating my achievement because I didn't see it as an achievement. After all, I had only passed through Springfield College as a history major, not exactly the school's signature degree. Then, too, unable to attend graduate school I had no idea what I would do with my degree.

Four years at Springfield transformed my aspirations. My brothers John and Bill also detoured from their former laid-out paths. Instead of joining the priesthood, John commuted to Providence College, where he majored in history and compiled an excellent academic record. After graduation, he joined the Durfee High faculty. He would serve as one of its most dedicated teachers for nearly four decades. In August of 1965, Bill and his wife Pat packed their car and set out for Charlottesville, Virginia, and the Institute of Textile Technology. But Pat was expecting their first child in a matter of weeks. They had difficulty finding housing. The August heat of Virginia didn't help, and then homesickness blindsided them. Bill turned his back on a well-deserved fellowship. He and Pat returned to Fall River, their three-week sojourn over. Bill eventually found a job as a technical editor for the navy in Newport. He would commute from Fall River for four decades during which he rose to the manager of his department, overseeing the work of eight editor-writers.

My brother Doc succeeded in Fall River against long odds. He studied at Bristol Community College for a year, then married, and went into a textile mill that made upholstery and fabric for cars. Through intelligence and hard work, he rose to a well-paying job as a production manager responsible for two hundred and fifty of the mill's six hundred workers. He was the only production manager without a college degree.

From Durfee student whose cerebral cortex activity was almost as flat-lined as a Kansas interstate, I somehow would become the most highly educated member of my family. Before I resumed my education, however, I found myself beached along the northern bank of the Quequechan River for two years. I taught in a Catholic Portuguese school in the heart of the Flint. Many times I wondered how this backsliding from an intellectual awakening and academic aspirations that were four years in the making had befallen me. With the Vietnam War raging and graduate school deferments abolished a year after I left Springfield, I also feared that my academic dream would turn into a mirage.

❧ Seven ❧

NATIVE GROUND,
AGAIN

I spent the summer after I graduated from Springfield reading, thinking, and chewing over what I might do next. My father must have wondered about the ten job offers that were supposed to be waiting for me after four years of effort. Instead, I was beholden to the federal government with no prospects on the horizon. After a six-month grace period, I would have to begin paying back student loans.

One afternoon in mid-August, Father Andrade appeared at our doorstep in his familiar summer straw hat ready to spend a couple of hours with my mother and titia. I happened to be home. I had no car, no money, and nowhere to go. When he learned that I had graduated and didn't have a job, he told me there was a fourth-grade opening at the school of Espirito Santo parish, where he was a curate. In the Azores, islanders prayed to Espirito Santo, the Holy Spirit, to ward off volcanic eruptions. The church, filled with old and new immigrants, had a reputation as one of the most Portagee in Fall River. The church and the school were in the Flint's far East End, pinched between the Quequechan River and triple-deckers shaded by John Flint's mills on narrow, winding Alden Street. The school made use of a dirt, city-owned playground that backed up to the turgid millstream and was named for Espirito Santo's first pastor. Father Travassos Park seemed like a bad consolation prize for a local religious pioneer. "Park" dignified the scant strip of dirt that bore his name. The Flint Portuguese had grown accustomed to accepting what they could get.

"Joe, the school needs a teacher urgently," Father Andrade informed me. "Classes are going to start in a little more than two weeks." He told me that the young Portuguese man who taught fourth grade had just been appointed to fill a vacancy in the public school system. This promotion meant better pay and benefits.

I didn't respond enthusiastically to the notion of teaching in the fourth grade and of doing so in a school that had been considered too Portagee for us Conforti kids to attend. "Joe, call the principal. Don't waste any time," Father Andrade prodded me. "I'll put in a word for you." Under his barrage, weighed down in debt, and with no job offers or money, I called the principal instead of running away with the circus.

Espirito Santo was staffed by the Franciscan Missionaries of Mary, the FMM, as they referred to themselves. They were primarily a foreign missionary order. Their training prepared them to accept an assignment in places like the Philippines or India on a moment's notice. The mother superior in Fall River had spent time in New Guinea and China where the Japanese imprisoned her in the late 1930s. In other words, the FMM were among the Catholic Church's most demanding orders. But St. Francis's accepting and charitable spirit, I would come to realize, leavened the FMM's obedience to Catholic dogma. In addition to their predominately foreign labors, the order did some work in the United States. Espirito Santo was considered a missionary field because of the poor immigrants who had formed the church and continued to augment the parish.

A card-carrying religious skeptic, I walked the plank to Espirito Santo filled with anxiety and with images of Sacred Heart's Millie ricocheting in my head. Fate or God had smiled down on me and executed Millie's revenge — or at least I fleetingly thought so. I introduced myself to Sister Mary Josetta, the name the principal took when, after completing a noviatiate and then temporary vows, she received a ring and became a permanent bride of Christ. She was neither Millie nor a poor desiccated nun who had poured out her life in service to the Church. I liked her immediately. She was young, smart, and personable. She also had a high-wattage smile. Never could I have imagined what lurked around the corner. In two years "former" Sister Josetta and I would be planning our marriage!

"I'll need a transcript from you," she said. "I understand you majored in history." "Yes," I replied, "and I minored in English." "Did you student teach?" she asked. "No, I was in secondary education and took some education courses," I explained, "but I became a liberal arts major and intended to go to graduate school." She asked me about my grade point average and then offered me the job. It paid $5,000, and there were no benefits.

She arranged for me to meet with the departing teacher. He was a dark-complexioned, young Portuguese man who happened to be cross-eyed. He spoke slowly and didn't strike me as someone capable of lighting up a classroom. He left me with the impression that Espirito Santo, given the pay, had just been a way station until his number came up on Fall River's political roulette wheel. "The kids are basically very good and well behaved," he assured me. "The nuns are wonderful to work with."

Anxious and disheartened, I began preparing for school. On credit, I bought two sports jackets and slacks and a few shirts and ties. I didn't own a car. Each morning for two months I walked more than a mile from Way Street, up Pleasant, and then down a hillside toward the Quequechan, whose granite bed seemed to be the lodestone of my life. After school I retraced my steps. By the time the weather started to turn cold, I had saved enough money for a used car, a small, six-cylinder, blue Ford Falcon. "That's a girl's car," the salesman had mocked, as he tried to sway me toward a bigger, more expensive hulk of steel boasting fins and a v-8 engine — the "muscle car" of the era, V standing for factory-installed virility. I settled for the powder blue Falcon.

The school was attached to the old church, a humble redbrick structure that now served as a parish hall. After decades of small contributions, what nineteenth-century Protestants used to gather through so-called Mite Societies, the parishioners of Espirito Santo financed a new church. It was one of those forgettable modern post–World War II buildings that tried to announce an immigrant church's movement toward the American mainstream. Father Andrade worked under an old Azorean pastor who entrusted the Franciscans with oversight of the school. The students' parents understandably revered the Franciscans. There were two other lay teachers besides me. As an elderly, loving single woman who was a member of the parish and had taught kindergarten for years, Miss Cabral was a nun who simply didn't wear a habit. The other lay teacher was an ex-seminarian. He was paid by the city to teach English to immigrant students.

The Franciscans were a mix of Irish and Italians, with one Portuguese and one French nun. Italian Sister Josetta hailed from Providence. She and her fellow religious were incredibly dedicated individuals. Their lives in and out of school were richly furnished with piety and self-sacrifice. Several of them were exceptionally smart, especially an Irish nun with a science background who taught the seventh grade and Sister Josetta who went on to earn a PhD. The nuns were surprisingly open-minded and tolerant. Only one had a glint of Millie. She was a tiny Franco woman who taught the eighth grade. She had grown up in insular Franco-dominated Woonsocket, Rhode Island. Near the end of my second year at Espirito

Santo, when she learned that I was going to attend Brown University, she raised her eyebrows. "Isn't that an atheistic, socialist place?" she asked with concern for my soul. I assured her that was not the case, though I doubt she was convinced.

Sister Josetta handed me a plan book where I was supposed to fill out my lessons hour by hour for each day of the week. Of course, I flew by the seat of my pants during the first months. I played hooky with planning. Every several weeks, a student messenger arrived at my door, usually at lunchtime. "Sister Josetta would like to see your plan book," the student announced. "Tell her I'll send it down in a few minutes." I scrambled to fill in the blank pages. She was astute enough to figure out what was going on. All she had to do was remove a paperclip and check the back pages, which held mostly scattershot planning for previous weeks. She was just trying to keep me honest. She didn't monitor me. After all, there were no reports of my defaming the Church or slamming kids against the wall. The nuns around me must have reported that I was competent enough to maintain order in the classroom and not have to bellow at my students—not continually at least.

My admiration for the Franciscans did not lead me back into the Church's fold. While I lived at home, I continued the charade of attending Sunday Mass out of respect for my parents and fear of my father's censure. I now had a car, which made dissembling easier. I drove to the corner drugstore and bought a couple of Sunday newspapers. Then I steered to a remote location and devoured news about the Red Sox in and out of baseball season. I felt like something of a hypocrite, never more so than when I taught religion out of a textbook with the Church's seal of approval. At least I didn't try to subvert my students' faith. That would have betrayed their parents and the Franciscans—and also imperiled my job.

My classroom window framed the mills that stretched along Alden Street and the Quequechan. At one point during my tenure at Espirito Santo, in my frustration with being stuck in Fall River, in the Flint, and in a school I had looked down upon as Portagee, I spitefully smeared my students with my own bile. "This is the only school," I scoffingly complained to Sister Josetta, "where the students can look out the window and see where they are going to work when they grow up." Most of my kids were second- and third-generation Portuguese Americans, some of them the products of mixed ethnic marriages. A handful of immigrants rounded out the class. They were overwhelmingly good, respectful kids. I had only a few discipline problems where I squared off with a couple of Flint hoodlums in the making. Most of the kids, especially the boys, were thrilled to have a lay male teacher.

I grew very fond of my students, the boys in crisp, white shirts and ties, the girls decked out in school uniforms. They gave one another colorful names. A very slight boy was known as "Twiggy." Two hefty fraternal twins, one bigger than the other, were known as "Beef" and "Little Beef." The emotional calluses formed at Sacred Heart School still had not softened. They prompted me to do things with the students that were unconventional for a Catholic school in the late sixties. At the time, there was a popular afternoon television show called *The Dating Game*. It featured three males or females separated by a screen from a contestant of the opposite sex. The three potential dates were questioned for several minutes. Then the contestant made a choice, and the date walked out from behind the screen for a face-to-face meeting.

The students loved the game when I staged it in class. Word circulated around the school, and some classes visited us to observe, perhaps enviously eyeing what took place. The Franciscans tolerated my unorthodoxy.

I hatched another activity, more of a lesson, based on television that the kids also loved. I watched the CBS *Evening News* each night with the ludicrous military reports of the number of Vietcong dispatched that day. We imitated the news program—minus the gore. When the *Scholastic Reader*, a small newsletter-like publication, arrived each week, we set up a news program. An anchor introduced all of the reporters and identified their geographical locations, just as CBS then did. The anchor then turned to the reporters individually. Each read their stories. Sometimes my irregular lessons would get a little raucous. Poor Sister Cordelia, the gentle, spiritual, Irish, fifth-grade teacher from Brooklyn, would open the door between our classrooms. I approached her and she would softly say, "Joe, can you keep the noise down a little bit. My students are trying to write." "My apologies, Sister," I would offer. "I'll quiet them down."

By midyear, my kids and their parents were no longer Portagees to me but members of decent, hardworking families. Most parents made financial sacrifices to send their sons and daughters to Espirito Santo because of the Franciscans and because the Flint's grammar schools had more than their share of bare-knuckle kids. My frustration originated not with the students or nuns. I just longed to be in graduate school, not teaching the fourth grade. I reported for duty every morning but found it increasingly difficult to kick-start the religion lesson that began each day.

My unhappiness and embarrassment over teaching the fourth grade at Espirito Santo came to a head in February 1968, a month after the shocking Tet offensive in Vietnam, when the enemy even attacked supposedly secure Saigon. Each teacher was assigned a month to decorate the bulletin board in the entrance foyer of the school. I drew February, without a clue as to what inspirational message to install. The second-grade teacher, Sister Queranus, sensed my dilemma. "I can help you with the bulletin board," this energetic, upbeat Italian colleague offered. "Thank you," I replied. "But I don't know what uplifting message to post." "Why don't we do something patriotic since Washington's and Lincoln's birthdays are this month?" Even though I had relegated my patriotism to the antiwar, countercultural slagheap of the late sixties, I hypocritically accepted the suggestion as a good idea. Then came the drum roll: "We can put up pictures of Lincoln and Washington," Sister suggested, "and how about the motto 'For God and for Country?'" My first thought was what would my Springfield pal Bill Stueck say?

We completed the bulletin board display, with Sister doing most of the work. When Father Andrade saw it and learned that it was credited to my handiwork, he was reassured that my education at a secular institution had not subverted my faith. His mossback politics closely aligned with archconservatives like South Carolina's Strom Thurmond. "'For God and for Country,' Joe, that is wonderful," he complimented me.

Instead of working on lesson plans, I read academic history at night. I made periodic trips to the Brown University Bookstore and purchased as many assigned books for American history and American studies courses as my finances allowed. I spent time on weekends teaching myself to read French so that I could satisfy the master of arts' language requirement. One of the embarrassing blemishes on my transcript was that Springfield College had allowed me to graduate as a liberal arts major without two years of a foreign language. This was the academic equivalent of receiving a diploma from what had been YMCA central without satisfying a swimming requirement. Having never studied French, I followed lessons in a college textbook, memorized vocabulary lists, and then progressed to reading short novels. In the spring, I took a standardized language exam for graduate students by the Educational Testing Service—of SAT fame. I surprised myself by scoring comfortably ahead of the minimum that good graduate schools, including Brown, established to gauge reading proficiency in a foreign language. By then I had been accepted to the only school I had applied to: the University of Illinois, which had a strong History Department. I sent the deposit that confirmed I would be attending in the fall of 1968.

Suddenly draft policies changed. Deferments for graduate students were abolished. The draft board ordered men my age to its headquarters in the downtown post office building to schedule a physical examination. When I went to the draft board's nerve center, I met a friend from the Flint. During our years at Lafayette Park, Danny O'Connell closely guarded the fact that he was not a full-blooded son of Erin. His mother was Portuguese. I wouldn't find out his true ethnic makeup until decades later—a startling reminder of Fall River's durable tribal hierarchy. Danny and I walked into the draft board office, and the secretaries gave us the once over. They had watched hundreds of young men parade by their desks. Danny grumbled to me, "I felt like a piece of meat being inspected by secretaries who seemed to think they have us by the balls. "

I took my physical and failed. The doctor said I had a hernia, but I didn't feel a thing. I knew it could be surgically repaired. Yet the doctor went by the book. "The guidelines exclude men with hernias." I was deemed physically unfit for duty, a former athlete and recent graduate of Springfield College! What a disgrace to dear old alma mater. I couldn't tread water to save my life or don my country's uniform!

I was now free to attend graduate school. My finances remained in a sinkhole, however, as I continued to pay down student loans. Then I learned that the federal government classified Espirito Santo parish as a poverty zone, which encompassed much of the Flint. If I taught for another year by the waters of the Quequechan, 50 percent of my student loans would be forgiven. In the meantime, I could save money, continue to read in preparation for graduate school, and pay off what remained of my debt. I was still living at home but not giving my father any money. I could tell this violation of customary Fall River ethnic tradition peeved him, though he knew I was burdened with debt. At one point he had said to my brother Bill, "Aren't you gonna pay me back?" in reference to his Durfee Tech education. My brother John and sister Betty Anne also continued to call 83 Way Street home. My father was sixty-four years old during my first year at Espirito Santo and still shouldering home expenses for three of his five kids.

The earth moved during my second year at Espirito Santo. Sister Josetta and I fell in love. The serendipity of what happened is perhaps a story for another time. I am tempted to place it among my classified files, which all memoirists maintain whether or not they acknowledge it. This story is my wife's too. She is understandably uneasy revisiting in print an intensely personal part of her past. I can never adequately convey the depth and complexities of her struggle with her religious vocation and the decision to leave the Franciscan community. Yet our love was such a startling, consequential twist in my life that mere hints of its flowering would open an unbridgeable chasm in my narrative.

My love story involving a nun, reader, is not a chapter out of *The Scarlet Letter*. I had no feelings for the Franciscan principal during my first year of teaching, other than to like and respect Sister Josetta for her smarts, her sense of humor, and her light touch when it came to my teaching. But the messy splendor that I experienced during my second year resembled the confounding intellectual awakening I had undergone at Springfield, of all places. My new feelings toward Sister Josetta began at the start of school that second year. She was deeply tanned after spending two weeks at the Franciscans' summer retreat house on the shore in Narragansett, Rhode Island. Her southern Italian skin was bronzed just like my Conforti grandmother's and aunts' in late summer. Her coffee-colored complexion accentuated her incandescent smile. Then for some reason the nuns had cast off for a day the dreary black and gray components of their habits. Sister Josetta was completely dressed in white, which created a striking silhouette of her browned face. In the twinkling of an eye, I found myself physically attracted to her.

From Durfee to Springfield the once dead-set course of my life had only landed me in a heap, sentimentally run aground on a bank of the Quequechan. I faced what had been an unimaginable dilemma after being worked over by the religious at Sacred Heart and after losing my faith in the institutional Church: I was in love with a nun who was married to Christ. "What a revolting development this is," Chester A. Riley used to say in the weekly punch line when he found himself in a comical predicament on *The Life of Riley*. I felt like the befuddled Chester, but there was no humor in my predicament. What would my friends say, especially atheist Bill Stueck? "For God and for Country" had been bad enough!

Little did I know that Sister Josetta had long struggled with her vocation and had already decided to leave the Franciscans. That vocation had been fostered by her attendance at an all-girls Catholic high school in the 1950s. She united with a phalanx of nuns who, perhaps more than priests, shaped moral habits in neighborhoods across New England such as the Flint. In addition to her work at Espirito Santo, Sister Josetta taught catechism at the Flint's Lebanese church. She would join thousands of nuns who poured out of the convents during the late 1960s and the 1970s, a devastating loss to the Church. Sister Josetta possessed a Catholic conscience that was less fraught with guilt than mine and more committed to service in the world. She had worked with underprivileged and abused kids in a temporary shelter in midtown Manhattan before coming to Espirito Santo.

By the time school started, Sister Josetta had already confided in some of her fellow religious that she intended to leave the Franciscans. She also told her supportive mother superior in Fall River. When she informed the mother provincial, this head of the order in the United States expressed sadness and disappointment more than displeasure. The Franciscans supported Sister Josetta's higher education, obviously grooming her for a leadership position.

I had no inkling that all this had happened. The Espirito Santo school year opened, and the weeks began to roll by. One day in October Sister Josetta approached me. "Mr. Conforti, would you be able to give me a ride to Westport after school tomorrow? I have an appointment with a priest, and our car has to go into the garage." "Sure, I'm free."

The next day was warm with the nearby Westport countryside ablaze in peak fall colors. Her meeting lasted about an hour and a half. After she climbed into my car, I asked her if she wanted a milkshake at a dairy restaurant next to the priest's rectory. As we were sipping our shakes, making small talk about the foliage, she casually informed me, "I'm planning on leaving the Franciscans at the end of the school year. I thought this priest might help me with that decision. I don't think he can." I couldn't believe my ears. Maybe I did have a chance.

A couple of weeks later, Sister Josetta approached me again. She needed a ride to Boston College to attend her graduate class. The Franciscans had only one car for the convent—a big, black station wagon. Most of the nuns didn't know how to drive. It became inconvenient when Sister Josetta made her weekly trip to Boston College. If I drove, the convent's car became available to shuttle nuns to doctor and dentist appointments as well as to other commitments. After that first trip to Boston College, I offered my services. "Sister, let me know if you need a ride again. I'm usually free after school." Several more times that fall I chauffeured Sister Josetta to Boston College.

On those trips, and when we stopped to eat at a Chinese restaurant in Dedham, we had plenty of time to talk. I learned about her family. Her parents had emigrated from Italy when they were very young children. Her mother worked intermittently in a textile factory while she raised six kids. Sister Josetta's father spent most of his working life at the UniRoyal rubber plant in Providence. He was a proud union man who kept his job through the Depression. I had fallen in love with an individual—a woman I found attractive, intelligent, warm, outgoing, and a pillar of integrity. But my marriage to former Sister Josetta would represent a kind of affirmation of or return to my background, at the same time that I was struggling to gain social and intellectual distance from it. Negotiating that tension, the stress I often kept to myself would sometimes surface as a strain in our marriage.

That fall of my second year at Espirito Santo, I gave Sister Josetta some other rides. She visited her mother, who was seriously ill in a Providence hospital, for instance. We usually stopped for take-out coffee on those trips. By then, of course, we both knew that, mostly from time in a moving car, something emotional had taken hold between us. Then, as we were returning from her last class at Boston College, in the midst of our conversation she gently said, "I think I have come to love you." I didn't veer to the side of the road and kiss her. I didn't even hug her when we arrived home.

Sister Josetta finished the year as principal while completing her master's degree at Boston College. She then left Espirito Santo and the Franciscans in June. The compassionate mother superior in Fall River gave her departing nun $300 and her blessing. She remained our friend until her death four decades later.

Sister Josetta reverted to her birth name, Dorothy Morelli. She had petitioned Rome for release from her vows of poverty, chastity, and obedience, which took a year to be granted. Bank Street College, a highly regarded graduate school founded during the Progressive Era and shaped by John

Dewey's educational philosophy, awarded her a fellowship. The college was located near Columbia University where Dewey had taught. In the fall of 1969, Dorothy went off to Bank Street and I enrolled at Brown, commuting from Fall River. I proposed to her on a fall Sunday afternoon in Providence's Roger Williams Park before she took the bus back to New York. I had no engagement ring that October. Still, the colors seemed even more radiant than they had been in Westport almost exactly a year earlier. We planned our wedding for the following September.

I had been admitted to Brown's master of arts in teaching program, the university's academic runt. The program had only two full-time education professors, who occupied a nook in one of the house-office buildings on campus. Given my collegiate pedigree, I didn't think I would be admitted to the master's in history. But I devised a plan. I would only register for American history courses during my first semester. If I proved myself, I would transfer to the History Department. I certainly didn't dazzle anyone that first semester. Yet I had performed well enough to move ahead with my plan.

I went to see the History Department chairman between semesters. "I am currently in the MAT program," I informed him, "and I want to transfer into history." "Well, well, you know, we have different standards," he responded grumpily. "Where did you do your undergraduate work?" "I went to Springfield College in Massachusetts." He squinted at me through his thick Harvard-tinted horn-rimmed glasses. "Get all your material in, and we will let you know in a couple of weeks." When I returned, he obviously had consulted with my professors. "It's all set. "It's all set," he greeted me.

Compared to Springfield, the workload at Brown was brutal—a book per week along with heavy reserved reading in the Rockefeller Library for each course; a paper mill of written assignments from five to twenty-five pages in length; and three-hour final exams. It was during that first year that I began to understand what reading critically really meant. I came to appreciate Thoreau's high-minded dictum: "Books must be read as deliberately and reservedly as they were written." What I took from him was that serious reading did not simply involve the acquisition of received wisdom; it entailed intellectual combat.

The reserved course reading in the Rockefeller Library was highly instructive on this score. One could borrow assigned books and articles for two hours. They had to be kept in the reserved reading room. Countless students had read the assignments and left their tracks behind. Few used mindlessly the yellow felt highlighter that was so popular in the 1960s. The astute readers resorted to marginalia: symbols (checks, asterisks, question marks, and exclamation points) and comments (including the not infrequent "bullshit"). In short, the good students had taken a kind of Thoreauvian intellectual possession of the reserved books and articles. I learned to make a reading assignment my own, to wield a pen or a pencil like a weapon. Brown's distinguished Revolutionary historian Gordon Wood later offered us a revision of Thoreau: "You need to learn how 'to gut' a book," he said, "to extract its entrails, to remove its vital intellectual parts." This was a far cry from reading every book from cover to cover and simply absorbing its information or its basic arguments. No one could stay abreast of scholarship in a field or prepare for PhD oral exams that plodding way.

At the end of the year I received an unexpected letter from the chairman of the History Department. "We have just completed the annual review of our graduate students," it began. I didn't even know that such a review took place, though I had heard that at least one doctoral student was asked to leave. The letter went on to say, "We invite you to apply to the PhD program." I found myself in something of a quandary. I was in the recovery phase from a rigorous year of proving my academic manhood to others, and to myself. I still had to write my thesis. I didn't have a farthing to my name, and marriage was bearing down on me. I had borrowed $500 from my brother Bill to finish my coursework at Brown, and I still owed him the money. I decided to sit on the chairman's invitation.

That summer I worked on my thesis. At the same time I returned to my roots. I took a part-time job tending soda, coffee, and snack machines in the Arkwright and Newport Finishing mills on the Quequechan River. I had actually worked in the latter for part of the summer after my junior year in college. I ran a machine on the second shift (3–11 p.m.) that spun cloth into large spools before they went to the dyeing room. I had to sew bolts of cloth together and then keep my machine rolling while trying to avoid breakage or snags. My fellow workers couldn't figure out how I managed to bag such a good Fall River job; it paid several bucks over minimum wage. My Uncle Tippy delivered again. On some nights I walked home along narrow, shadowy Quequechan Street. When I reached the Quequechan Café, idle chatter and the stench of stale beer spilled out of the open doors into the summer night. "What was she doing fucking the lawyer?" a throaty woman asked through the frame of one door. "Don't bust balls," a surly male voice sounded as I passed another. Under the shroud of night, I barely resisted the impulse to finally join the profane Flint's goings-on.

While working on my master's thesis I spent mornings in the Arkwright and Newport Finishing mills and afternoons in Providence conducting research. I continued to live at home, writing my thesis chapters on the small desk wedged into the bedroom that I no longer shared with my brother John. He had married the previous summer.

In mid-September of 1970, Dorothy and I were married in a Catholic Church ceremony with no Mass and a small family reception at her parents' house in Providence. I had scraped together thirty-five bucks for a ring. We had visited a jewelry factory outlet in Fall River's North End. Dorothy picked out a plain gold band in my price range. Our honeymoon consisted of a weekend on Cape Cod. We returned to our one-bedroom apartment in Cranston, a heavily Italian city-suburb bordering Providence with a population of approximately seventy-five thousand. Dorothy had paid for its inexpensive furnishings with money she had saved from her fellowship. We chose Cranston because it was approximately halfway between the University of Rhode Island, where she was appointed as an assistant professor of education, and Fall River, where I searched for a teaching position. Two weeks into Fall River's school year, I was offered a job that taught me how personal influence served as legal tender in the city's public school system and how the dug-in local culture hobbled the education reform efforts of one Great Society program.

⋈

I was asked to take over an out-of-control third-grade class in Project Follow Through, which was an experiment in extending Head Start into the lower school grades. The class was running roughshod over a temporary teacher, a young Englishwoman who was about to return home. I was offered a substitute teacher position with the promise of a regular full-time appointment as soon as approval was secured from the school committee.

Little did I know that the permanent appointment would never come to pass. Little did I realize that I had personal resources available to have made it happen.

Project Follow Through was in the experimental stage with a limited number of programs across the country. Institutions of higher education provided consultants, teacher workshops, and evaluation. Fall River was one of the pilot sites, and Bank Street College served as its higher education partner. In fact, during the previous year, Dorothy had served as a consultant to Follow Through in Fall River as part of her fellowship work. Thus, I knew something about the project. I was aware, for example, that Follow Through faced resistance even before it was up and running. The entrenched, politicized ethnic fiefdoms that dispensed education in Fall River would never cotton to progressive reformers from away, especially from New York City. In part, at least, Fall River welcomed Great Society money as a means to bolster and expand its educational patronage system. If change around the edges came along for the ride, it would be tolerable. I became a pawn in a political struggle over who had the power to make teaching appointments in federal government programs. I was a local boy who had made no significant enemies. I held political cards. Instead of playing them, I miscalculated and took matters into my own hands.

Follow Through enrolled at-risk kids and established demonstration classrooms in some existing Fall River schools. In this way the project attempted to encourage movement away from teacher-centered education with students lined up in rows of desks. Follow Through also took over a defunct Irish Catholic school, St. Louis, in the South End of the city near the Portuguese enclave that rose up from the waterfront on Columbia Street. St. Louis contained the third-grade class in disarray where I would appear suddenly like an educational paratrooper. I quickly gained control of the class. The incredibly dedicated and determined principal, a young energetic man, even slapped me on the fanny, as was then common with baseball players, when I was conducting a successful lesson with the students fully engaged. But my early victories proved fragile.

I soon came to realize that, in part, Fall River principals saw value in Follow Through because it took special needs kids off their hands and provided more support services than were unavailable in regular public schools. St. Louis consisted of an entire school of at-risk youngsters; perhaps more than a third of them were second-generation or immigrant Portuguese. Some of the kids came from broken homes. Most of the Portuguese kids were the product of intact patriarchal families.

The city's principals ran their schools with strict discipline and traditional forms of instruction born of Fall River's insular working-class, Catholic, ethnic culture. I heard stories of principals who were openly antagonistic toward Follow Through and its progressive ways. One Bank Street consultant, a tall blonde, told me that a principal propositioned her. "He figured I was a liberal Jew from New York and therefore readily available," she explained. In effect, some locals in positions of authority extended a hostile invitation: "Here, you know-it-alls from New York, see if your progressive coddling can shape up these kids from traditional ethnic communities and troubled families." Dedicated teachers, caught up in the educational ferment of the era, volunteered for Follow Through knowing it would be no walk in the park. The idealism of one or two of my St. Louis colleagues wilted as the year progressed.

Some of my third graders were not markedly different from my Espirito Santo kids. Others were more hardened, many of them obviously the victims of neglect as well as verbal and physical abuse. Life had already cheated them of affect, except mistrust and hostility, which in the boys sometimes detonated in my classroom.

I had been warned by the Englishwoman substitute that Tony, a Portuguese kid from below the hill, was a powder keg, easily ignited. I had no significant difficulty with him during the first few months. He admirably befriended and looked after Dinizio—a respectful, hardworking son of Azorean immigrants who suffered from cerebral palsy. Just as I was patting myself on the back for my classroom skill, Tony went into a rage. He got into a fight during class. I ran to break it up and pulled him away. He slipped to the floor, a kind of knockdown that only provoked his fury. I put my knee gently on his chest as he flailed against me. I talked to him calmly, and when I thought he had cooled off, I let him up. He stormed out of the school.

Within minutes he was back, accompanied by his burly immigrant father whose flared nostrils all but emitted steam. He kept saying in broken English, "Why you have put knee on chest?" Tony had only told his father one side of the story. After some tense moments, the principal and I explained to the father what had actually happened. His indignation subsided, but not completely. He kept returning to the knee on the chest. Nevertheless, he saw to it that Tony gave me no more problems.

Coming close to getting my jaw broken by an enraged parent the size of a New Bedford harpooner was not the most harrowing incident I experienced in Follow Through. An attempted suicide topped the confrontation with Tony's father. I agreed to take a boy from a Follow Through classroom in another school. His female teacher had tried repeatedly to work with him, but she was unable to control his behavior. He had an arm that had been badly disfigured when it was caught in a car door. He was a physically wounded, deeply disturbed boy, and far more than I bargained for when I agreed to take him.

The first few weeks were uneventful. And then one day, as my class was returning to our third-floor room after recess, my student with the mangled arm and maimed psyche erupted without provocation. He mounted the banister and threatened to jump down the stairwell. The attention he attracted made him giddy. "Don't come near me or I'll jump," he warned as he pranced on the railing. This little drama lasted about fifteen minutes as the principal and I gently coaxed him down from his perch. His father was called and arrived shortly thereafter. He humiliated his son in front of us, berating him and forcing him to apologize as the whimpering kid bowed his head. I am sure worse things happened later that day at home. I had witnessed another dimension of this boy's troubles. I never saw him again.

The fall wore on, and I still did not receive my appointment despite repeated reassurances from the director of Follow Through in the city. I came to understand that Miss Mary Cullen, the director of elementary education for the school system, single-handedly stood athwart my appointment. An Irish spinster, Miss Cullen had worked her way up the public school system to the crowning position of her career, where she had acquired some clout. She jealously guarded that hard-earned power, especially against outsiders who believed they had a better way of educating Fall River kids.

The director of Follow Through and my principal thought that Miss Cullen might be appeased and assured if she observed my teaching. She was invited to my classroom, a way of showing her respect, bowing to her authority, and symbolically kissing the hem of her dress. After all, she had long risen above the dirty job of observing nontenured teachers. She spent about an hour in my classroom, and as she was leaving she said, "Mr. Conforti, that was a very good lesson."

I was hopeful. Yet my recommendation to the superintendent, who would bring it to the school committee, didn't materialize. I decided it was time to lift the veil that mystified opposition to my promotion. I made an appointment to see Miss Cullen in her lair—a small office in the public schools' administrative building. It was a large, handsome redbrick structure in the Highlands that fell just short of the former mansions surrounding it. A slight, birdlike, seemingly frail woman in her midsixties with white hair and rimless spectacles, Miss Cullen held fast to her power in the twilight of her regency. She constantly resisted challenges to her authority by so-called experts from away. In her small office it was just she against me, and Miss Cullen was obviously nervous. "I'd just like to know why I haven't been appointed," I began. "Well you don't have the appropriate degree or certification," she replied. "But I have two years of successful elementary school teaching experience, and you've observed me in the classroom. Besides, I took over a class that was in turmoil, and I was promised an appointment at that time." She stammered a response that focused on who had made the promise—certainly not her.

Then the exchange turned more personal, and she grew increasingly uneasy. I don't know why, but I played the Bedford Street–Up the Flint card. "I worked my way through college and graduate school," I told her. "My parents couldn't afford to pay." She rose to close the door to her office. "You weren't poor," she countered. "Your father is a businessman." "He had five kids to support and we had nothing," I responded. She wasn't buying it, this notion that I deserved an appointment because I was a Flint ethnic who had pulled himself up by the bootstraps.

By Fall River standards my meeting with Miss Cullen represented bad form. It was too confrontational and not the way things were done in the city. She may have seen me the way old Mrs. McCready had viewed the Bedford Street kids at Brown School. With her authority at stake Miss Cullen probably never cared a copper for me. After our encounter, I suspect she vowed not to accede to my appointment as long as she possessed a shred of authority.

Finding that Miss Cullen was immune to my charms, I moved up the chain of command, turning to the superintendent. I soon discovered that

I was a dead man talking as far as he was concerned. The superintendent wore his trademark bow tie, as he had as principal when I was a student at Durfee. We called him "Bow-tie Bob." I remembered when students wired the cafeteria doors shut from the inside, causing chaos at lunchtime as hungry, furious Hilltoppers began to pile up at the entrance. Bow-tie Bob cut to the quick. "If students have enough time to spend on disruptive activities," he growled on the school's intercom, "then maybe the lunch periods are too long and we will shorten them." There were no more lunchtime problems at Durfee while I was there. Bow-tie Bob was an administrator not to be trifled with. There was no bluster behind his neckwear. After all, the Sacred Heart protected his back.

He was very gracious when I arrived at his office; he hung my coat on a rack and invited me to take a seat in front of his desk. He sat opposite me under the large image of the Sacred Heart. "I keep being promised that I'm getting an appointment and it never comes," I related what he already knew. "I've been working month after month as a substitute with a challenging group of kids." "You need a recommendation," he responded. I probed further, but he stuck to his script, repeating the same line in different ways. Miss Cullen's name never came up. Still, it was clear that he would not go over her head unless he had to, that is, unless a candidate had political capital such as a patron on the elected school committee. I shook his hand, thanked him, and left.

Many years later I would come to know the man who oversaw all Great Society education programs in Fall River. He was an outsider—an evangelical Protestant who had taught at Barrington Bible College in Rhode Island and who was appointed by federal authorities. He would tell me, "I constantly had to negotiate with the superintendent. He was well intentioned, but he felt limited by the political realities of the system." I wanted to believe the former federal administrator, a Social Gospeler who tried to look for the good in people. Yet I doubt Bow-tie Bob sought to tamper with the customary way of doing things in Fall River. They had enabled him to rise to the school system's place of honor. He was not about to shit in his own nest.

Toward the end of March, on a beautiful spring Friday, when my promised appointment again misfired, I walked out of my classroom in protest and drove home to Cranston. I had already been accepted into the doctoral program at Brown. I just wanted to express my anger over an illusory appointment—a promised position that no one seemed able to deliver. And the school year was now in the home stretch.

The head of Follow Through in Fall River called me and angrily asked, "What are you trying to prove walking out? Do you intend to come back on Monday?" He soon realized, I think, that he was not the untainted moral conscience of Follow Through. The director was a few years older than me, a business administration graduate of Durfee Tech who apparently knew the right people and fell into a federal job with a fat salary. He then hired a friend from Durfee Tech as business manager. From my CYO days, I recalled that he had played on the St. Louis basketball team. Follow Through had taken over the grammar school in the director's parish—the school that he had most likely attended. I wondered if he had negotiated the deal with his pastor or the diocese. There was more. In the middle of the year the director's brother suddenly appeared as a part-time, do-little janitor at St. Louis, where we already had a custodian. The Fall River school system's political culture wormed its way into Follow Through.

The previous spring, as a meteor shower of Great Society funds descended on the city, a small incident illustrated the "get what you can" mentality that too often prevailed in Fall River. "Project Process," a federally financed program, was conceived to address Fall River's historically supersized school dropout problem. Every Saturday morning twenty-five teachers convened to engage in preliminary discussions, raising issues and exploring practices that might stanch the flow of students from the school system once they reached the age of sixteen. I was fortunate to join the discussion group, whose members were paid an attractive hourly wage. I represented the Flint—an intractable dropout red zone—and the Catholic school perspective, even though I was no longer teaching at Espirito Santo. My good fortune was apparently the handiwork of Sister Cordelia, my former Franciscan colleague, who was some kind of Catholic school liaison to Project Process.

At one point, we were asked to visit a progressive educational resource center near Boston between meetings. A pleasant, unpretentious, female participant in her midthirties and I decided to drive to the center together. A former teacher, she was now raising a family in Somerset. Her husband was an elementary school principal in Fall River. He had been a business teacher when I was at Durfee, and I'm sure he remembered me as a knucklehead jock. I picked his wife up at a new split-level ranch house. He gave me a worried look from the doorway as we left. His furrowed brow and penetrating gaze seemed to say, "I hope he brings her back with body and virtue intact." We drove back and forth on my tank of gas. At the end of next Saturday morning's blather, we were asked to fill out forms for travel expenses. In our case it included only mileage, which required no documentation. I was shocked when I saw my traveling companion submit the form for reimbursement. Grab the free loot while it was available, even if it added up to less than twenty bucks!

In the end, I only pocketed some loose change from the federal cash that poured into Fall River. Despite the string of promises that included benefits, I was never allowed to step off the substitute treadmill. Near the end of the year, I mentioned to my father what had happened. "Why didn't you tell me?" he asked in frustration. "Tommy Cullen is a good customer of mine. I woulda spoken with him." Tommy was a likeable guidance counselor at Durfee; he was also Miss Cullen's brother. Perhaps the matron of elementary education in Fall River feared having her arm twisted by brother Tommy. After my visit to her office, she could dismiss me as disrespectful—a hotheaded Flint ethnic.

About the same time I also relayed what had occurred in Follow Through to my politically connected uncle and godfather Tippy Carreiro, the business agent of the Steamfitters Union who was a crony of former mayor John Arruda. "Ah," he said, throwing up his hands. "You shoulda let me know. The superintendent owes his appointment to John Arruda," he informed me. The mayor served ex officio as the chairman of the school committee. "We woulda gotten to him," my uncle assured me of the superintendent. In other words, there had been influence-peddling ways around the turf battle between Follow Through and top school administrators that probably would have secured my appointment.

As a native son I should have been more aware of the lubricants that made this other "Fall River System" operate smoothly. I should have consulted Uncle Tippy and outsourced my case to a third party rather than taking things into my own hands. After all, I hadn't secured good summer jobs on my merits. Nor for that matter had I gained entrée to Project

Process's Saturday morning gabfests without Sister Cordelia's intervention. Perhaps the moral haze of the era and my Brown credential deceived me into thinking that I could get a teaching position on my own.

I finished the year in Follow Through. I worked for the program during the summer: "compensation," the director said, for the money I lost from teaching yearlong as a substitute. The next time I entered the classroom as a teacher, two years later, my students would be Brown undergraduates.

∢ *Eight* ⊱

LEAVING

I lived in Fall River, at home, for three years after I graduated from Springfield. Then I moved twenty-five miles away to Cranston, just south of Providence. In retrospect, the distance was much less than that. Grey, grim, ethnic, Catholic Providence in the 1970s resembled Fall River. The city even had its own Quequechan — the inky Providence River. This putrid stream separated downtown from College Hill and the East Side, the leafy streets and tasteful neighborhoods with eclectic architecture that spread east and north of Brown University and the Rhode Island School of Design. More than once when an East Sider learned I was from Fall River, a question quickly followed: "What would you have if you took Brown University and the East Side out of Providence?" The answer: "Fall River." As the Bradley Hospital psychiatrist would later suggest to me, I had really not left home. I came to understand my father's affinity for Providence, whose paper he scoured every day. It was not only the place where for years he had doggedly peddled Hoffritz Blades. Providence was also where he bought crates of California grapes each October for his wine press. I realize now that Providence served as the Italian capital for southeastern New England. I also better understand how Fall River was connected to Greater Providence's cultural constellation more than to Boston's.

⊰⊱

When I reapplied to Brown after completing my master's, I wasn't sure that I wanted my life to be consumed by doctoral studies. "I'll only go back if they give me enough money," I vowed to Dorothy. Brown delivered. They paid for all of my tuition the first year, followed by teaching assistantships for the next two years.

I reenrolled at Brown in September of 1971. Within two weeks our daughter Antonia was born. After three weeks of recuperation, Dorothy returned to her job at the University of Rhode Island. I became the primary caregiver, as they now say, for our daughter. I bathed her, dressed her, fed her, and later read to her constantly. I pushed her through our work-ing-class neighborhood in a carriage, which sometimes turned heads. In the era before "house husbands," I was something of an oddity. Occasionally, I stopped to talk to neighboring women who were discussing the price of hamburger at the local Star Market or swimming lessons for their kids at the nearby YMCA. As Antonia napped, I turned to my schoolwork. When I had to attend classes or conduct research, I took Antonia to her grandparents' house across the city from Brown. On Sundays, I worked a thirteen-hour day at the local Cumberland Farms store to earn book and spending money. Dorothy and Antonia paid me a visit in the middle of the afternoon and brought me something to eat.

I surprised myself as a parent; having not read Dr. Spock or his traveling companions, I learned on the run. It helped having a wife who was a spe-cialist in early childhood development. My years raising Antonia gave me respites when I relished being an off-duty academic. I loved fatherhood even more than my tobacco pipe, to adapt a line from "Ichabod Crane," where Washington Irving describes Dutch patriarch Baltus Van Tassel's relationship with his daughter.

If parenting was a heady experience, so too was returning to Brown — this time with a measure of confidence and affirmation. It helped that Bill Stueck, my best friend from Springfield, enrolled in Brown's doctoral program in history the same year. In 1971, the University on College Hill was in the midst of rebranding itself as something of a "granola" or coun-tercultural institution, the "non-Ivy, Ivy League school." The so-called New Curriculum, introduced in 1969, redefined undergraduate education. All course requirements outside of one's major were abolished. The grading system was transformed. Students could elect either "Satisfactory/No Credit" or "ABC/No Credit." The freedoms of the New Curriculum en-couraged intellectual exploration across disciplines as well as double, triple, and self-designed majors. Applications soared. The university attracted marquee names, beginning with Amy Carter and then John F. Kennedy Jr. Brown's reputation grew as a place that was increasingly difficult to get into and also difficult to flunk out of. There were no "D" and "F" grades outside of one's major, just "No Credit" for slackers.

When I returned to Brown, I joined the American Civilization Program rather than the History Department. It was the fulfillment of a dream that, like my determination to play football for Durfee, took flight in my imagination at a particular moment in time. During my junior year at Springfield, I worked in the library. The second floor had a small, glass-enclosed room filled with graduate catalogs. I scanned those with American studies programs. I thumbed through Brown's white catalog with black letters and a crimson Brown emblem on the cover. I fixed on American Civilization 201, a required introductory course for doctoral candidates that focused on a single topic. *The House of the Seven Gables* was the simple listing of the subject for the semesterlong course. I found this intriguing, using a single major work of fiction as a springboard for explorations from a variety of disciplines.

I thought my peers in "Am. Civ." were stronger and more creative than history graduate students. The program, which was almost exclusively a doctoral degree on the graduate level, attracted individuals primarily from first-rate liberal arts colleges and universities. Many of my Am. Civ. peers would become highly accomplished scholars. One woman who graduated a year before me went on to win the Pulitzer Prize for a biography of Harriet Beecher Stowe.

Like many classmates, I was drawn to the Am. Civ. Program because it most resembled the new undergraduate curriculum in its freedom. There was only one required introductory course. Students then had the freedom, and the intellectual responsibility, to define their program by selecting courses from other departments. For oral exams one could delineate four fields either chronologically or thematically or a combination of the two. One had to corral graduate faculty from more than one department to oversee the fields.

With my master's degree, I was required to complete only one more year of full-time coursework. I spent my second year reading for oral examinations and serving as a teaching assistant responsible for my own freshman seminar. I received no pedagogical preparation. No one choreographed my leap from Fall River grade school teacher to seminar instructor of superb students at an elite university.

The New Curriculum had created "Modes of Thought" courses focusing on a topic of interest to an instructor. The courses were designed to introduce freshmen to cross-disciplinary seminar study. They were supposed to be taught by senior faculty. But departmental demands did not free up enough accomplished faculty members to staff the seminars. American Civilization graduate students helped fill the vacuum; our major credential was enrollment in an interdisciplinary program. We also arrived on the cheap, since our courses were a "profit" rather than a "cost center" in the lingo of contemporary higher education.

Provoked by the tumult of the times, I was fascinated by how diverse individuals become radicalized. I taught a course titled "American Radicals: Some Studies in Motivation." I still have the catalog. My course is listed as number 8 among 56 Modes of Thought entries. The students were very responsive—and sharp. They occasionally read assignments more perceptively than I did and tripped me up. In those moments, I could hear the tinny sound of my voice. My students' parents had paid thousands of dollars for a Brown education, I mused, and their sons and daughters had ended up with me—a shaggy graduate student who had not taught above the fourth grade!

One day early in the semester, as I struggled to convey my own ideas and not simply to take out the laundry of others, a man with a camera appeared in my doorway. He slowly moved into the classroom, adjusting his camera lens. Was this some scheme to get the goods on me and give me the hook so early in the semester? "May I help you," I enquired? "Oh, I'm just a university photographer, and I'm taking pictures for publicity purposes." I felt assured and continued with class, ignoring him as best I could while he clicked away. I then forgot about what happened.

The following fall, 1973, a picture of my classroom surfaced in a sixty-five-page booklet titled *Brown*. It described the New Curriculum, provided detailed information on the university and its admission requirements, and contained application materials. The booklet was mailed all over the country and overseas. It was also distributed to prospective students who visited campus.

A series of pictures break up the text. There is the requisite photograph of a touch football game on the university green. Scenes of academic life dominate the booklet. Leon Cooper, Brown's Nobel Prize–winning physicist, appears in a three-piece suit standing before a blackboard explaining a mathematical formula to students. Forty-eight pages later, I step in for a bow attired in the graduate student uniform of the era: a blue work shirt, blue jeans, and boot-like, industrial-grade shoes, an accessory option to sneakers. I am standing with one foot on a chair and gesturing with my right hand. The photographer caught a student looking at me intently, as if enraptured by what I was saying. Perhaps. But this bright, intellectually aggressive student would later respond to one of my points with a dismissive, "That's totally ridiculous!" Nevertheless, the photograph made good copy. I was probably taken for a student actively participating in a small seminar. I dressed like them, had long hair like them, and sported a mustache that trailed off toward Pancho Villa territory.

Images aside, the *Brown* pamphlet's text accurately describes the intellectual ethos that the New Curriculum cultivated and that imbued both the undergraduate and graduate American Civilization Programs. "Only you can evaluate the extent to which your education satisfies the needs of personal development," the booklet huffs in rhetoric redolent of the era, "and Brown therefore urges you to assume complete responsibility for your own education." Another passage begins with a verb that served as an incantation in the seventies, the decade when, as someone has observed, most of the sixties actually occurred. "Brown *feels* that traditional curricula, under the pretext of insuring [*sic*] a 'liberal' education, are too often filled with an excessive number of irrelevant course requirements. Such requirements too often preclude the personal choices essential to a personal education."

For all this over-the-rainbow rhetoric of the sixties and seventies, there is something enduring, and not just quaintly endearing, to Brown's intellectual manifesto. It harks back at least to Emerson and Thoreau and to Dewey who followed them. No wonder the New Curriculum remains Brown's higher education signature.

My academic interests when I first enrolled at Brown leaned toward urban and immigrant history, a fledgling field that was just beginning to gain altitude from the work of historians with backgrounds similar to mine. Brown had only one urban historian, a newly appointed professor whose specialty was not immigration. I quickly capitulated to Brown's strengths: early America, New England, and cultural-intellectual history. I wrote my master's thesis on an influential but neglected mid-eighteenth-century theologian who was a leading disciple of the formidable Jonathan Edwards and an early antislavery reformer from his pulpit in Newport. I delved deeper into Puritanism's theological thickets for my doctoral studies.

After a year of teaching freshman and devouring books that were stacked up like cordwood while changing diaper after shitty diaper, the time for my oral examination had arrived in late May of 1973. I combined chronology and themes to define my four fields: colonial and Revolutionary America; American religious history from 1800 to the present; the Puritan conversion narrative in American literature from the seventeenth to the mid-nineteenth century; and theories of history in modern American fiction. Each field had a bibliography of fifty books. These areas of study tilted toward early America, New England, and religion. In 1973, American religious history meant Protestantism. Unlike now, the existing meager scholarship on Catholicism inhabited the backwater of the field. I didn't realize it at the time, but I had defined my fields in reaction to what Fall River and my ethno-religious background represented: a cultural terrain residing on the margins of the "real" New England and America as territories of my imagination.

I got a haircut, scrapped my jeans and blue work shirt, donned a sport coat, and showed up the next morning, nervous the way I had been before football games. But like them, once the contest began, once intellectual contact was under way, I downshifted to a tense but determined stance. Each faculty member was allotted a half hour of questioning and probing. The first fifteen minutes went well, and then I was the recipient of some academic "chin music," to use a baseball term for a high inside fastball intended to rattle a batter. After a series of interpretive questions, a colonial historian sitting in for Gordon Wood, who was on leave, quickly changed tactics. "Where was John Adams in 1783," he asked pointedly. I answered correctly and felt relieved. "Where did he go from there," the inquisitor countered quickly. Again I knew the answer and thought I had fended off his probing of the depth of my knowledge and his attempts to challenge my poise. He persisted. "And where did he go from there?" I was tempted to hazard an educated guess, but I changed my mind in a flash, hoping that composure would redeem me. "I don't know," I responded calmly, my hands folded on the seminar table.

I finished with the first field and still had an hour and a half to go. It took all the discipline I could muster to stay focused and to respond coherently, the gristle in my answers seeming to increase field by field. Then the examination was over. My adrenaline continued on high alert—fight or flight, evolutionary survivalism still coursing through my body. I had remained steadfast, but I was far from sure it had been enough. I was asked to leave the room.

Emotionally spent, I paced the corridor convinced that if I failed all or part of the examination, I couldn't face the ordeal again in the fall. I knew that a classmate, an alumnus of Colgate who would go on to a distinguished academic career at Berkeley, Virginia, and UCLA, had failed part of his exam the day before with two members of my committee. If that happened to me, I feared my hard-earned intellectual confidence would dissolve, dropping the curtain on my academic career.

A recent film, *Getting Straight*, grabbed me by the throat. It starred Elliott Gould as a Vietnam Vet and student radical with a mop of dark, curly hair, a Jewish Afro it was sometimes called in the 1970s. He returns to campus to complete his master's thesis. The final hurdle is an oral defense. Gould's character becomes increasingly frustrated with what he sees as a kind of academic inquisition. And then he crosses swords with a particularly pedantic professor. Gould's character finally boils over. He launches into a tirade against his tormentors and storms out of the room. I had cheered when Gould's character exacted some revenge. But I resisted the temptation to do that, even when niggling questions about John Adams came my way. With a wife and a child, perhaps I had too much at stake. Maybe the discipline I had learned from sports kicked in. Possibly, I remained the compliant Flint ethnic boy-student I had always been, except for the one lapse at Durfee. In all likelihood each of these facets of my life saw me through the ordeal.

After about twenty drawn-out minutes the door to the seminar room opened and my chairman invited me to enter. I took my seat and the verdict came quickly. "Congratulations, you have passed all four fields," the chairman announced. "Not only that, you have passed with distinction." Stunned yet relieved, I thanked the committee members and we shook hands. I made tracks from the room trying to reconcile my perception of my performance with the committee's.

I rushed home to tell Dorothy. We went out to dinner that night to celebrate. It took me weeks to recover from the intensity of the examination and mostly from the dread of failure.

In the fall I taught a seminar to senior American Civilization majors. I felt more confident in the classroom with these seasoned students, most of them headed for graduate school. At the same time I settled on a dissertation topic and drafted a prospectus for approval after my advisers critiqued it and I made revisions.

I decided to expand my one-hundred-page master's thesis into a book-length study. I examined two generations of developments in Calvinist theology and the New England Congregational ministry. The study focused on the influential Samuel Hopkins and other disciples of Jonathan Edwards, whose importance had essentially been dismissed because a liberal Protestant narrative dominated the study of New England religious history. The dissertation broke new ground, but it was rushed and flawed. I was anxious to test a job market for humanities PhDs that deteriorated year by year during the 1970s. It didn't help that I wrote about dead, white, elite males, who had seemingly passed their academic shelf life at the time. Social history and the lives of ordinary people had overtaken the historical profession and especially the study of early New England. A new academic holy trinity composed of class, race, and gender begat a tide of books and articles.

Before I chose a dissertation topic, no one adequately explained to me that there are actually two almost disconnected parts to a doctoral program. First there is one's coursework and oral examination. Next comes the dissertation. One might falter at the first stage, failing parts of the oral exam along with a foreign-language test, as some of my classmates did. After they passed on the second attempt, they might fully recover at the dissertation stage by choosing a timely, ambitious topic that appealed to search committees and showed promise of leading to an important book. I had encountered no significant turbulence in the first phase of my studies. Then I settled on a specialized topic. I discovered around me an all too common academic species known as "ABDS," "All but Dissertations." This classification embraced the individual who labored for years on a dissertation, which turned into a ball and chain, to the student who ultimately arrived at the calculation that an investment in a dissertation would not yield a commensurate return given the dismal state of the academic job market. I feared being reduced to an ABD, which influenced my choice of a dissertation topic.

I finished my dissertation at the end of 1974, four and a half years after I started at Brown—excluding my time in Follow Through. To pay for the dissertation to be typed professionally and also to earn some pocket money, I took two menial, part-time jobs. The first was at Temple Emmanuel, a large, affluent, conservative synagogue on Providence's East Side. I worked under Louie Pacheco—a Portuguese man from Fall River whose daughter I had taught at Espirito Santo. We got along exceptionally well;

our relationship was grounded in ethnic and hometown ties that trumped educational differences. We worked at all hours, cleaning and preparing the synagogue's large function room for various activities. On Saturday we served as "Shabbat Goys." We put on yarmulkes and passed out prayer books as worshippers entered the synagogue. We also did anything that the members apparently were unable to perform on the Sabbath.

The members of the congregation were mostly kind to Louie and me. The lay director of the temple was a nice older man whose business had failed and who had been rescued by his fellow Jews. One Saturday I was standing at the back of the temple. He gestured for me to come over to him. "Would you pick up that and get rid of it?" he said as he pointed to a dirty tissue at his feet. I did so without a complaint or any hostility. But I had just about earned a doctorate from an Ivy League institution and here I was picking up a snotty tissue and doing other scut work. After several weeks, word got around the temple that I was completing a doctorate at Brown. I now acquired a new status. The young rabbi even stopped me one day and said, "You know, we have strong ties to Brown."

I left the temple after several months because the hours were so unpredictable. I found another humbling job with "Mr. Panel," an outlet store that was part of a national chain. Imitation wood paneling was popular in the sixties and seventies, a kind of suburban-inspired appointment for "dens" and "finished" basements. I worked in the warehouse, carting sheets of paneling to customers' cars and trucks. Mr. Panel ran newspaper advertisements with a bespectacled little man wearing a mortarboard who was called "Professor Panel." He announced sales and lent his authority to the merits of paneling. When my manager and assistant manager learned of my educational background after they hired me, I became the real "Professor Panel," as they took to calling me. What had all my effort earned me, I often brooded during those months, but Shabbat Goy and Professor Panel positions, and prior to that a Cumberland Farms clerk. At one point I even applied for a job as a debt collector. I received a phone call but no interview.

I defended my dissertation in February of 1975 while I was working at Mr. Panel. My doctoral work was then complete. I soon finished my tenure as Professor Panel. A New York publisher who had a contract with the East Providence Bicentennial Committee "rescued" me. I received a meager stipend for what I was asked to do: research and write in time for the bicentennial a two-hundred-page history of the city of approximately fifty thousand that was situated across the Seekonk River from Providence.

East Providence, I discovered, had an interesting history with connections to Fall River. Like so much of Narragansett Bay's eastern shore, what became East Providence had belonged to Plymouth Colony and then to the colony and state of Massachusetts. East Providence was part of Seekonk, Massachusetts. It shifted to Rhode Island in 1862 as part of the boundary settlement that partitioned from the Ocean State the town that created Fall River's extensive South End.

East Providence, like Fall River, developed a thriving Portuguese community after 1900. By the 1930s, East Providence surpassed Providence and Bristol to claim the largest Portuguese population in Rhode Island (5,500 or 18 percent of the city's approximately thirty thousand Depression-era residents). Like the Azores, southeastern New England boasted its own "archipelago" of Portuguese communities. This chain stretched from Fox Point on one side of the Seekonk River to East Providence on the opposite side; to Bristol, Rhode Island; and on to Fall River, New Bedford; and smaller points beyond.

Brown commencement took place in June, when I was fully engaged in the East Providence project and when unemployment stood at 12.3 percent in Massachusetts and even higher in Rhode Island. As I had with my bachelor's and master's degrees, I decided to skip commencement, selfishly depriving my wife and parents of the opportunity to celebrate and participate in my achievement. That achievement rang hollow to me because I didn't have a professorship, and with the country, and especially New England, mired in deep recession, the academic job market was bleak. I collected my third sheepskin via the mail.

My father was especially proud that I had earned the PhD from Brown and done so relatively quickly—and without any cheating, he must have assumed. "Often it takes people ten years to get a doctorate," he said. The tools of my trade were supposed to have been a clipboard, a whistle, and a drill-sergeant's voice. My unforeseen educational success called for a family celebration with lobsters as the main course. My brother Bill called. "Dad wants to have a party for you on Sunday afternoon," he reported. "It'll be at my house." I thought it strange that the party was not going to be held at 83 Way Street.

Dorothy, Antonia, and I showed up early in the afternoon. My father and my siblings were there with their children. My mother and titia were missing. "Where's Ma?" I asked. "She's not coming," my brother Bill informed me. "Why?" He was reluctant to say anything. I persisted. My mother refused to host the party or to join the celebration at my brother's house. Mother's Day had occurred two Sundays earlier. Dorothy had baked a plate of cookies for her. Whenever we presented my mother with gifts, she would insist, "You shouldn't have spent your money." Dorothy and I had very little cash in June of 1975. Two years earlier we had bought a Cape Cod house in Cranston. After the down payment, we were left with only $300 in the bank. My mother had a conniption because we only brought her cookies and not a gift. Titia had no choice but to join my mother's boycott of the party.

My mother and I never said a word about what happened. Family life went on as usual. I overlooked her behavior, chalking it up to the kind of snit she often directed at my father and the Confortis. At least I thought I had put this episode, and others, to rest. Nearly three decades later, she would be on her deathbed barely conscious from the Alzheimer's disease that ruled the last decade of her life. I just could not pull myself away from Maine, drive for three hours to Fall River, and say a final goodbye. The nun at Catholic Memorial Home told my brothers to call me. "Your mother is holding on until he arrives," she claimed. I didn't believe her, or I persuaded myself that it couldn't be true. My mother had long lost contact with reality. One time when I visited her and extended my arms for an embrace, she resisted. "Don't you touch me," she exploded. "I don't know you." She was in and out of consciousness during her last days. I made excuses. I was too busy. It was the end of the semester. I was writing a book. These were evasions. Like some of my Follow Through kids, affect had seemingly abandoned me.

Several years after my mother's death a tidal wave of guilt washed over me: for not visiting her more often at Catholic Memorial Home; for feeling no compulsion to say one last goodbye; and for resenting the emotional dependencies she cultivated. I wrote her a long love letter. She had unfailingly cared for us and cooked wonderful meals. She stretched the family budget. She worked to pay for our Catholic education and pushed us to fulfill the respectable social aspiration that she and Titia imposed on themselves. In our jobs and our family lives we all turned out successfully.

And yet, I am a historian and sadly I cannot pin down precisely the year my mother passed away.

My father died in January of 1993, four months short of his ninetieth birthday. Over the decades after we had all left home and grandchildren kept arriving, he increasingly mellowed. On his deathbed, he occasionally cracked open his eyes. I kissed him on his cheek and broke down in tears. I cried halfway home to Maine.

⊰⊱

My advisor, Professor William G. McLoughlin, then the dean of American religious historians, strongly supported me. He continued to recommend me for positions and encouraged me to revise my dissertation for publication. When I finished my doctoral work in 1975, he said that I didn't "push myself enough in the profession." He was right.

During the first few years after I graduated, I received several invitations to interview at the American Historical Association's annual meeting, which was held after Christmas. The usual practice was to winnow a short list of interviewees at the meeting down to three or four candidates who would be invited to campus for daylong interviews. I resisted attending professional meetings. I did show up at the Organization of American Historians annual meeting when it was held in Boston. I was put off by the new harvest of PhDs in a free-for-all to score interviews for the handful of jobs that were available. To me the meeting resembled a cattle call, with us professional outsiders being so much meat on the hoof. But something else was at play in my tentative search for an academic position. Physically and emotionally, I hadn't yet left Fall River.

Dorothy, Antonia, and I had begun to put down roots in Cranston. Soothing memories of fall walks, of winter sledding, of Sunday visits to the Roger Williams Zoo began to pile up on the Rhode Island landscape and to occupy my psychic terrain. Then, too, Dorothy's family of good, hardworking people, just like the Confortis of Beattie Street, surrounded us. Her years in the convent had deprived Dorothy of regular contact with her family.

After we had settled into our densely built 1930s neighborhood of Capes, colonials, and bungalows, I encountered a throwback to St. Anthony's parish several blocks away. A small Italian enclave had formed around "Knightsville," one of Rhode Island's older mill villages. Many of the Italian families traced their origins to Itri, a town between Rome and Naples. I learned that in the eighth century the townspeople believed that the Blessed Mother appeared to a deaf-mute youth, who was miraculously cured.

The commemoration of Mary's apparition passed down through the centuries. It crossed the Atlantic in the steerage of immigrant ships and spanned generations in Knightsville. Every third weekend in July my neighbors celebrated the Feast of Our Lady of Itri. Surprisingly the Sunday morning procession tugged at me. Mary's statue was paraded through the streets as people ran up to her figure and attached money. One year the French bishop of the Rhode Island diocese, which Fall River had been part of until 1904, joined the procession. The St. Mary's parishioners were obviously pleased that he had seen fit to recognize their tradition's importance. He marched with a bounce in his step, making the sign of the cross to the left and right and pronouncing "God bless you, God bless you."

I felt like an intruder, a trespasser on a sacred ritual that had been transported across time and space. Perhaps the procession beckoned me out of sheer nostalgia for a simpler time when my faith had been undisturbed by doubt. With Antonia in tow, I remember feeling more envy than cynicism toward my Cranston neighbors. They cherished a tradition and ritual that conferred meaning and continuity on their lives. Never more than on those sparkling July Sunday mornings in Knightsville was I aware of how my education had been a devil's bargain: it had rewarded as well as robbed me.

On my doorstep I had been given an impressive story of faith, tradition, and ritual. Yet it never occurred to me, a specialist on American religious history, that the Feast of Our Lady of Itri represented an important subject worth studying. I seemed to need a miraculous intervention to restore my perspective.

My alienation from the Church stirred disagreement with Dorothy when it came to rearing Antonia within the faith. I supported her baptism and passively accepted Dorothy's preparation of Antonia for First Communion. Sunday Mass was another matter. Dorothy drove Antonia to Providence where they attended Mass at an inner-city chapel run by Franciscan priests for the poor and disenfranchised. It represented a place of worship that should have appealed to me. But we lived in the most Catholic state in the country. I adopted a contrarian religious stance. Graduate school sowed the seeds of a secular humanist outlook as I was continually whipsawed between parochial Cranston and cosmopolitan Brown. Without my support Dorothy eventually gave up her efforts to raise our daughter fully within the Church. My trips with Antonia to Roger Williams Park became the new Sunday morning ritual.

I am still haunted by my failure to back Dorothy when she tried to introduce Catholicism to our daughter through the Franciscans. It is perhaps my biggest failure as a parent. Dorothy had no intention of force-feeding Antonia churchly doctrine. She wanted to instill a moral and spiritual awareness. I shortsightedly deprived my daughter of a valuable religious tradition.

We were enveloped by an all too familiar ethnic Catholicism: Dorothy's family was near at hand in Cranston, and we also remained attached to my family, and thereby to Fall River. Every other Friday night we had dinner with my parents and some of my brothers and their families, enjoying a blend of Portuguese and Italian food. In addition, special days—Christmas Eve, parental birthdays, and others—found us in Fall River. The old hometown bled into our lives, just as southeastern Massachusetts melded into Rhode Island, and like the Taunton River simply widened into Mount Hope Bay. State boundary signs on I-195 proved meaningless, a convenient and historically contested political partition of what cohered as a cultural subregion. The scraggly scratch of boundary lines on the map had shifted over the centuries; swaths of southeastern New England had switched colonies and then states.

As I was bringing the East Providence book to a close, I began teaching part time at Rhode Island College. This public institution in Providence was a small university with several large departments: twenty-four full-time faculty members in history and thirty-four in English, for example. It kept its identity as a college to remain distinct from the University of Rhode Island.

A month after I started teaching at the college in the fall of 1976, the History Department's specialist on early America was diagnosed with stomach cancer. She went on extended sick leave, and I took over her colonial and Revolutionary history courses. She sent me the course syllabus and the required books, along with a kind note: "I know the students are in good hands." The poor woman died slowly over more than a year while I continued to teach colonial and Revolutionary America. I never met her.

Another agonizing death affected me at this time. A Bento family curse paid an unwelcome call on poor Titia in the late winter of 1976. She suffered a devastating stroke that left her paralyzed, unable to stand or talk. For the better part of a year she lay in a hospital bed, hooked up to a catheter, in the room I had shared with my brothers. Hours on end she stared up at the badly cracked ceiling, listening to the rumble of cars and trucks on snug Way Street and feeling the tremors that had always raced through the house that Cerce built. In silence, she probably continued her daily recitation of the Rosary and leaned on St. Anthony and her unflinching faith for solace. She smiled when we kissed her hello and goodbye on our visits to Way Street. From the Azores to her deathbed, Titia seemed to accept that life's choices were always beyond her reach.

My mother refused to commit Titia to a nursing home. She went into overdrive, caring for Titia around the clock and for my sister's youngest son three days a week. She reverted to the kind of intensity, with its complex wellspring of emotions, that had guided her parenting: devotion to her sister; a sacrificial sense of duty; pride that no close blood relative of hers would die in a nursing home as had my Conforti grandmother; and a daily mission that sidetracked her from dealing with my father.

A second massive stroke in the fall of 1976 snuffed out what remained of Titia's life. Regretfully, I didn't attend her funeral, though I joined family and friends for the lunch that followed. I was in my first semester of part-time teaching at Rhode Island College and feared I would jeopardize my temporary position and future prospects by canceling classes. I think Titia would have understood, or at least accepted, my calculated, if not twisted, priorities.

When a national search to fill the Rhode Island College position took place during the 1977–1978 academic year, the department was inundated with applications. I made it down to the final three candidates. After the interviews were completed I was offered the position. It helped that I had begun publishing pieces of my dissertation, including an article in the leading journal of early American history. When I submitted the essay I referred to my dissertation in a footnote. One of the outside readers who evaluated the submission for the journal's editor wrote, "I see Conforti has recently been un-caged from a doctoral program." Welcome to the sharp elbows and big egos of academia.

When I joined the Rhode Island College (RIC) faculty in the fall of 1978, Dorothy had already been there for five years after transferring from the

University of Rhode Island. She was a tenured associate professor. Antonia even attended the laboratory school on campus. After two years, my position was changed to a joint appointment with the English Department. I had the luxury of drawing on my American studies background by teaching colonial and Revolutionary history in one department and early American literature and autobiography in the other. It was an ideal arrangement. I even had graduate students in both departments. In a short span, we Confortis had built up a cozy relationship with the college. In the end, RIC's ivy-less walls closed in on us.

On the whole, I liked and always tried to respect my RIC students. They were mostly my Espirito Santo kids grown up: working-class ethnics and some immigrants, usually the first members of their families to attend college. Still, from Espirito Santo to Follow Through and to RIC, there were always a couple of serious dustups with students. Teaching at RIC, a diverse, comprehensive urban institution, was not always a tweedy affair with mutual respect an accepted rule of the realm. Fortunately, I was far more mature and confident at RIC than when I muddled through two years at Espirito Santo and my teaching assistantships at Brown. Yet, when combustible friction arose at the college, I remembered what I had learned from Sister Cordelia during my first year of teaching: remain fair, firm, and self-composed.

My two major clashes with RIC students during my nine years on the faculty left me feeling like Professor Panel with tenure. They took place in night courses offered in a block of time once a week. There one encountered a few characters who moonlighted as students. Some chose a class for convenience, not for their interest in the subject. If the course was not in their major, they could take it for pass/fail rather than a letter grade. The instructor was not supposed to know. But from body language to attendance and to written work, these slothful members of the class quickly revealed their stripes as they tried to calculate how little they needed to do just to pass.

One semester a couple of sweethearts enrolled in a history course I taught at night. The young man sat in the back of the classroom, his girlfriend in the front. He began to miss class every other week; she was never absent. When her beau graced us with his presence, he had a scowl on his face that seemed to say, "I'd rather be guzzling Budweiser and watching Monday night football." His first written assignment suggested that, even with possible coaching from his girlfriend, he just mindlessly slapped something together. He reckoned, as I was soon to find out, that all he had to do to get credit was to submit a paper that wasn't written in a Magic Marker.

He failed to show up when I returned the papers. The following week, he approached me during the short break I gave students before the last hour of class. He asked for his paper, and I handed it to him. He was a lanky fellow, easy to spot in class. I could tell he was agitated and itching for an argument.

He approached me at the end of class after all the students had left except his girlfriend, who hovered just outside the door. "Why did you fail me?" he demanded. "Your paper showed no evidence that you had read any of the assignments or even heard lectures and discussions." "But I turned in a paper. Shouldn't I pass the assignment?" "It shows no evidence of work," I countered again. "But I did the assignment. I deserve more than an F," his voice grew louder as he towered over me. "You just can't turn anything in and expect to pass." He headed for the door, rolled up his paper, and threw it at me. "Here, shove this anywhere it fits," were his parting words. Trailing behind, his girlfriend looked in the door and mouthed, "I'm sorry." Maybe this incident discouraged her from marrying the lout.

A much more serious incident took place near the end of my short career at RIC when I was teaching a required general education course on classic Western literature. One year I offered the course during a seven-week summer session. The course met for two and a half hours twice a week. At the first class I looked across the trench and saw a student resting his head on a desk with his eyes closed. Boldly, he sat toward the front of the class not the back. I could tell that the students wondered what I was going to do about this flagrant class misconduct. I ignored it for the first week. Little did I know that it was the opening round in an escalating campaign of intimidation.

The student confronted me outside the classroom building before the start of the second week. Dressed in a soiled T-shirt and pants and scuffed construction boots, he kept within six inches of me, even as I tried to step back. With this physical harassment he made me an offer. "Look, I work construction all day. How about if you give me a break? I'll do all the reading, write the papers and take the exams. You excuse me from attending class." "I can't do that," I replied, defending the moral high ground that he might understand. "It wouldn't be fair to the other students."

He was an industrial arts major who just needed a D to pass the course and graduate. I had some sympathy for his having to read Voltaire, Wordsworth, and Yeats, among a host of other great writers. But I wasn't the curriculum czar. When I returned the first written assignment after class one night, he waited until all the students had left to "discuss" his F grade. He reverted to bodily intimidation and the old saw, "Why'd I get an F? I turned in a paper." I parried his efforts to get me to change the grade. I also refused to backpedal from his ruffian demeanor. He must have thought that a little rough play might soften up the hidebound professor. He shoved me. I immediately opened the door to an adjoining classroom for witnesses and yelled, "I have been assaulted by a student!" The instructor shouted, "Call security!" The student scurried from the room with a baffled look on his face.

Because I made the charge of assault, the off-campus police had to be notified. A burly officer arrived to sort out what happened. With the details in hand, he asked me, "How big was this guy?" "He was a little taller than me and a little heavier." The cop looked at me quizzically. "Why didn't you just cold-cock him?" "I couldn't do that. This is a college. It happened in a classroom." The student was ultimately expelled from RIC. I found out that the industrial arts faculty had been sick of his bullying behavior for years.

Despite these incidents, I generally established good relationships with RIC students as I had at Espirito Santo and even Follow Through. Some RIC students remain my friends to this day. A handful of faculty became more than just colleagues. I wasn't eager to leave RIC, even though I grew increasingly uneasy after tenure was secured. I faced another twenty-five years at the same place.

During the little more than a decade that encompassed study at Brown and my receiving early tenure at Rhode Island College, Providence was nearly as economically spent as Fall River. Rhode Island as a whole was dispro-portionately affected by the decline of defense spending with the winding down of the Vietnam War. The navy significantly reduced its footprint in Newport and shut down its large air station at Davisville on the opposite side of Narragansett Bay. The Arab oil embargo of 1973 sent gasoline and home-heating oil prices skyrocketing across New England. Soon un-employment climbed to nearly 14 percent in Rhode Island. Providence's triple-decker neighborhoods resembled Fall River's: fading paint, peeling surfaces, and sagging porches. A 1960s downtown pedestrian mall was as deserted at night as Fall River's Main Street. Both cities continued to shed population, as people fled to the suburbs.

Of course Providence most resembled Fall River in the dominance of ethnic Catholicism. The city also had an entrenched ethnic spoils system that sometimes spilled over into blatant political corruption. One Irish mayor, Providence's variation on Chicago's boss Daley, bragged that he didn't know where the East Side was until after his election. His successor, the infamous Buddy Cianci, rode a platform of reform straight to public disgrace and resignation (and later to jail).

Then there was Governor Ed DiPrete. I had supported him when he was mayor of Cranston. I worked the phones for him when he ran for governor. An RIC colleague and I wrote a letter to the faculty urging them to vote for DiPrete. I never sought anything in return, but that was not how things were done in Rhode Island. The governor appointed me to the State Committee for the Humanities, another way I found myself surrendering to life in Rhode Island.

DiPrete turned out to be one of the shadiest politicians in Rhode Island history. At one point, he received a bribe in a paper bag at his family insur-ance business several blocks from my house. Later in the day he mistook it for his lunch bag, crumpled it up, and tossed it in a restaurant dumpster next door. When he discovered what had happened, His Excellency the Governor climbed into the dumpster and pawed through the trash until he found the paper bag with his prize.

Something gnawed at me during this corrupt, depressed era as I finished at Brown and pursued my academic career at Rhode Island College. All the lofty rhetoric of Brown's New Curriculum—what I would charac-terize as Emersonian individualism and intellectual self-reliance—was at odds with the world that bounded my life. I had not distanced myself from Fall River, as the Bradley Hospital psychiatrist would point out. I was still enmeshed in identities of descent, not consent, while fashioning a place-based comfort zone in Cranston, an extension of Providence, of Fall River. The liberation theology of Brown's New Curriculum seemed little more than intellectual filigree, ornamentation, on my academic credentials. And then a festering feeling took hold that I had failed some test of authentic American individualism represented by the Protestantism that I had made my life's study. I reproached myself for inhabiting some tinsel town of the mind.

About to be made a full professor, another name for a "lifer," at Rhode Island College, I decided to leave. Dorothy and I gave up tenure to resettle in Maine. "It's a gutsy move," some of my colleagues observed. Translation: "You're crazy!" Staring into the Depression's maw in a battered, bankrupt city, my father still opened his barbershop. That was a gutsy move. My Azorean and Calabrian grandparents exiled themselves from the only homelands they knew. Those were gutsy moves. If I bear a shred of my forebears' tenacity, I offer it up to the memory of their silent heroism. My move to Maine represented a real uprooting of my place-bound identities. It precipitated an emotional crisis, and a first-ever visit to a psychiatrist. Yet the risks I took in leaving security and the known behind are trifling in the shadow of my grandparents' lives.

When I first settled in Maine I used to say to some people, "I am not a native New Englander. I was born and raised in Fall River, Massachusetts." I was only half joking. Fall River didn't seem to belong, and neither did I. From the region's geographic margins, however, I would come to see my hometown more clearly, as I explained in *Imagining New England* (2001). Once again the earth shifted under my feet as it had during my academic rebirth at Springfield and my falling head over heels for a nun. I gradually came to understand that Fall River was far more a part of the real New England than I had ever imagined.

Among many other things, as I have already suggested, I learned that in the 1950s New England was the most immigrant-ethnic region in the country. I realized that New England has been a majority Catholic region for a century. I also became aware that the redbrick mill city teeming with triple-deckers represented a distinctive, defining landscape in much of the region. To all the transplanted Bay Staters I met in Maine, I now readily identified myself as a Fall Riverite, a native New Englander who had always resided in the region and who always will. Warts and all, Fall River is my New England hometown, not just Lizzie Borden's, B. M. C. Durfee's, John Flint's, or Matt Borden's. You might even call me a "Hilltopper." You have my consent.

◁ *Epilogue* ▷

I had never visited the Fall River Historical Society, except to drop in to its Museum Shop to buy works of local history as I mused over writing this memoir. Such societies are important custodians of history, interpreters of the local past to adult visitors and school groups. I wanted to know if the Fall River Historical Society offered a prospect of the city's history from above or below the hill or from some vantage point in between. After all, academics and especially local organizations such as New Bedford's Spinner Publications have been documenting the non-Yankee history of southeastern New England for more than two decades.

A few years ago, Dorothy and I visited the Historical Society on a hot, humid mid-July day. It was the kind of weather that might have raised the spirits of mill owners and managers. The humidity would have reduced thread breakage and boosted the production of cotton cloth. The Historical Society is located in the Highlands, in a former mansion on Rock Street. When we toured the building, a window was open on the second floor, the location of the bedrooms. Even on a still, stifling July day, a breeze swept up from the Taunton River and Mt. Hope Bay. It rustled the long, heavy Victorian drapes, giving one a sense of the benefits of living on Fall River's summit during the summer.

The former mansion was built of Fall River granite in 1843. It was located below the hill on Columbia Street in what is now designated as a cultural district in Fall River's oldest Portuguese enclave. In 1870, the second well-to-do owner of the mansion decided it belonged in the Highlands. He dismantled the building, loaded its granite onto oxcarts, and transported the blocks a mile uphill to its present site on what had been Fall River's Easy Street. He rebuilt, expanded, and updated the mansion in high Victorian style. David Brayton, the brother of Mary B. Durfee Young, later acquired the mansion. He was the agent of the Durfee Mills and the owner of a country estate on the shores of Mt. Hope Bay in Somerset, where I worked in the Brayton Point Power plant in the summer of 1963. The mansion remained in the Brayton family until 1937. By then Fall River's textile empire had cratered and much of the remaining trust fund money had fled the city. The mansion was handed over to the Historical Society and became its headquarters.

The society's colorful brochure plotted the narrative of Fall River's history that we were about to hear on our hourlong tour. The first page featured the Fall River Line Pier, two of its magnificent steamships, and a well-dressed couple leaning over a rail on deck. Below this historic scene there was a photograph of Lizzie Borden as she appeared at the time of her trial. She had an axe superimposed across her chest. Inside the brochure was a large staged picture of Victorian-era high tea in the mansion's opulent music room. A sample of the society's art collection followed, along with more Lizzie memorabilia, including a photograph of her father's shattered skull. Without a cushy endowment, the society obviously capitalizes on the principal historical asset at hand to underwrite a chunk of its budget. Lizzie Borden temporarily diverts visitors headed for the Cape, Newport, or Plymouth. For the price of admission, the society tosses in a taste of Spindle City's history from the perspective of the Victorian-era Highlands. As the brochure put it, the mansion "will give you an intimate feeling of the lifestyle of an affluent family in nineteenth-century Fall River."

A nice seventyish lady who was a native of the city served as the tour guide for Dorothy and me. She began with the music room, described its historical furnishings, and talked about the ritual of high tea. She made the first of her two comments during the tour that revealed a trace of class consciousness. "I'm English and Scotch," she announced. "We had tea all the time. Tea was just tea. I don't know what all the fuss was about."

We moved on to the dining room. Historic paintings hung on walls throughout the mansion. One was a large portrait of Matthew Chaloner Durfee (M. C. D.) Borden on the first floor. The tour guide seemed unsure of his major role in the city. She referred to him as "Andrew," which, of course, was Lizzie's father's name. She told us "the portrait had been rescued from the Boys' Club where it was used by kids as a dartboard." How far the greatest Borden and premier industrialist of Spindle City had fallen. The Boys' Club, whose basketball teams once donned uniforms emblazoned with his name, had long found a new home. The portrait of a mighty, muttonchop-whiskered, late middle-aged Victorian man, who no longer seemed to matter, or to be remembered, had been recycled as a dartboard. I wanted to quote the wisdom of the Puritans' *New England Primer* when it came to teaching the letter *T*: "Time cuts down all, both great and small." But when I entered the Historical Society, I parked my occupational hazard—reflexive academic pronouncements—at the door.

Images of Bradford Matthew Chaloner (B. M. C.) Durfee outnumbered the single portrait of his much more robust and accomplished cousin, M. C. D. Borden. B. M. C. Durfee kept cropping up in various guises. There was a romanticized portrait of him as a young boy. Another painting of him as a young man offered a side-glance that made him look much handsomer than he had been in real life. There was his death mask. Victorians often shrouded the face of the deceased, we were informed, and the mask was placed beside the head of the corpse. Finally, there was an impressive white alabaster bust of B.M.C. that was sculpted in Florence, Italy, and ennobled his visage. Like the wife of General George Armstrong Custer, Mary Brayton Durfee Young cultivated her son's memory for private consolation and public consumption.

On the first floor we were escorted into the room that served as the society's draw: the Lizzie Borden Exhibit. Our guide suddenly turned peremptory. "Don't interrupt me while I am talking," she ordered us. "I will answer questions when I am finished." Given the interest in Lizzie Borden, guides had apparently been peppered with questions to the point where the exhibit could not be adequately interpreted and the tour time was exhausted by preoccupation with the axe murderess. Renewed interest in the case, the tour guide told us, began with the made-for-television movie of 1975 in which the well-established actress Elizabeth Montgomery played Lizzie.

The sensational exhibit included a vial with a sample of Lizzie's blood taken as evidence; a hatchet with a broken handle that was found in the Borden basement and whose blade had been wiped cleaned; drops of her stepmother's blood on pillowcases from the bedroom where she was murdered; a braided hairpiece that Abby Borden was wearing when she was attacked; and other items such as photographs of Andrew Borden's bludgeoned skull. The Historical Society also preserves a bulky archive of evidence for researchers interested in what may have been New England's crime of the century. Our tour guide refused to take a position on Lizzie's guilt or innocence. She did, however, offer a class-inflected view of the controversy. "If Lizzie had been a mill girl, she surely would have been convicted."

From the Lizzie exhibit we were directed to the second floor, where another guide greeted us. She was a friendly local woman about twenty years younger than our host downstairs. After the Lizzie exhibit, I imagine visitors to the second floor posed a serious challenge to tour guides. We viewed the Victorian-appointed large bedrooms and the bathroom. A room devoted to the Fall River Line was temporarily closed. Nevertheless, we were offered concise histories of that Fall River glory, of the second-floor quarters, and of the mansion's inhabitants.

We headed for the exit. I assume some visitors walk the two blocks to see Lizzie's badly faded Maplecroft, where she took up residence after her acquittal with her miserly father's modest fortune in hand. Many curious out-of-towners drive the half mile to the scene of the crime. Now a bed and breakfast, the original Borden house also has a popular souvenir shop. It sells things like golf balls inscribed "Keep Hacking Away." Once they have tarried long enough to satisfy their Lizzie interest, most tourists forsake Fall River like the high-living Yankees who left the city in shambles.

I mused over the massive exclusions from the Historical Society's story of Fall River: generations of immigrants; vibrant ethnic neighborhoods; the overwhelming Catholic majority; distinctive granite mills; abounding triple-deckers; the historic, if befouled, Quequechan River; and the wreckage left behind by people who lived the life of luxury in the Highlands, right in the Historical Society's headquarters. In other words, the familiar world that I shared with legions of Fall Riverites was all roped off from view. In defense of the Historical Society, the staff has a house museum to interpret and a notorious event that is their meal ticket. Still, there is nothing to prevent guides from at least nodding toward a more inclusive narrative of Fall River's past. After all, the city's historical significance extends far beyond Lizzie Borden and the Highlands to the Fall River manufacturing "system" that produced rivers of coarse cotton cloth and to the character of the people who labored and lived in what was a singular New England place—a gray granite industrial city situated above open ocean. Fall River represented a radically different New England "city upon a hill" from what Puritan governor John Winthrop had envisioned with that famous utterance in 1630.

From the Historical Society and the Highlands, Dorothy and I drove down below Fall River's hills to Columbia Street, a few blocks from the site of Matt Borden's old American Printing Company. We stopped at the first Portuguese bakery we found. I asked for sweet bread using its

Portuguese name. A young girl stepped into the room behind the counter and returned with two freshly baked round loaves for us to take back to Maine. The bakery was filled with the bread's sweet aroma. We couldn't resist. We bought two small rolls to satisfy our sudden cravings. As soon as we returned to the car, we began devouring the rolls. Savoring the taste of the Fall River to which I belonged and that Dorothy had come to know, we made our way to the interstate. We headed toward Maine, to the wonderful bayside city where I have lived for many years—but true north is not the direction of home.

᪳ A Note on Sources ᪾

I consulted numerous books and newspaper articles for the more historical sections of this memoir, particularly the first chapter. Some of this material is available online at the Keeley Library (www.sailsinc.org/durfee/fulltext. htm). Philip T. Silvia Jr. has edited three invaluable collections of newspaper accounts. His bulky volumes with numerous photographs also contain informative introductions: *Victorian Vistas: Fall River, 1865–1885* (Fall River, MA: R. E. Smith, 1987); *Victorian Vistas: Fall River, 1886–1900* (Fall River, MA: R. E. Smith, 1988); and *Victorian Vistas: Fall River, 1901–1911* (Fall River, MA: R. E. Smith, 1992). The definitive, detailed history of Fall River was written by Arthur S. Phillips, *The Phillips History of Fall River*, 3 vols. (Fall River, MA: Dover, 1944–1946). Also helpful, especially for its biographical sketches, is Henry M. Fenner's *History of Fall River* (New York: F. T. Smiley, 1906).

There are other works of local history that I found helpful. Ellen Fletcher Rosebrock's *Historical Fall River* (Fall River, MA: Preservation Partnership, 1978) is an informative architectural-preservation history. Judith Boss's *Fall River: A Pictorial History* (Norfolk, VA: Donning, 1982) is more than a picture book. Alfred J. Lima and colleagues' *A River and Its City: The Influence of the Quequechan on the Development of Fall River, Massachusetts* (Fall River, MA: Green Futures, 2007) reviews much of the city's history. Carmen J. Maiocco has produced two pamphlets that stimulated my memory: *Up the Flint* (Fall River, MA: n.p., n.d.) and *The Granite Block: Downtown Fall River in the Mid-Twentieth Century* (Fall River, MA: n.p., 1994). Equally helpful was *The Fabulous 1950s as Recorded in the Fall River* Herald News (Fall River, MA: Historical Briefs, 1991).

On the Italian community, I have drawn on my brother's master's thesis of 1975, which was later published: John J. Conforti, *Fall River's First Italians, 1872–1914* (Fall River, MA: privately printed, 2003). Helpful on the Portuguese is Marsha McCabe, Joseph D. Thomas, and colleagues' *Portuguese Spinner: An American Story* (New Bedford, MA: Spinner, 1998). For a mid-twentieth-century Yankee perspective, see James Chace's *What We Had: A Memoir* (New York: Summit, 1990).

Three academic works provide detailed portraits of the city's textile industry and labor strife. I am particularly indebted to Mary H. Blewett's exhaustive *Constant Turmoil: The Politics of Industrial Life in Nineteenth-Century New England* (Amherst: University of Massachusetts Press, 2000). See also John T. Cumbler's *Working-Class Community in Industrial America: Work, Leisure, and Struggle in Two Industrial Cities, 1880–1930* (Westport, CT: Greenwood, 1979) and Philip T. Silvia Jr.'s "The Spindle City: Labor, Politics, and Religion in Fall River, Massachusetts, 1870–1905" (PhD diss., Fordham University, 1973).

The best study of the triple-decker focuses on New Bedford: See Kingston W. Heath, *The Patina of Place: The Cultural Weathering of a New England Industrial Landscape* (Knoxville: University of Tennessee Press, 2001). On the Boston Associates I have found very helpful Robert F. Dalzell's *Enterprising Elite: The Boston Associates and the World They Made* (Cambridge, MA: Harvard University Press, 1987). In places I have drawn on my own work, especially *Imagining New England: Explorations of Regional Identity from the Pilgrims to the Mid-Twentieth Century* (Chapel Hill: University of North Carolina Press, 2001). Finally, on Fatima and the Church's interpretation of the final secret, see Cardinal Tarcisio Bertone, *The Last Secret of Fatima* (New York: Doubleday, 2008).

ᓚ Notes ᕼ

7   *It is our opinion:* quoted in Alfred J. Lima et al., *A River and Its City: The Influence of the Quequechan on the Development of Fall River, Massachusetts* (Fall River, MA: Green Futures, 2007), 218.

15   *Fall River Industrial System:* Mary H. Blewett, *Constant Turmoil: The Politics of Industrial Life in Nineteenth-Century New England* (Amherst: University of Massachusetts Press, 2000), chap. 9.

20   *hardy peasants:* Herman Melville, *Moby Dick* (1851; repr., New York: Bantam, 1981), 117.

21   *"Serious Results":* The headline from April 24, 1896, is in Philip T. Silvia Jr., ed., *Victorian Vistas: Fall River, 1886–1900* (Fall River, MA: R. E. Smith, 1988), 64. For another local newspaper account of a "race war," see ibid., 509–10.

22   *half Negroes anyway:* The businessman is quoted in Donald R. Taft, *Two Portuguese Communities in New England, 1910–1920* (1923; repr., New York: AMS Press, 1967), 33.

22   *their group as a whole:* ibid., 188.

23   *landed on our shores:* Harriet Beecher Stowe, *Poganuc People* (1878; repr., Hartford, CT: Stowe Foundation, 1985), 31.

31   *macaroni and lazzaroni:* Samuel Adams Drake, *Our Colonial Homes* (Boston: Lee and Shepard, 1893), 19.

36   *"Man Swill Carts":* The headlined controversy over the swill carts was reported on June 8, 1899. It is reprinted in Silvia, *Victorian Vistas,* 105.

38   *her agonizing shrieks:* The newspaper story from January 1, 1901, is reprinted in Silvia, *Victorian Vistas,* 159.

38   *brown skinned immigrants:* Jack London, quoted in Miguel Moniz, "The Shadow Minority: An Ethnohistory of Portuguese and Lusophone Racial and Ethnic Identity in New England," in *Community, Culture and the Makings of Identity: Portuguese-Americans along the Eastern Seaboard,* ed. Kimberly DaCosta Holton and Andrea Klimt, 409–30 (North Dartmouth: University of Massachusetts Dartmouth, 2009), 415.

110   *go to the mother:* Bernard of Clairvaux, quoted in Andrew Greeley, *The Catholic Imagination* (Berkeley, CA: University of California Press, 2000), 101.

113   *there were Puritans:* Greeley, *Catholic Imagination*, 62.

123   *that iron string:* Ralph Waldo Emerson, "Self-Reliance" (1841), reprinted in *The Harper American Literature*, ed. Donald McQuade et al., vol. 1, 1032–48 (New York: Harper & Row, 1987), 1033.

123   *lost self-respect:* James Joyce, *A Portrait of the Artist as a Young Man* (1916; rpt. New York: Viking, 1964), 243–44.

131   *branches of industry:* Henry M. Fenner, *History of Fall River* (New York: F. T. Smiley, 1906), 61.

137   *Callahan, you got none:* Bill Reynolds, *Fall River Dreams: A Team's Quest for Glory, a Town's Search for Its Soul* (New York: St. Martin's, 1994), 13.

147   *voices in the bright air:* Thomas Wolfe, *A Stone, A Leaf, A Door: Poems* (New York: Scribner, 1945), 125.

162   *they were written:* Henry David Thoreau, *Walden and Other Writings* (New York: Bantam, 1962), 180.

177   *a personal education:* Brown University, *Brown* (Providence, RI: Author, 1973), 8.

182   *"archipelago" of Portuguese:* Clyde W. Barrow refers to the "Portuguese Archipelago" of Bristol and Plymouth counties in Massachusetts. See Barrow, "The Political Culture of Portuguese-Americans in Southeastern Massachusetts," in Holton and Klimt, *Community, Culture and the Makings of Identity*, 294.

195   *both great and small:* *The New England Primer* (1727), ed. Paul Leicester Ford (New York: Teachers College, Columbia University, 1962), 31.